FUTURE LIBRARY TECHNOLOGY

FUTURE LIBRARY TECHNOLOGY

By
Deepak Kumar
BLISc, MLISc
Librarian
Sardar Patel Subharti Institute of Law
&
Subharti Institute of
Fine Art & Fashion Design
Subharti University, Meerut (U.P.)
(India)

DISCOVERY PUBLISHING HOUSE PVT. LTD.
NEW DELHI-110 002

Published by:
Namit Wasan
DISCOVERY PUBLISHING HOUSE PVT. LTD.
4383/4B, Ansari Road, Darya Ganj
New Delhi-110 002 (India)
Phone : +91-11-23279245; 23253475; 43596065
E-mail : discoverybooksindia@gmail.com
discoverypublishinghouse@gmail.com
namitwasan9@gmail.com
web : www.discoverypublishinggroup.com

***Reprinted:* 2019**

***First Edition:* 2014**

ISBN: 978-93-5056-421-9

Future Library Technology

Printed at:
Infinity Imaging Systems
Delhi

Preface

As we all know that library science is one of the most important topics in today's world. After two decades of continuous library technology increases and a budget crisis that has affected nearly every library in the world. What is the new normal and what are customer expectations? These expectations are not driven by what libraries want to provide or tradition. They are driven by the new ecology of the web and big players like Facebook, Bing, Hulu, YouTube, Amazon, Google and more. Where we are going is where we are at. Foursquare has been called the next Twitter, location-based social networks are all the rage this year, and even our interaction with places, people, and information is being affected by the emerging 'check in' culture. Explore how they may impact the future of libraries and discover how libraries stand to gain from this new trend of engaging and leveraging the power of place.

—Author

Contents

1

The Future of Library Technologies: An Introduction

THE FUTURE OF PUBLIC LIBRARIES IN AN INTERNET AGE

With the Internet reshaping so many aspects of our lives, it has become common for prognosticators to speculate about the ultimate demise of all sorts of institutions that many of us have come to take for granted. So when Public Agenda set out to investigate public and civic leaders' thinking about public libraries today, we were not at all certain what we would hear. The first message that came was loud and clear: there is a future for public libraries in the Internet age. Even with the vast and growing amount of information available on the Internet and more competition for public funding, Americans say that public libraries will continue to play a vital role in communities.

A strong majority say that if their public library were to shut down, they would feel "that something essential and important has been lost, affecting the whole community" (78 per cent). The feeling that libraries are central to healthy communities is even more common among those who are most actively engaged in communities: the voters, volunteers, and contributors who make communities strong and can usually be counted on to raise a ruckus when things go wrong. In our recent report on the research, "Long Overdue: A Fresh Look at Public and Leadership Attitudes About Libraries in the 21st Century", Public Agenda documents the strong beliefs people have that their communities must have wellfunctioning public libraries in order to be healthy and strong. Large majorities said that all children should have a good, safe, appealing library in their neighbourhood; that libraries play a crucial role in preserving permanent and unalterable records; and that government should support the wiring of libraries so that low-income people can have access to the Internet.

AMERICANS SAY LIBRARIES ARE A GOOD PUBLIC INVESTMENT

At a time of broad concern about wasteful public spending, and as we hear of communities refusing to pay more taxes for public education or "essential services", 71 per cent say that libraries spend public money well. Fifty-two per cent say that if their local library needed additional funding, they would favour a tax increase to generate the necessary resources— significantly more than the number who favour charging users (32 per cent) or reducing services (16 per cent) as options for solving a financial shortfall. In many ways, people believe that libraries are more essential now than ever before. Americans say that since so many businesses are selling information, we absolutely need public libraries to provide vital information free of charge to anyone who needs it.

They also strongly agree that libraries are an important, quiet oasis from fast-paced, stressful lives. In an age when people are often deeply cynical about the performance of all sorts of public services, from public education to the police to cultural institutions, public libraries are rated A more often than any other public service we asked about. Indeed, public libraries seem almost immune to the distrust that is associated with so many other institutions. More than one hundred years ago, the philanthropist Andrew Carnegie saw the potential of the public library to be the center of enlightened learning in every community. He offered to build libraries if communities would contribute land, furnish money for annual maintenance, and exercise governance and oversight.

He gave communities the incentive to participate in a national movement and between 1881 and 1917 invested the equivalent of $3 billion to build 1,689 libraries across the nation. The result of Carnegie's investment and the involvement of communities helped educate generations of Americans. His commitment helped fix the library in the American consciousness as a significant public institution that needed and deserved broad public support. A century after this compact with American communities, nearly 90 per cent of library funding derives from local public dollars—which can be seen as either a curse or a blessing.

LIBRARIES FOR TODAY, LIBRARIES FOR TOMORROW

When people think about their expectations of libraries today, they generally think about the traditional services that most libraries carry out so well. Topping the public's list of priorities is that the basic services they have come to expect from libraries remain free of charge to the public. They also expect libraries to have enough current books for children; numerous reference materials; and friendly, knowledgeable librarians available. Libraries should offer convenient reading hours and special programmes for children, and they should have well-maintained buildings along with books and information that are organised for easy self-service. The top-ten list of public priorities for libraries also includes making available safe and productive gathering places for teenagers, being open on evenings and weekends, and having plenty of current books for adults.

For the most part, these public expectations are matched by libraries' performance, the public told us. People give especially high grades to their public libraries for having buildings that are well maintained; comfortable places to read; and enough friendly, knowledgeable librarians to supply help when needed. Although people clearly want libraries to ace the basics—materials, hours, and service—they also expect more and more from libraries in this age of the Internet. "Long Overdue" reveals a great deal about libraries and technology. Libraries are anything but relics of the past. They are viewed as key players in our digitised future.

Two-thirds of survey respondents say that having enough computers and online services for people should be a high priority for their local library. Seven in ten favour wiring libraries so that those who might not be able to afford a computer in their home can learn computer skills and get online. Those who think that libraries are merely becoming "information resources of last resort" for those who can't afford a home computer seem to be mistaken. Advanced computer users and families with higher income are even more likely to use public libraries and the technology services they offer. But, not surprisingly, people with few computer skills are the most likely to say wiring libraries to provide for "have-nots" should be a high priority.

WHERE IS THE LOVE

Public libraries are beloved institutions, but they can't survive on accolades alone. With the advent of computers and search engines, digital libraries, and the Internet, some question if libraries are essential and whether they should command priority in the competition for public dollars. Public Agenda's research shows public libraries are not seen as objects of nostalgia, but rather as essential community players in the effort to increase equity, opportunity, and community development in the information age. A growing number of communities are determined to keep their libraries at the leading edge of technology: affording small businesses the resources to compete globally; giving residents access to credible, current health information; and making libraries vital information access points for everyone.

These communities reveal the vast potential of libraries for the future. But only a small percentage of communities invest in public libraries to the extent necessary to produce maximum dividends. In those communities where the case for libraries is less clear and competition for public funds is high, there are disturbing indicators that support for libraries is slipping. The precarious financial condition of the nationwide public library system (to the extent that there is a cohesive system at all) that we heard about from library advocates was reinforced in our interviews with civic leaders across the nation.

Civic leaders do see the great strengths of the public library as being an information center in the digital age, an important resource for those who have the fewest resources available to them, and the "go to" place for all manner of public functions (including health information, job services, immigrant acculturation, and adult literacy training). But they also see challenges for libraries that need to be addressed by library supporters. Many civic leaders pointed to public libraries' seemingly infinite variety in governance structure as a major stumbling block. Public libraries' lack of marketing, impassive advocacy, and isolation from the community were also cited as shortcomings in library performance. Our research identified four specific areas where civic leadership, public citizens, and library leaders all seem to agree that there is a major opportunity for public libraries to step in and address community needs:

- Developing better programming and services for teens,
- Addressing illiteracy and poor reading skills among adults,
- Offering ready access to information about government services (including making public documents and forms quickly and easily available), and
- Permitting much greater access to computers for all.

Yet venturing into these areas would likely require financial resources that many libraries do not currently have. The civic leaders we spoke to questioned whether a groundswell of citizen support for public libraries would emerge in their communities. "Long Overdue" suggests that there is, in fact, strong potential for vocal support from activist citizens who could argue effectively for consistent and reliable financial support for public libraries. But library supporters, especially leaders with governance responsibility, must take the steps necessary to harness this potential and make it a reality.

LEVERAGING PUBLIC GOODWILL FOR FINANCIAL SUPPORT

There are people in every community who make things happen but don't necessarily hold any official post. These are the folks we refer to in our research report as "community soldiers", because no battle can be won without them. The good news for libraries is that these citizens—who nearly always vote in local elections and involve themselves in community organisations and activities—are heavy users and big fans of libraries. But even though they may be considered champions of libraries, currently they are not very aware of the potential financial vulnerability of their local libraries. Although 45 per cent of the civically engaged think their local government has not furnished enough money and assistance to the public libraries in their communities, 42 per cent think they have, and 13 per cent say they simply do not know. It appears that those citizens who can be counted on to rally to the cause if libraries are in financial peril are no more likely than the general population to be aware of the challenges facing libraries today.

Public lack of awareness of the financial challenges libraries face aside, there are other reasons everything is not milk and honey in the land of libraries. Libraries face real challenges today. Only 35 per cent of survey respondents say their local library gets an A when it comes to having convenient hours so people can use the services; only 28 per cent give libraries an A for offering access to catalogues and databases through the Internet; 26 per cent give an A for having enough computers and online services in the library for the people who want to use them; and just 24 per cent give an A for making available reading hours, homework help, and study space for children and teenagers. These are services that the public rate among the highest priorities for libraries. Clearly there are opportunities to improve service delivery on the part of local libraries.

Library leaders would like to do much more in the way of customer service and innovative programming. But as our interviews with public leaders attest, finances are always a challenge. The civic leaders we interviewed generally share the public's high regard for libraries but are more conscious of the tenuous financial condition of many public libraries. Some public libraries are comfortable with the funding they receive, but the vast majority are not so well supported. Though the public remains largely unaware of the fiscal pressures on libraries today, civic and business leaders believe that public libraries are often first on the chopping block when state and local budgets are cut.

Recent history in Salinas, Calif., a community that closed almost all of its libraries (and is profiled in our study), points to the passion for libraries that can emerge when a funding crisis imperils a treasured institution. But since the vast majority of the public do not sense that their own libraries may be at risk, most people do not see a reason to raise their voice in concern. It is simply not something on their radar screen today. The "canary in the coal mine" metaphor has a place here. Leaders have pricked up their ears to the distressed calls of the canary, but the public seems to hear only a sweet song and no hint of impending trouble.

LIBRARIES: ESSENTIAL COMMUNITY PROBLEM SOLVERS

To identify the most favourable potential opportunities for libraries to strengthen public support, Public Agenda asked the public about their priorities for urgent action in their communities and in which areas they think government should be more effective because current performance is relatively poor. Researchers explored the same terrain in the interviews with national and local leadership.

Four areas of opportunity resonated most with the public and leaders alike:

- *Providing stronger services for teens*: The public is greatly concerned about teenagers and feels (72 per cent) that offering safe and productive activities for teens should be a high priority for their communities. This is also an area where the public potentially holds local government accountable, believing local government both can and should do more for teens. In the public's reckoning, libraries can potentially fill the gap: three out of four Americans (74 per cent) believe providing services for teens should be a high priority for libraries.
- *Helping address illiteracy and poor reading skills among adults*: Another major opportunity for libraries to fill community needs is with supplying literacy and reading programmes for adults, which many civic leaders tied to strengthening workforce skills and economic development. Sixty-eight per cent of the public said adult literacy programmes should be a high priority for the community, very few said it was something their community was doing a very good job of providing, and a large majority (68 per cent) said it should be a high priority for their local library.
- Affording ready access to information about government services, such as making available government forms or information on literacy programmes.
- Ensuring even greater access to computers for all. Almost two-thirds of Americans say having enough computers and online services for the people who want to use them should be a high priority for libraries.

For public libraries today, the greatest challenge is not in convincing the public of their worth—in the present or for the future. People clearly see many valuable roles for libraries to play. Our research yields ample evidence that libraries are highly valued public institutions serving multiple needs that, the public notes, will certainly continue to be needed with changing times.

A TIME OF RECKONING

America's public libraries are facing a pivotal time in their history. There is a rich tradition of public service that infuses citizens with great respect for the mission of libraries. Libraries have received significant public and private financial support over the years, ranging from local property tax support to state budget funding and a high level of private philanthropic funding. But funding level and mechanisms vary tremendously from one community to the next—and that's part of the problem. During the past several decades, there has been a major effort to upgrade technology and Internet access to bring the benefits of these new technologies to all citizens, regardless of economic circumstances. This has added further to public approval of the allimportant contributions of libraries.

Of course, libraries have also long held a position of special importance in educating schoolchildren and older students. The kind of action required for libraries to position themselves securely in the future will demand active and engaged governance. When change happens in communities, it is often a product of the passion of engaged citizen leaders who demand change from elected officials. But our research into a variety of library environments would suggest that libraries may suffer in some cases from a kind of "benign neglect" on the part of those who are most civically engaged. The reasoning here may be a variation on the theme that if it ain't broke, don't fix it. Although the public's strong feelings about how well libraries are doing their job make clear that libraries aren't broken, this doesn't mean there aren't cracks in the foundation.

Those who are most passionate about the importance of libraries in communities, if they are to secure their future, must make certain that the local and state governance structures that determine funding understand all that libraries are able to do for citizens and just how successful their constituents perceive them to be.

E-BOOKS AND THEIR SUCCESSORS

Publishing is going through several huge, related changes. Bestselling books are critical to the success of local bookstores but many bestselling novels are more popular as ebooks than they are as printed books. This trend, combined with the fact that so many people buy their books on-line, means that some bookstores have disappeared and more will follow. Publishers are losing physical places where printed books can be sold. A Canadian reality makes this situation even more critical. Since most on-line bookstores are not housed in Canada, Canadian publishers receive even less revenue from the titles they distribute. If we want a strong Canadian publishing industry, libraries and publishers need to work more closely together. This may include finding ways to allow customers to buy printed books through library web sites and for local bookstores, where they exist, to fill these orders. We need to become more active partners with the industry which is critical to our existence.

E-BOOKS USERS

Many people who currently express distain for electronic books will soon be reading them.

Amongst those who migrate towards some use of electronic books will be:

- *Avid readers who love works of fiction and have wide ranging tastes in books and authors*: This is an easy prediction. Backlist titles, literary fiction and books by new authors often lose money for publishing houses. The president of one large publishing house has said on many occasions that publishing such material only in ebook formats might allow publishers to develop new writers and re-print books that ordinarily would be unavailable to readers. Serious readers will have to move to ebooks or accept that they may lose access to writers they love. Readers who discover a good author and want to read past titles may discover that these books are only available in ebook formats. The good news for writers and for readers is that books will remain more accessible than at any time in the history of publishing. The bad news for writers is that their books will face even more competition for reader attention.

- *Readers of large print material and those who use spoken books*: E-books offer the opportunity for any book to become a large print book. Technically, any electronic book can also become a spoken book, although some publishers are currently blocking this capability. Rights management should and will address this issue. The arrival of accessibility capabilities in ebooks is happening at the same time as record numbers of tech savvy seniors are beginning to retire. ebook readers are the first digital technology where an older demographic is proving to be early adopters.

A US report on the future of academic libraries states that the world of ebooks has reached a *tipping point* and that ebooks will become more dominant than print in an academic setting. If we accept this fact, then it is critical for schools to provide access to ebooks, preparing students for college and university. It will also become important for public libraries to provide material in formats that students will be learning to use.

WHAT COMES AFTER E-BOOKS

It is possible that ebooks have the same relationship to books that horseless carriages once had with horse-drawn buggies; ebooks are the first form of a new product that takes its name identification from the immediate past. This product will soon begin to morph into something far different from the printed book, just as the horseless carriage developed into something far different from the horse-drawn buggy. To glimpse the next stages of this new product and the opportunities that electronic learning and creative media represent, we should look more closely at graphic novels and at "apps" and at the rise of visual forms of information portrayal.

Graphic novels and apps are well-known. Visualisation of information is not. Visualisation attempts to convey complex ideas and thoughts through interactive graphics. Visualisations may help to teach complex ideas to students that think more visually than previous generations. In fact, one of top tech trends is listed as "The Visual Web". The fact that the younger generation both thinks visually and learns through play is well documented by the scholars.

The image to the below is an example of information presented through Visualisation. The bubbles are arranged to convey, with few words, a visual image of the scientific evidence that supports or criticizes various natural remedies and cures.

The higher the bubble on the chart, the more evidence exists to support claims that the holistic medicine inside the bubble can at least ease problems with the targeted ailment. The interactive version of this chart allows readers to explore the research behind each bubble and to set personal parameters about gender or unique circumstances. Bubbles sink or climb with each unique qualifier. To an extent, this image is one prototype of a new Table of Contents, one that can be customised to fit the reader.

PRIVATE PUBLISHING

We will also see a rise in the acceptance and the popularity of personally produced and published books. The qualitative difference between books produced by private sector publishing houses and by individuals will begin to blur. Book equivalents of YouTube videos will challenge traditional publishing for reader attention, just as YouTube is challenging traditional television. School and public libraries will face an opportunity to "publish" outstanding creative material to the web and to help these works find an audience. Although library print circulation remains strong, books will soon constitute less than half of the circulation figures for many library branches. This is already happening in some cities, particularly in more economically challenged, urban neighbourhoods.

It is important that libraries embrace the fact that their mission is not connected to a type of container (print) but to the ability of residents and students to access the best of the world's intellectual property, no matter the format in which it is presented. There are plenty of cautionary tales around us. For example, when downloaded music became popular, music industry did not establish its own digital network; they were too focused on trying to sell physical material through stores. The music industry forgot to focus on the customer instead of their own infrastructure and allowed a computer company, Apple, to create iTunes Clayton Christensen's book *The Innovator's Dilemma*, written before the music industry's radical changes, provides a cautionary tale for libraries and librarians who assume our business is immune to change or that the public will always protect us.

TECHNOLOGY AND TELECOMMUNICATIONS

Less than two years ago industry projections suggested that there would be 150,000,000 tablets, smart phones and e-reader devices sold in North America by the year 2015. The North American market passed the 150,000,000 milestone last fall. It took less than half the time that industry experts had predicted. Estimates suggest that there are now more than 200,000,000 devices in the hands of North American consumers and that by the end of 2016, there may be 8 billion cellphones worldwide. This trend will affect public libraries. Data plans for these smartphones and other devices are more frequently bought by wealthier Canadians. There are also more free wi-fi zones in wealthier neighbourhoods. There is an implication for libraries. It is possible that libraries might provide more users with information access by supplying wifi outside their walls than by offering some current services inside their walls. Public libraries have a unique opportunity. Canarie (the Canadian Advanced Research and Innovation Network) has partners in every province.

The British Columbia partner is BCNet. Canarie recently changed its definition of research organisations (those allowed to use their service) to include both public libraries and school boards. In some provinces, Canarie, along with a provincial partner, now helps to provide inexpensive, high-speed Internet access to K-12 school boards and to public library systems, provided they can reach a Canarie hub. A Canarie programme called the Infrastructure Extension Programme has a statement of purpose which says they are to... enable national and international collaboration, improve access to knowledge, and contribute to the development of cyberinfrastructure and e-research in Canada. Specifically, connections to government laboratories, educational institutions and other facilities are to be supported.

Very few K-12 school boards or public libraries currently take advantage of this amazing opportunity. Canarie/BCNet may be able to provide British Columbia K-12 school boards and public library systems with improved bandwidth at a reduced cost. In Ontario, one public library system is planning to use Canarie access (through the Ontario partner, Orion) to provide recreation centers with free wifi zones. Recreation centers are open more hours than public libraries. Technology and technologically-based solutions to problems will be peppered throughout this report. The most important message is that school boards and public library boards need more knowledge about how people use technology when they seek information, and libraries need to ensure that their mandate fits that world. As an example, the Cleveland Public Library has just started to offer library card holders free cloud storage space that is protected from commercial invasion and that ensures privacy is preserved. Wow.

FROM CONSUMPTION TO CREATION

An emerging trend, with a youth focus, is shifting the role of public libraries from a place focused only on information that is consumed (usually by taking it home to read or view) towards places where people gather, learn from each other and then use new skills. This trend is reflected in the American Library Association report mentioned in the Introduction. The shift towards library as community creativity hub is more developed in northern Europe but some initiatives are taking place in North American.

The Fayetteville Free Library in New York is receiving deserved attention for its Fab Lab, featuring a 3D printer that people can use to *print* plastic objects. The 3D printer is not expensive (less than $2,000) but is having a huge affect on how youth and older customers view their library system. The District of Columbia Public Library has a recording studio in its Central Library teen area. The Chicago Public Library has a YouMedia Center where young adults can:

- *Hang out* (talk to each other in informal sessions with no adults telling them to be quiet or to take their feet off the tables),
- *Mess around* (Experiment with new technologies),
- *Geek Out* (Teach each other about ways they have learned to use music and video editing equipment, etc.)

These three "goals" come from research conducted by the MacArthur Foundation. The research identifies ways that teens and youth can learn from each other. YouMedia labs are now being established in other U.S., cities. The provision of creation spaces in public libraries is pervasive in northern Europe. Researcher visited a Swedish library where people bring projects to the library, learn how to use relevant software tools and then reserve large blocks of computer time for weeks into the future. In contrast, the North American model for public computer use is based on shorter blocks of daily time and an assumption that people are using the computers to search for information. The Helsinki Library system and other Scandinavian libraries provide video and music editing rooms as well as staff expertise. The Finnish creation movement started with a national initiative to reconnect alienated youth. The public library portion of this initiative has proven remarkably successful.

COMPUTERS AND INDIVIDUALISATION

Library computer areas are often designed to resemble quiet reading rooms, but:

- School boards and teachers stress group projects and collaborative work. To complete their work, young people want to cluster and want to talk as they work.
- Some computer applications have noisy, interactive elements.
- People do not always want to use computers while sitting in chairs and at the same kind of desks as the people next to them. They want options.
- The presence of wifi in libraries means that one area cannot be set aside for computer use. Instead, all areas of the library now house technology and all staff need to provide assistance.

The photos to the below tell the story. The first photo is from the Amsterdam Central Library and shows one of their many seating options available to people using library computers. The Amsterdam photo shows an option designed for teens and the way they sit. The second photo is from Mohawk College in Ontario and it shows one of many types of collaboration spaces where teams can work together on projects.

Today, the computer is a phone, a gaming device, a movie screen, a radio and a videoconferencing tool. These are not quiet uses.

OPEN DATA, INTERNET RESOURCES WEB SITES AND LITERACY

The public, graphic Internet is a young technology. It is so young that it has only endured one significant change.

It has morphed from being a passive information tool where large companies and organisations posted documents and has become, as well, a place where anyone can and does contribute opinions about events and thoughts or their personal lives. We are beginning to see a third major change in the web. This change is characterised by people being sent information that their profile suggests they might like to receive. Singles Around Me (SAM) is a dating app for smartphones. It links to social media profiles and lets users know when single people who match their interests are physically close, in any city. This is a huge shift from a web that provided passive web pages waiting to be viewed.

FOUR PRIORITIES FOR THE 21ST CENTURY PUBLIC LIBRARY SERVICE

- Place the library as the hub of a community.
- Make the most of digital technology and creative media.
- Ensure that libraries are resilient and sustainable.
- Deliver the right skills for those who work for libraries.

The key issues emerging in this research are similar to those we handle with the wider arts and cultural sector. It is because there is such a close fit with the Arts Council's five long term goals that we will be able to develop solutions to these challenges from which both libraries and arts organisations can benefit.

Place the Library as the Hub of a Community

We know that, in future, many people are likely to lead more isolated lives. More will work from home and more will live alone. Opportunities to meet in free public spaces for a wide variety of purposes will be increasingly important. Our findings show that libraries will continue to be valued as trusted, safe, democratic places that offer valuable resources and expertise to support the activities of the people who use them.

Libraries' physical space will be more flexible and integrated with a virtual presence that includes web-based reading groups, social networking and links to other online resources. People will engage in creative and cultural activities as well as reading and learning, exchanging ideas, conversation and knowledge.

Space shared with community based services (such as council, health, business support, and learning organisations) will be better for local people, and will bring benefits such as skills exchanges, reaching more people and cutting costs.

The challenge: the use of a library's space:

- Re-think the way library spaces are used to encourage shared and creative activity while continuing to welcome those who want to explore on their own
- Integrate the library's physical and virtual spaces
- Sustain enough spaces offered by libraries to meet the needs of their communities

Make the most of Digital Technology and Creative Media

Digital technology is developing rapidly and will continue to have a major impact on the way we obtain and consume information, culture and the written word. Beyond the library building, people will expect a more interactive experience and to be able to gain access to library services all day, every day, particularly while on the move.

Libraries should be at the heart of digital innovation. They should develop their role in actively connecting communities and helping people to experience, experiment with and master new technologies. Digital technology will be the key to future library service delivery but our research points out that its true potential will not be achieved unless the principle of an open, enabling ICT infrastructure is agreed by local authorities and library services.

This would allow libraries to innovate, and to share or jointly adopt services more efficiently. By making it easier to develop national services and enable local innovation, people will get access to more resources, information and support. Many assume that digital information sources and online services are accessible to everyone. But a digital divide still exists because a significant number of people lack the confidence, the necessary skills or the desire to make effective use of technology. Some who do, are held back by poor digital connections or can't afford them. Public libraries will ensure that no-one needs to be left behind or excluded.

The challenge: using technology:

- Improve the quality and consistency of the virtual library experience
- Develop an open ICT infrastructure that encourages innovation and better service
- Enable libraries to lend the full range of e-books, including remotely

Ensure that Libraries are Resilient and Sustainable

Our research, along with reductions in public expenditure, makes clear that libraries will need to reduce costs and find other sources of funding to supplement local authority support. Alongside this, communities are becoming more involved in the design and delivery of library services. To find the right solution, councillors in local authorities are considering whether they should change the way their library service is governed, or whether they can share aspects of their service with others.

Our research indicates that, as with many other public services, this trend will continue and grow, and the debate about community involvement in public libraries needs to be seen in this wider context. We do not suggest that any one approach is the right one in all circumstances but we have published guidance, based on experience to date, that we suggest should be taken into account.

Some library services are already doing this and we believe that they could be role models, not just among libraries, but for all public services. This kind of community involvement will become seen not as a cost-cutting tool but as a normal way of working, with staff and users developing ideas and creating services together.

The challenge: cutting costs, finding new sources of funds and new ways of working:

- Create a positive environment for communities and individuals to become actively involved in the design and delivery of their library services
- Encourage the development of new approaches to governing and managing libraries that make it more likely that they will survive and succeed
- Equip libraries to be commissioned to deliver other public services, and to commission other organisations to deliver library services

Deliver the Right Skills for those Who Work for Libraries

Our research indicates that one of the major challenges facing public libraries in the future is ensuring that library staff have effective leadership and delivery skills for a rapidly evolving service. Librarians will need to be active in their communities, encouraging people to get involved with their library. That involvement will include local people identifying what their priorities are as well as volunteering and community managed services.

Supporting people in using digital resources competently and confidently will become increasingly important. Those who work in libraries will need to improve their skills in organising and helping users to find their way through complicated information sources. They will become more pro-active in inspiring new services in partnership with others, and their leaders will need to be more entrepreneurial and adept in communicating and marketing their services.

Our research indicates that not enough people working in libraries are equipped to tackle these changes and take on these roles, and that current training is not always relevant for the current and future needs of those working in public libraries.

The challenge: developing the skills of those who work in libraries:

- Ensure those responsible for libraries have the right range of skills and experience to lead their services successfully

- Encourage those working in libraries to offer creative and innovative ways to use library spaces, books and other resources
- Ensure that library staff have the skills to develop and respond to digital developments and to support digital users

THE ROLE OF THE ARTS COUNCIL IN DEVELOPING THE LIBRARY OF THE FUTURE

We also recognise that to build an effective 21st century library service, we will need to work in partnership with a range of agencies, who have their own distinctive responsibilities:

- Department of Culture, Media and Sport where the statutory oversight of public libraries in England sits.
- Local Government Association who represent the local authorities with the statutory responsibility and democratic mandate to ensure public library services are provided.
- Society of Chief Librarians who are the leaders of public library services.
- Chartered Institute of Library and Information Professionals who are the professional organisation for librarians.
- British Library the national hub of knowledge, information and expertise.

This is only the start and we will be inviting other partners from across the library, cultural, commercial, voluntary and academic sectors to work with us to make real this ambition for public libraries in England. We are confident that we now have a robust set of evidence to provide a framework for what happens next. We want this evidence to inspire a collaboration that will make it possible for the public library service to change and develop with confidence.

By combining our resources we expect to be making progress on a shared programme of activity by the end of the year. So we invite all those involved in libraries and those who care about their future to embrace the findings and to work with us on the next stage of their development.

VISION AND THE CHANGING ROLES OF THE FUTURE ACADEMIC LIBRARY PROFESSIONAL IN THE E-LEARNING ENVIRONMENT: CHALLENGES AND ISSUES

The information atmosphere around the world is changing every minute and growing at a tremendous speed due to the emergence of the web based Information and Communication Technologies (ICT), globalisation of networks and Internet. Hence ensuring and organising access to educational materials in the electronic environment is an important factor in determining realistic requests for development and advancement of education. The information revolution and the pervasive thinking that everything is available on the Web have created new challenges to the traditional library professional ethics. Acquiring and providing access to electronic knowledge resources require library professional to change their role from traditional librarian to information scientist by learning and applying new skills to understand the evolving technologies to manage and provide quality on-line information service to the patrons of the knowledge society. Since, almost all the educational institutions, organisations, universities and academic associations have created their own web sites with the digital repositories on Internet, the global networked environment has paved the way and opportunity to eliteracy. The impact of web based e-learning and teaching environment has influenced very much on every facets of library and information services in Academic Libraries and providing new opportunities and challenges to the library professional.

VISION OF THE FUTURE ACADEMIC LIBRARY PROFESSIONAL

Technology will continue to change, and libraries and librarians have to use the changing technology to provide the best access and service to their patrons. Electronic information creates challenges for the library community at its very foundation, moving it away from the traditional paper-and-print format to an ethereal world of circuits and connectivity. The library is no longer defined simply as a building or a physical repository that houses information. So the essential future vision of the academic library professional to achieve the necessary information transformation and to face the digital information needs of the user should concentrate on the following:

- The vision of the future academic library professional must be to create a World Class Networked Global Library and Information Centre to provide web based quality information service to the user in time in the e-learning environment.
- The librarians must change the library environment as pathways to high quality information in a variety of electronic media and information sources.
- Library professional must assert their evolving roles in more pro-active ways, both in the context of their academic institutions and in the context of increasing competitive markets for information dissemination and retrieval.
- *The vision for the 21st Century librarians* must offer electronic teaching and learning both to guide and beckon the library profession as education leaders. They should shape the library programme and serve as a tool for library media specialists to use to shape the learning of students in the academic institutions.

REVIEW OF EARLIER LITERATURE ON CHALLENGING ROLES OF LIBRARIANS IN THE E-LEARNING ENVIRONMENT

The concept of a digital library and its usages for faculty at the university and the changing role of librarians in creating and managing digital libraries are described by Joseph Janes, Assistant Professor at the University of

Washington Information School. He also presented a case study of the Internet Public Library developed between 1994 and 1995 by the then School of Information and Library Studies at the University of Michigan which illustrated how a digital library can support education. Christine Dugdale in her presentation on Electronic Library System which offers access to electronic reservation systems, current awareness service, has shown how short loan collections can provide access to a great quantity and range of material for a larger distribution of learners.

Bank, reviews the trends in online e-literacy programmes in colleges and universities both in the United States and around the world, which describe the desire of teachers to empower the learner, the power of future developments such as simulations and virtual world technology in education. Karen Jurasek says that libraries must uphold professional standards and a commitment to service Also he describes that along with its services, resources, and technology, the library is both a physical and virtual space for the 21st century. He also concludes that the academic library professional must develop a virtual electronic learning system to enhance the user's knowledge and to accommodate an increasingly diverse group of users.

John MacColl's presentation was on virtual learning environments (VLEs) and the aim of his project was to integrate open library resources and closed learning environments. Also he describes that since Virtual Learning Environment contain links to resources, both licensed and free, overlaps with electronic reserve systems, and has a dynamic linking potential with library, librarians should be involved in creating and maintaining VLEs as resource managers in this new environment of web-based courses. Kasperek, Johnson, Fotta, and Craig, found that ". . . continued involvement with play participants outside the library increased student comfort level both with the library in general and the librarian for their major…and that students are more comfortable with librarians once they have the opportunity to get to know them."

Kinnie similarly found that increased involvement with faculty outside traditional library responsibilities also improved his subject specialty liaison work. Dewey likewise promotes the embedding of academic librarians into as many campus venues as possible as a way of "advancing colleges' and universities' strategic priorities through constant collaboration" and Gamble argues for the recognised presence of academic librarians on university governance committees, faculty unions, clubs and student activities as legitimate modes for providing university service that ought to be valued and rewarded by library administration.

E-LITERACY/VIRTUAL LEARNING ENVIRONMENTS IN ACADEMIC INSTITUTIONS AND THE DIGITAL FUTURE OF THE ACADEMIC LIBRARIES

E-learning is a means of becoming literate, involving new mechanisms for communication, such as: computer networks, multimedia, content portals, search engines, electronic libraries, distance learning, and web-enabled classrooms. Different web based applications such as e-mail, real-time conference, Web Cam, etc. are being used as important tools in the process of e-learning. Technological innovations have brought tremendous changes in the whole education process and have led to a paradigm shift from teacher based education to a learner based education system. Developments in the electronic networking frontier have changed the whole dimension of the education system.

This has brought a shift from the 'just in cast education' to 'just in time education' system. Internet, another cost-effective solution of reaching out to the learners at a distance, is gaining ground throughout the world. It is acting as a catalyst for change in the education process. It has taken education beyond the classroom and lecture hall into a new era of networked and collaborative learning. Since the aim of e-learning environment in education is to enhance students' learning opportunities by enabling them to partake in global, team based educational projects, in which they directly experience different cultural contexts and access a variety of digital information sources via a range of appropriate Information and communication technology, the future academic library professional should change their role by developing new standards and skills accordingly to meet the future digital information needs of the users.

Today almost all the academic institutions, universities and college libraries have been automated by library software and have become connected with Internet, intranet and extranet facilities and through which they are providing access to relevant e-journals and e-books by proxy-server based networks. So the future of the academic library services may be changed accordingly to fulfill the needs of the patrons in the e-learning environment. Libraries have an outstanding potential as the third place, after home and work with learning, inspiration and entertainment. Hence it is very essential to change the environment, structure and interiors of the academic libraries according to the digital information needs of the user and the future library should not have collection storage as its main function. E-learning opportunities must be enabled by the library professionals to the user in global level to access a variety of digital information sources via a range of appropriate World Wide Web technology. E-Learning is a catch-all term that covers a wide range of instructional material that can be delivered on a CD-ROM or DVD, over a local area network (LAN), or on the Internet. It includes Computer-Based Training (CBT), Web-Based Training (WBT), Electronic Performance Support Systems (EPSS), distance or online learning and online tutorials. The major advantage to students is its easy access. So, providing access to online e-journals and e-books through networks will enhance the self-learning knowledge of the user.

TRENDS AND CHALLENGES BEFORE THE FUTURE ACADEMIC LIBRARY PROFESSIONAL IN THE ELEARNING ENVIRONMENT

The first and foremost challenge before the library professionals to face the future academic needs of the user in the e-learning environment is to provide electronic access to all relevant information and integrate it on networks across the world. The second challenge is to create a new physical library premises with computer network facilities, abandoning the old concept of library as a storehouse, and, the third challenge to future library professionals is to develop new standards and skills for the library profession to meet the user needs in a proactive way. In this elearning and e-publishing environment, electronic reference services and other support services with various expertise and digital repositories are becoming a must. The most pressing and pervasive issues and challenges that the library and information science professionals face in the present digital era for providing digital information service to the knowledge society are:

- New generation of learners
- Copyright
- Privacy / Confidentiality
- Online/Virtual crimes and Security
- Technology challenges
- Manpower
- Collection of digital e-resources
- Organisational Structure
- Preservation/ archiving of digital e-resources
- Lack of clarity in vision.

The New Generation of Learners

Today's students are grown up with latest information and communication technologies. They are coming to higher education with aptitude, knowledge and expectations that have been shaped by the use of the Internet, digital media, and portable communication technologies. Students often begin their search for information with Google or similar commercial or social search engines. The academic library professional must develop a virtual electronic learning system to enhance the student's knowledge and to accommodate an increasingly diverse group of users.

Copyright

An important issue that the present day library professionals are facing in providing electronic/digital information service is the large scale of piracy of software and plagiarism. The cost and timeliness in retrieving the information are also considered. When negotiating access with a publisher, the librarian must agree to certain restrictions on photocopying or distribution of electronic materials. Despite copyright notices and efforts to educate employees and users about intellectual property rights, electronic publications can be easily forwarded to people outside the licensed user group. The library is responsible for maintaining the awareness of all users about copyright issues.

Privacy/Confidentiality

Maintaining privacy and confidentiality is another problem in accessing online information. To control pirating of software, copying or downloading all the contents of any e-resource at a time, right to obtain information and right to withhold or ban the access is essential and so there is a delicate challenge between privacy and rights to information. Now a days almost all the users are having their own e-mail accounts and they are often sending and receiving important information and even secret programmes and databases through e-mail itself and storing them for future usage. So maintaining privacy from e-mails is a great issue. Protecting one network from another to maintain confidentiality of information is another problem in securing databases on Internet and Intranet.

Online/Virtual Crimes and Security

Privacy and security are two sides of the same coin," said Kurtz. "If we can improve Web security, we will be able to have a positive impact on privacy as well." Presently, Web/cyber crimes have become a common threat on internet. To overcome this issue, compulsory Virus Proof procedures should be adopted while downloading e-information from any other system. To secure the system from viruses, the databases can be modified by hacker proof procedures. Separate login and password systems are to be compulsorily adapted to the Network systems.

In the LAN environment, the real danger is the gradual erosion of individual liberties through the automation, integration, and interconnection of many small, separate recordkeeping systems, each of which alone may seem innocuous, and wholly justifiable. To overcome the above database security problems and issues, it is essential to install a database security software or firewall technology like Norton Anti-virus software and IBM e-network Firewall technology to protect the databases.

Technology Challenges

Technology provides challenges to access information. The ALA's 1995 Code of Ethics clearly states that everyone should have access to information. The recent explosion of information available on the Internet presents challenges to the traditional American Library Association (ALA) code of ethics that is taught in library school. Librarians make ethical decisions every day on the basis of the culture of their organisations. Some organisations limit access to particular levels of employees by requiring a username and password; others may institute behind-the-scenes filtering software or restrictive policies for providing access to the entire Internet. Because these steps challenge the very essence of librarianship, the librarian must step in and voice concern for the patron's rights. Establishing well defined access policies will help to clarify who has access to the Internet, under what conditions, for what purposes, and with what restrictions. Policies should consider how to integrate the new technology and how its use reflects the objectives and values of the library.

Manpower Issues

Lack of skilled manpower to maintain the e-resources and to provide proper e-information service to the knowledge society is another main problem. Core competencies of library staff are expanding to include technology skills, personal skills, learning and teaching capacity, team skills, commitment to ethics, leadership skills, communication skills, creativity skills, designing and implementing skills etc. Hence library education must be redesigned to meet the new challenges and issues evolving in the knowledge society. Adequately skilled staff should be recruited to meet the increased demands of the knowledge society. With a rapidly changing environment both within and outside the library, staff development programmes are crucial to the continued success of the organisation.

Organisational Structure

Technology has broken down the rigid hierarchical structure of the organisations which is another important issue in changing the roles of the librarian in the knowledge society. Far from emulating the organisation of conventional libraries, the organisation and structure of digital libraries, and the division of labour within them, are open to considerable experimentation. For example, as publishers and professional societies disseminate works electronically, they are testing how far their investments should incorporate the full range of library functions, and the digital libraries license content from publishers and professional societies that manage their own repositories.

Collection of E-resources

Collecting the materials and making it available to all current and future users is another core value of librarianship. The challenge is for the librarian to contribute to establish realistic collection-development policies covering acquisition of and provision of access to electronic resources for users now and in the future.

With the increase in electronic resources, librarians and libraries are no longer just collecting and caring for print materials. Unlike a print book or a journal, electronic resources cannot be considered a permanent addition to a collection.

Payment for a product covered by a license is a payment to use the information product for a period of time that is usually specified in a contract. This payment is not for the outright purchase of the product or for ownership of all the rights to that product. A digitised collection means that libraries share the use of the collections with other institutions, not only locally, but also globally. It is the publisher who dictates how much access will be provided, which issues will be available, and how much that access will cost.

Preservation/Archiving of E-resources

To preserve the e-resources for access would be a contradiction in an electronic environment for librarians, where there is unlimited and continuous access, but performance is not there in such an environment. This leads to the conflict on what is to be preserved and what is to be accessed. If we need to preserve electronic resources/ documents, we need to preserve all the software and hardware also to read the documents that we create. Currently, there are two radically different solutions for preserving digital information: migration and emulation. Neither solution is without some risk.

Migration may not work for specialised, proprietary formats. It may save the content of a file but lose or diminish the internal relationships or contexts of the information. The second strategy, emulation, assumes future access to multiple data objects. If one or more of the components were missing, this complex environment would most likely fail. Distribution and archiving through digital repositories will insure that the library has a viable system for sustaining digital content. Digital repositories also will facilitate the long term conversion and preservation of print materials, and create new opportunities to structure learning activities around the content.

Lack of Clarity in Vision

The biggest challenge that the librarians are facing in the knowledge society, seems to be lack of clarity in vision and a general lack of direction. A general vision is needed and the general integrated plan should be shared among the library professional, which should bring unity of purpose. The Library professional should become capacity builders and facilitators to the knowledge society. The vision of the library professionals should emphasize on the quality of services provided to support teaching, research and public service activities, to enable the users to become self sufficient and to make the library both a place and gateway for accessing information within and beyond the walls of the library.

Impact of Web-based e-Learning Systems

The emergence of web-based e-learning systems through Internet facility has great impact on every facet of library activities and information services. Library and information professional of the future academic libraries face the following paradigm shifts due to the rapid developments in the ICT and WWW technologies:

- Transition from procuring and managing print media to electronic media.
- Changes from passive user to active user in the e-literacy environment.
- Concept of web-based networked environment.
- Disseminating information on demand to proactive digital information services.
- Providing information service to facilitating access to e-information service.
- Transition of developing the normal collection to e-resources (e-books and e-journals).
- Individual works to team works.

CHANGING ROLES OF FUTURE ACADEMIC LIBRARY PROFESSIONALS

The changing role of library professional implies a set of updated skills needed for facing the challenges created by the latest web technologies in the elearning environment. The emphasis will shift from technical skills in the library to communication, facilitation, training and management skills. Although technology presents the librarian with ethical challenges, the librarian is to be ready for the role of information professional in the connected networked world and they have to acquire skills that can be contributed to success in their new roles.

Leadership Role

One primary role of librarians is to provide leadership and expertise in the design, development, and ethical management of knowledge-based information systems in order to meet the information needs and obligations of the patron or academic institution. In the future, as now, we can expect the virtual library to be the organisation that identifies, selects, negotiates for, and provides access to an incredible range of information resources on our behalf. At present, lot of virtual libraries have been created and managed by various institutions and organisations for e-learning and teaching professional. Hence library professional should enrich their management skills to play leadership role in the digital future, for organising, managing and disseminating e-literacy to users.

Proactive Information Professional Role

The modern trend is for the role of the librarian to move from that of a passive intermediary role responsible for guiding patrons to appropriate information resources, towards that of a much more proactive professional role which includes analysing and repackaging information, content information management systems and institute digital repository management systems.

Role of Librarians as Masters of Web

To face the challenges of the virtual learning environment in educational institutions, librarians are becoming masters of the Web. Librarians create powerful web sites such as the National Library of Medicine's PubMed database. They create their own web site as an easier way to share with others what they know. They gather electronic information and create electronic pathfinders and front-end search tools to help users for accessing the required information. Academic Library professionals create online tutorials and instructional web pages to help patrons for performing the best searches. They provide links to web sites on specific topics and lead patrons to these evaluated sites as a starting point for retrieving related and relevant information.

Role of Information Scientists in Digital Libraries and E-Literacy

Librarians have to change their role in the e-learning environment by participating in e-learning experiments and becoming involved in universities' e-learning centers. They should invest in procuring e-learning tools and software and should develop their e-learning and ICT skills. Hans Roes addressed changes in education in general, and then focused on strategic opportunities in education for libraries.

The opportunities for libraries, he mentioned, included:

- Developing digital libraries as natural complements to digital learning environments to support educators with respect to the selection of adequate resources for a given course;
- Managing and indexing digital student portfolios and integrating them with other information resources offered by the library;
- Teaching information literacy to educate future knowledge workers, in traditional ways or via Internet-based instruction modules;
- Collaborating as part of multidisciplinary teams of experts to design courses;
- Providing a learning center to serve as a physical learning environment suitable for more active learning styles

Role of Digital Space Manager of Academic Institutions

The librarian has an important role in making digital space accessible to members of an academic community on campus and beyond, in addition to providing physical space for assembling communities of interest.

A number of faculty members have data sets that they may wish to post for review and comment by colleagues on or off campus. Some academic and research libraries have expanded the concept of providing access to scholarly work by becoming electronic publishers of faculty projects and by providing institutional repositories, where faculty can store their scholarly work under the stewardship of the library.

Librarians also can participate in the institution's e-portfolio programme, in particular, by providing advice and expertise on information policy issues and preservation strategies.

Role of E-Resource Managers

Academic and research libraries have a major role in ensuring that they and their home institutions remain vital players in the changing terrain of information and education. Faculty may not aware of copyright issues and do not know what material is electronically available or licensed by the library. Virtual learning systems can be connected to library systems, through the integration of library systems at the back end via the technology components, and through the close liaison and involvement of library staff in VLE development, *i.e.* the human component. MacColl says that:

- "VLEs are changing the way learning and teaching is delivered and will soon be ubiquitous. Libraries must assert their traditional role as resource managers in this new environment of web-based courses".

A MOBILE FUTURE FOR ACADEMIC LIBRARIES

In the past few decades, some technological changes have appeared gradually and their impact on higher education has been incremental. In other cases, over relatively short periods of time, technological changes, such as the introduction of Web browsers, have had a major, and some would say revolutionary, impact on higher education as well as the broader society. Which will it be for mobile devices? Will their impact be gradual and incremental or sudden and revolutionary? There is a case for both points of view. Since individuals have been using devices such as laptops and mobile phones for decades, one might argue that the impact of the use of mobile devices on peoples' behaviour in general and on higher education in particular has been relatively gradual.

On the other hand, as devices with compelling new features emerge and wireless connectivity is almost ubiquitously available, we may be on the verge of a revolutionary phase of mobile device impact on higher education and libraries. This stage will examine trends and developments for mobile devices and will discuss what impact they may have on the future of academic library services. The stage focuses on a few types of mobile devices (particularly smartphones and e-book readers), selected applications for mobile devices, and provides some thoughts on the implications for library information and services. While many academic libraries are experimenting with various types of reference services for users of mobile devices, fewer are thinking of the potentially dramatic changes that the uptake of devices with sophisticated capabilities may have on their user community and more specifically on the use of digital information resources.

Keeping abreast of this rapidly changing arena can be challenging, and this stage attempts to provide an overview of developments of significance to academic libraries. The 2010 edition of the annual and influential Horizon Report, sponsored by the New Media Consortium and the EDUCAUSE Learning Initiative, came out at the time of the writing of this stage. Mobile computing was the first trend they identified, with an adoption timeframe of one year or less. The 2010 report marks the fourth appearance of mobile computing on this annual list of key technology trends for higher education. The report is compiled through a process to first identify a wide array of current and emerging technologies, which are then ranked in importance by an international advisory board using a modified Delphi process.

Therefore, many individuals around the world who are involved in developing, using, and monitoring technologies in higher education believe that mobile computing has great significance for our education institutions. Last year's report commented, "Over the past several years, we have watched mobiles become ever more capable and more common. The rapid pace of innovation in this arena continues to increase the potential of these little devices, challenging our ideas of how they should be used and presenting additional options with each new generation of mobiles". The students that we serve in higher education often own a variety of mobile devices, including laptop computers, cell phones, and MP3 players or other audio player devices.

The annual EDUCAUSE survey of undergraduates' use of technology stopped asking about student ownership of cell phones because they are so ubiquitous. However, they have been asking about ownership of Internet-capable handheld devices for the past few years so that they can monitor this emerging trend. In another survey, about half of students reported owning an Internet capable handheld device and around 12 per cent said they plan to purchase one in the next year. Many students do not use the internet capabilities of their devices at present, primarily due to cost considerations. In order to better understand how students might want to use internet-capable cell phones, the survey asked this year about potential uses.

Only 14.8 per cent selected "library services" as one of the top three institutional services they would most likely use from a smartphone. While librarians might feel discouraged by this number, I think it is likely that students do not yet understand the full range of library content and services that they might potentially reach via a smartphone.

DEVICES

Mobile devices include laptops, netbooks, notebook computers, cell phones, audio players such as MP3 players, cameras, and other items. This stage will focus on smartphones (and assumes the inclusion of the iPod Touch, which has the features of a smartphone minus traditional telephone capabilities) and on e-book readers. The array of names used for telephone handheld devices can be confusing, *e.g.* cell phone, mobile phone, handheld device, smartphone, etc. The use of the term "smartphone" has become popular to identify devices that have Internet capability and functionalities that are similar to computers, although there is no industry-wide standard definition of the term. The capabilities and uses of smartphones have gone well beyond the simple cell phones of 20 years ago.

When Americans first bought cell phones, they used them for communication on-the-go and the communication was solely via voice phone calls. While Europeans, Asians, and Africans have long used their mobile phones for text messaging, many Americans were much slower to move into this different mode of communication via the phone device. Only when the service became more predictably affordable and teenagers in households quickly adopted the mode of communication did texting begin to take off in the US. The third way that individuals use some cell phones – smartphones – for communication is e-mail; internet-capable models such as Blackberries and iPhones make checking and writing e-mail from many venues possible and more convenient than carrying a laptop computer in all travel situations.

In a period of around twenty years, mobile phone devices have become much more versatile, allowing communication between and among individuals in at least three ways that are now considered mainstream, *e.g.* voice, texting, and e-mail. In addition, other modes of communication, such as the use of Twitter or communicating updates on a Facebook page, are becoming popular activities on cell phones. While this range of communication capabilities has significance for libraries, especially in the provision of reference service, it is possible that it will actually be the use of smartphones for reading, watching, listening to, and producing digital content that will have the most impact on libraries. The lightning pace of development of new applications, or apps, for smartphones such as the iPhone, is enhancing the ability to use a wide range of information resources in various formats on handheld devices.

At MIT, with the introduction of the iPhone in spring, 2007, they found that the functionalities "spurred mobile web access on the MIT campus, especially among students. For many users, the mobile device was no longer just a telephone; rather, it was quickly evolving into a handheld information retrieval device." The 2010 Horizon Report states, "Third party applications for all kinds of tasks can now be developed once and ported to a variety of mobile platforms... It is these applications that are making mobiles such an indispensable part of our lives. Tools for study, productivity, task management, and more have been integrated into a single device that we grab along with car keys and wallet." It is truly remarkable to consider the kinds of activities one can engage in today using a single handheld device, including:

- Voice and video calling.
- Sending and receiving e-mail.
- SMS text messaging.
- Searching the internet.
- Searching databases of scholarly information.
- Organising citations.
- Accessing a course management system.
- Reading or listening to books and articles.
- Taking photos.
- Playing videos.
- Making videos.
- Setting an alarm clock.
- Using a GPS navigation system.
- Playing games.

In effect, the smartphone can provide capabilities that are very similar to laptop computers. One of the questions for the future is whether individuals will prefer to own one device that has many functions but may not perform all of them well or own a number of devices. It is likely that individuals will vary in their reliance on a smartphone for various functions. For example, a serious photographer will likely own and use a separate camera, and someone who writes lengthy documents (*e.g.* college students and faculty) will likely continue to have some type of computer that has a larger monitor and keyboard. Another question is what other types of devices will emerge and win popularity. Roy Tennant reports on prototype wearable technology devices that include cameras that can record information and use it to find information related to an item and then project that information onto a surface.

A library user could aim the camera to a code on a book in the stacks, software could connect the code to information or reviews about the book, and then project that information onto a surface. We may see more use of codes on labels, similar to bar codes that will link physical objects to information on the internet. Lorcan Dempsey reports that the University of Bath in the UK is already using codes -- specifically a type called QR codes in its catalogue. A user can scan the code into his or her phone and go into the stacks to find it with the call number readily available on the phone. In addition, the user can save the information provided by the code to begin compiling a bibliography. Libraries have traditionally served as a public good, providing resources and services to all, including those who could not afford to purchase some types of content or services on their own. While it is unlikely that libraries will provide smartphones, either for use within the library or for loan because most would agree that provision of telephone service is outside the scope of library service, many libraries are already loaning a wide variety of mobile devices.

For example, laptops are one type of mobile device, and many academic libraries have laptop loan programmes. Some libraries also loan cameras, video cameras, MP3 or similar audio player devices, headphones, etc. A small number of libraries are loaning Internet-capable devices such as the iPod Touch. It is also possible that more departments or institutions will begin to require that students have a mobile device that can be used for a variety of purposes in their coursework. The library will want to be part of campus discussions on such decisions so that they can ensure that library content and services will be able to interoperate with the device and platform selected. The proliferation of mobile devices will have implications for library space configuration and services. For example, libraries may want to offer large monitors and keyboards that students can use with their personal mobile devices. They may want to install lockers with electrical outlets so that students can recharge their devices while they go to class or take a break.

And, they may want to change the ratio of desktop computers to open tables as more students rely on their own devices. Currently, many students who own laptops do not bring them to campus, but students almost always bring their cell phones wherever they go. In fact, this is true of people of all ages and nationalities. In an international survey, three quarters of respondents said they never leave home without their mobile phones. A market researcher affiliated with the survey commented, ". . . the mobile is part remote control, part security blanket. Mobiles give us safety, security and instant access to information. They are the number one tool of communication for us. . . They are our connections to our lives." As smartphones become our users' key information devices, libraries will want to have a significant presence in offering content and services suitable for those devices.

E-BOOKS AND E-BOOK READERS

E-books, or books in digital form, may be purchased or freely downloaded in formats that will enable individuals to read them on standard computers, or they may be configured in proprietary formats for particular devices. Most academic libraries already offer e-book content that users can download and read on standard computers. Amazon's Kindle device and SONY's e-book reader will soon be joined by the nook from Barnes and Noble; these are purpose-specific handheld mobile devices. These devices are linked to content purchase programmes that limit what may be put on the device and in some cases, what may be shared with others. Both companies that produce e-books for computers and companies that produce e-books for their proprietary systems are now offering or promising to offer content configured for Smartphones. Some academic libraries are already experimenting with lending e-book readers loaded with content or providing specific content to fulfil interlibrary loan requests on an e-book reader. It is difficult to predict whether such devices will grow in popularity or will cede their market share to smartphones. The larger screen makes these devices more acceptable for some users to read online materials they might have formerly preferred to have in print. However, the current limited functionality, for example inability or poor capability for annotation or note taking, has made them less acceptable in some areas of higher education, particularly as textbook substitutes. The app for smartphones, released by Eucalyptus in fall, 2009 may be a harbinger of some trends. First, it has a page-turning function that gives the feeling that one has when turning the pages of a physical book; readers may like this feature.

Second, it makes available books from Project Gutenberg, one of the earliest projects to digitise books and make them available to the public; all books are out of copyright. The Eucalyptus homepage even advertises one of its functions as "Search like a librarian", a positive attribute of their system. The availability of a large collection of digitised books, Project Gutenberg, also brings to mind the potential impact that the Google Book Settlement may have on the availability of e-book content. Will collections of content be marketed through the e-book reader producers? Will the content, either public domain or in-copyright, be repackaged in collections and made available to libraries or the general public in formats for various devices or with enhanced functionalities for particular devices? E-books may be seen as a mechanism to promote environmentally friendly practices.

Princeton University has launched a small experiment in which around 50 students enrolled in three courses have been given Kindles in order to determine whether the use of the device reduces the amount of printing by students. The university estimates that 10 million pages were printed by students in computer labs in a year, and they believe that much of that printing was of materials on electronic reserve from the library. The experiment will help the university determine whether e-book readers reduce the cost of printing and conserve resources. While the experiment was developed primarily for financial and environmental reasons, at least one of the professors whose course is included is also interested in whether the e-book reader can enhance student learning. The library, computer center, and faculty are collaborating on this project.

MAKING PAYMENTS VIA DEVICES

Another trend that may have an impact on libraries and other areas in higher education is the capability to use mobile phones for payments for goods and services. In particular, there is an emergence of applications for contactless mobile payments that use radio frequency identification technology (RFID) to enable mobile subscribers to make payment by waving their device directly in front of a terminal or automated device, such as a vending machine. Globally, the payments made via these systems have exploded, from $3 billion in 2007 to $10 billion in 2009. Libraries will want to keep abreast of any campus initiatives to move to this type of technology for vending machines, printers, etc. so that their needs can be taken into account. This will be yet one more activity that mobile phones may be used for by our community.

MOBILE DEVICES, STUDENTS, AND LEARNING

As librarians work with students as part of information literacy classes, at service desks, and in cyberspace, it is important to realise that for students, the mobile device will increasingly become an instrument for creation of digital content, and not just a device for access to content. Students can use smartphones to create short videos, to type a blog entry for a class assignment, to "tweet" in response to a question posed by a professor or to create a group poem, or to take photos or record audio to embed in a Powerpoint presentation or text document. Some of this content creation may be in connection with independent assignments and some may be developed as part of coordinated class field work.

In describing the potential use of mobile devices for elementary students on field trips, the researchers wrote, "Mobile devices can capture authentic educational multimedia data, in context, that have previously been unavailable. Data captured in context allows for sharing and remembering experiences upon return to the classroom. Using multiple forms of data capture, for example, supporting photographs with audio recordings and student notes can assist students and teachers in seeing the whole picture of a learning experience." Librarians can teach students about the availability of access to information from their mobile devices in the field, to support research. They can assist students in learning about software to organise their information on their smartphones or how to develop mash-ups using geographic applications and other information resources

They can support students' creative work with mobile devices. This requires an awareness of innovative assignments, outreach to faculty, and the skills to teach these technologies. In one application developed for students with laptops and targeted for science classes, LectureTools allows students more functionality than a typical personal response system or "clicker." The professor can ask students questions beyond multiple-choice, enabling them to work with images or respond to more complex questions. In addition, a student has developed some applications for LectureTools, including one that enables students to connect with others, finding which students may live in the same dorm or share particular interests.

While LectureTools is employed on laptop computers, these types of functionalities may be adapted for smartphones in future. The incorporation of active learning functions along with social networking capabilities makes this a particularly interesting tool. One can imagine librarians incorporating the use of such tools in information literacy classes. Another model is the Hotseat application, which allows students to use either their laptop or their mobile phone to comment or ask questions during class. Faculty involved in pilot classes using Hotseat have found that the application encourages participation by more students when controversial issues are discussed, enables students to share information among themselves and to set up ad-hoc study groups, and encourages more interaction between professor and students.

As more and more students buy internet-capable phones and when phone plans that include internet access become more affordable, students will seek streamlined ways to locate the kinds of information they need. Campus information portals for mobile devices are one emerging model, and some academic libraries are already represented in these venues. Another model will be the development of applications, sometimes by members of the university community, including students. At Stanford University, two undergraduates along with friends built an iPhone app "iStanford" that provides some of the features of standard university portals, *e.g.* access to the course catalogue. In addition, they are releasing features that will allow students to access grades, add and drop courses, and perform other activities usually restricted to the secure campus network.

The students have worked with the Stanford information technology unit to integrate, with university approval, their application into core computer systems at

Stanford. Librarians should seek faculty on their campuses who are developing or using innovative tools like those described here and begin experimenting with them in partnership with faculty and students. Mobile devices can offer more opportunities for students to be actively engaged in their learning and to fully participate in the social nature of learning. Librarians might encourage, through contests or other means, student development of apps that make library content and services more useful for specific groups of users.

DIGITAL LIBRARIES OF THE FUTURE AND THE ROLE OF LIBRARIES

Research on digital library (DL) systems started in Europe in the mid-nineties. At that time DLs were seen essentially as repositories of digital texts accessible through a search service which was operating by indexing information stored in a centralised metadata catalogue. The construction of a DL was very resourceconsuming since, for each new DL, both the content and the software providing the DL functionality were built from scratch. As a result of this development approach, only powerful user communities or user communities with in-house computer science technical skills could afford the building up of DLs. These DLs were created to serve end-users only as consumers of information. They did not provide any functionality for submitting the documents.

The submission was usually performed either by the author or by a librarian operator by means of specific procedures residing outside the DL. Today, the requirements imposed on DLs are very different from that early time. A novel notion of DLs, also referred to as "knowledge commons" has recently emerged, whose fulfilment requires new technologies and new organisational models. This paper focuses on such new DLs by first discussing the motivations for their introduction, then presenting an innovative DL technology, called DILIGENT, and, finally, illustrating the role that libraries can play in this new scenario.

DIGITAL LIBRARIES OF THE FUTURE

According to the most recent understanding, the DLs of the future will be able to operate over a large variety of information object types - far wider than those maintained today in physical libraries and archives. These information objects will be composed of several multi-type and multimedia components aggregated in an unlimited number of formats. These, for example, can mix text, tables of scientific data and images obtained by processing earth observation data, or they can integrate 3D images, annotations and videos. These new information objects will offer innovative and more powerful means to researchers for sharing and discussing the results of their work. In order to be able to support these objects, the DL functionality has to be appropriately extended far beyond that required to manipulate the simple digital surrogates of the physical objects. In order to support these objects the DL may need considerable resources.

For example, the creation and handling of the new documents may require access to many different, large, heterogeneous information sources, the use of specialised services that process the objects stored in these sources for producing new information, and the exploitation of large processing capabilities for performing this tasks. New DLs are also required to offer a much richer set of services to their users than in the past. In particular, they must support the activities of their users by providing functionalities that may range from general utilities, like annotation, summarisation or co-operative work support, to very audience-specific functions, like map processing, semantic analysis of images, or simulation. The availability of this new DL functionality can, in principle, change the way in which research is conducted.

By exploiting such types of DL, for example, a scientist can annotate the article of a colleague with a programme that extracts useful information from a large amount of data collected by a specific scientific observatory. This programme, executed on demand when the annotation is accessed, can complement the content of the paper with continuously refreshed information. In the new DLs users are not only consumers but also producers of information. By elaborating information gathered through the DL they can create new information objects that are published in the DL, thus enriching its content. The new DLs are thus required to offer services that support the authoring of these new objects and the workflows that lead to their publication. In parallel with the evolution of the role of DL systems, we are now observing a large expansion in the demand for DLs.

Research today is often a collaborative effort carried out by groups belonging to different organisations spread worldwide. Motivated by a common goal and funding opportunities, these groups dynamically aggregate into virtual research organisations that share their resources, *e.g.* knowledge, experimentation results, or instruments, for the duration of their collaboration, creating new and more powerful virtual research environments. These virtual research organisations, set up by individuals that do not necessarily have great economic power or technical expertise, more and more frequently require DLs as tools for accelerating the achievement of their research results. This new potential audience demands less expensive and more dynamic DL development models.

They want to be able to set up new DLs that serve their needs for the duration of their collaborations in an acceptable timeframe and with an acceptable cost. The current DL development model cannot satisfy this large demand; a radical change is needed if we want to be able to address these new emerging requirements. A great contribution towards the satisfaction of all the requirements can certainly come from the introduction of mechanisms that support a controlled sharing of resources among different organisations. Sharing in this context is not only applied to repositories of content, as is usually meant today, but can be extended to any type of resource needed to build a DL, *i.e.* language and ontology resources, applications, computers and even staff with the necessary skills for supporting the DL development, deployment and maintenance.

Supporting this type of sharing requires the introduction of appropriate solutions at both the technological and organisational levels. These two levels are not independent; instead they strongly influence each other. In fact, the availability of a good technological solution favours the creation of an appropriate organisation, and vice-versa, a successful organisation stimulates the development of new supporting technologies. We present the DILIGENT infrastructure as an example of a technological solution for these new DLs. The organisational aspects stimulated by the introduction of this technology are briefly discussed afterwards.

DILIGENT

DILIGENT (DIgital Library Infrastructure on Grid ENabled Technology) is a three-year Integrated Project funded by the European Commission under the 6th Framework Programme for Research and Technological a Digital Library Infrastructure that will enable members of dynamic virtual research organisations to create on-demand transient digital libraries that exploit shared resources. Resources in this context are multimedia and multi-type content repositories, applications, and computing and storage elements. Following the understanding of DLs expressed in Borgman *et al.*, this project focuses on the development of DLs that "are not ends in themselves; rather they are enabling technologies for digital asset management, electronic commerce, electronic publishing, teaching and learning, and other activities".

From an abstract point of view, the DILIGENT infrastructure can be understood as a broker serving DL resource providers and consumers. The providers are the individuals and the organisations that decide to publish their resources under the supervision of the broker, according to certain access and use policies. The consumers are the user communities that want to build their own DLs.

The resources managed by this broker are content sources (*i.e.* repositories of information searchable and accessible through a single "entrance"), services (*i.e.* software tools that implement a specific functionality and whose descriptions, interfaces and bindings are defined and publicly available) and hosting nodes (*i.e.* networked entities that offer computing and storage capabilities and supply an environment for hosting content sources and services).

Providers register their resources and give a description of them by exploiting appropriate mechanisms provided by the infrastructure. The infrastructure also automatically derives other properties of the resources that are used to enrich the explicit description. The infrastructure manages the registered resources by supporting their discovery, monitoring and usage, and by implementing a number of other functionalities that aim at realising the required controlled sharing and quality of service. A user community can create one or more DLs by specifying a set of requirements. These requirements specify conditions for the information space (*e.g.* publishing institutions, subject of the content, document types), for the operations that manipulate the information space (*e.g.* type of search, tool for data analysis), for the services for supporting the work of the users (*e.g.* type of personalised dissemination, type of collaboration), for the quality of service (*e.g.* configuration, availability, response time) and for many other aspects, like the maximum cost, or lifetime.

The broker satisfies the community's requirements by selecting, and in many cases also deploying, a number of resources among those accessible to the community, gluing them appropriately and, finally, making the new DL application accessible through a portal. The composition of a DL is dynamic since the DL broker continuously monitors the status of the DL resources and, if necessary, changes them in order to offer the best quality of service. By relying on the shared resources many DLs, serving different communities, can be created and modified on-the-fly, without big investments and changes in the organisations that set them up.

In order to support the transactions between the providers and the consumers, the DILIGENT infrastructure exploits the virtual organisations (VOs) mechanism that has been introduced in the Grid research area. This mechanism models sets of users and resources aggregated together by highly controlled sharing rules, usually based on an authentication framework. VOs have a limited lifetime, are dynamically created and satisfy specific needs by allocating and providing resources on demand. Through the VOs mechanism the DILIGENT infrastructure glues together the users and the resources of a DL.

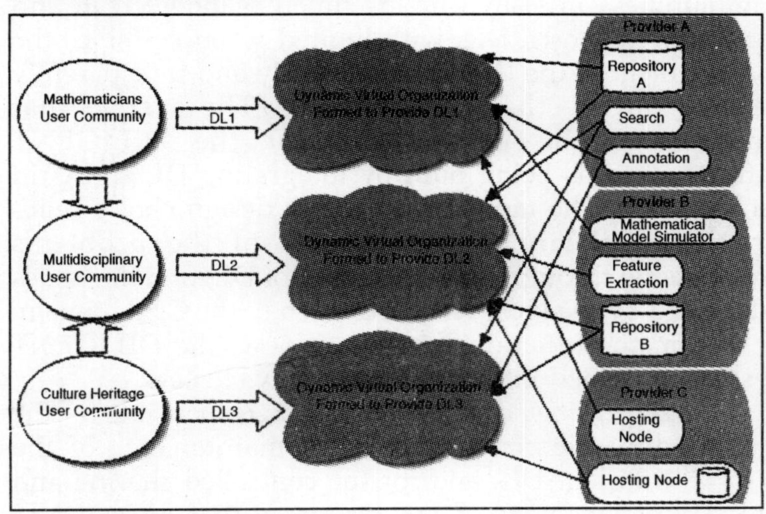

Fig. 1.1 The Role of Virtual Organisations in DILIGENT

Figure 1.1 graphically illustrates the role of VOs in supporting the brokerage model. The consumers, *i.e.* the user communities that require DLs to support their needs. The providers, each of which makes a number of resources available, are on the right. The infrastructure acts as a mediator by maintaining a framework where multiple virtual organisations, active on the same shared resources, can co-exist. The DL development model proposed by DILIGENT is radically new. Within the described framework each DL consumes the required resources only for the time it needs them.

This opens a lot of new opportunities for the creation of the functionalities required by the new "knowledge commons" environments. In particular, the exploitation of more effective, but also very computationally expensive algorithms becomes viable at an acceptable cost for many communities. For example, thanks to sharing, the use of the high processconsuming algorithms that automatically extract features from multi-media objects can be exploited in a large number of DLs. Moreover, in the framework established by the new development model, the user communities can easily, and in a timely manner, create and maintain their own DLs with limited resources since the management of the DL is automatically and transparently carried out by the infrastructure. The system that implements the functionality of the DILIGENT infrastructure is being built by integrating DL and Grid technologies. The motivation for this design choice relies on the similarity between many of the problems encountered through our new notion of DLs and the issues addressed by the most recent research in the Grid domain.

From the functional point of view, the DILIGENT system is divided into five functionality clusters:

- *DL Creation and Management:* is responsible for the dynamic construction and maintenance of the transient DLs and for the controlled sharing and management of the resources that are used to implement them. The functionalities offered by this cluster allow users to express the requirements that the DL must fulfil. Moreover, they automatically identify and arrange the pool of resources needed to satisfy these needs.
- *Content and Metadata Management:* implements the handling of DL content and related metadata, the consistent and distributed management of annotations, and the integration of external content and metadata sources.
- *Process Management:* manages the creation of user processes composed of existing services, the

validation of their correctness, the automatic optimisation of their definition according to the resources available and the service characteristics, and their reliable execution. Thanks to this feature, the DILIGENT system can easily be enriched with additional operational workflows to meet new user requirements.

- *Index and Search Management:* is responsible for enabling cost-efficient search and retrieval of information in DLs, while satisfying the level of quality required for the overall data retrieval and delivery operations.
- *Application Specific Functionality:* provides the functionality needed to support user-specific scenarios, like portals, document visualisation, or features extraction.

From the architectural point of view, the DILIGENT system is designed as a Web Services Resource Framework (WSRF) application built on top of the gLite Grid middleware released by the Enabling Grids for Escience in Europe (EGEE) project. gLite hides the heterogeneous nature of the computing elements (*i.e.* services representing a computing resource) on the one hand and storage elements (*i.e.* services representing a storage resource) on the other hand by providing an environment that facilitates and controls their sharing. The DILIGENT services are being initially deployed on a project-proprietary gLite infrastructure. Architecturally, this infrastructure is completely interoperable with the EGEE infrastructure. EGEE is currently the largest European Grid infrastructure ever built.

A number of other recently funded projects will extend this infrastructure to other geographic regions, like Mediterranean countries, Latin America, or China. The interoperability with the EGEE infrastructure will allow any authorised virtual community that wishes to create DLs to also exploit the resources made available by this vast Grid infrastructure. During the project timeframe, the DILIGENT infrastructure will be populated with a number of important archives and software applications provided by the two communities that are participating in the experimentation with the results of the project, one from the environmental e-science domain and one from the cultural heritage domain.

The first community is ImpECt (Implementation of Environmental Conventions) and includes leading players in the environmental sector. This community will use DILIGENT to support the organisation of conferences and the preparation of projects and periodical reports. Through DILIGENT this community expects to improve accessibility, interoperability and usability of environmental data, models, tools, algorithms and instruments, integrating the distributed data sources with specialised data handling services. The second community, ARTE, is a community of scholars located in different parts of the world, working together to establish a new discipline that merges experiences from research in medicine, humanities, social sciences and communication.

In order to achieve their objectives, these researchers require instruments to ease the construction of multimedia artefacts and to improve support for education. At the time of the writing of this paper initial experimentation with the features of a DILIGENT DL has already been conducted by implementing simplified services for preparing environmental reports, as required by the ImpECt environmental agencies. Through the exploiting of rich information sources, ranging from raw data sets to maps and graphs archives, these agencies periodically prepare reports on the status of the environment. Currently, this task is performed by first selecting the relevant information from each of the multiple and heterogeneous sources available, then launching complex processing on large amounts of data to obtain "products", like graphs, tables and other summarised information and, finally, producing the required report by assembling all the different parts together.

This process, which is repeated periodically, requires a lot of work due to the complexity of interfacing the different sources and tools. Despite the effort expended, the resulting reports do not completely fulfil the requirements of their readers, who would like to have a picture of the environmental status which is updated at the time the report is accessed. A DILIGENT DL offers a more effective framework for the creation and maintenance of these reports. In our experimentation, for example, we have built a DL which exploits content maintained in both repositories including textual documents and archives of Earth observation raw data provided by the European Space Agency. In this DL, which is accessible through a single user interface, all the different kinds of information necessary for creating the reports can be found.

By combining this information and by defining how to derive the associated "products" (images, tables, or graphs) from raw data, the users can create their reports much more easily. Moreover, a specialised user interface allows authorised users to access these composite reports by choosing static or dynamic generation. The selection of dynamic generation triggers associated process workflows which, by combining appropriate applications, generate the required products on demand by processing both the raw data and other intermediate products stored in the DL repositories. The dynamically generated products are obtained by running those applications that are computationally intensive on the Grid.

In this way the complex processes required to generate the products are executed in few minutes at a limited cost to the community that is exploiting them. In order to obtain the same performance without the Grid, an institution would have to equip its digital library with a great number of computers, while in the case of DILIGENT the institution can also exploit computer capabilities made available by third party organisations. The same is true for storage capacity. Maintaining raw data, intermediate products and high resolution images requires a large amount of storage capacity. By exploiting the Grid technology, part of this information, especially the temporary part, can be maintained in third-party storage systems.

THE ROLE OF LIBRARIES IN FUTURE DLs

In the framework envisaged by DILIGENT, libraries play an important role at the organisational level. In particular:

- As providers of resources, they can help to enhance the amount of available resources by making stakeholders aware of the importance of sharing. In particular, as far as the sharing of content is concerned, they can operate by promoting digitisation campaigns and the Open Access approach. These actions may result in a vast amount of new digital information accessible online which can be exploited by advanced services.
- Also within a digital framework, libraries are certainly the best candidates for carrying out content description, maintenance and preservation of resources. By exploiting their large experience acquired in the past, they can contribute to the long-term availability and to the quality of the resources disseminated by the DLs.
- Long-term availability also requires the implementation of models able to support the sustainability of the resources provided. Libraries, either alone or as members of library consortia, can also act as the organisations deputed to define and put in place these models.
- As main resource providers, libraries can work jointly on the definition of common policies and standards. An agreement on these aspects would strongly contribute towards facilitating the design and development of the new complex services required to fulfil the emerging user needs.
- In the future envisaged by DILIGENT, libraries can also play an important role as mediators between the infrastructure and the user communities. In particular, they can proactively promote and facilitate the creation of DLs that respond to the

needs of the user communities. They can also assist users by providing, if necessary, the skills required to select, update and exploit the DL content and services.

CONCLUSION

So we can expect to see a shift from a service *provided* to a community to one in which *local people are more active and involved* in its design and delivery. Libraries will be recognised as connecting individuals, communities and organisations to innovate, create and provide new library based services and ideas. People will be using libraries to do more with each other and this activity will cross over between physical and virtual spaces. They will be creating new content, having conversations and using new technology for their own benefit, for their community or their business. Those working in libraries will be less occupied in straightforward transactions and more involved in linking people and organisations together in using library spaces and resources for new activities.

There will be a greater emphasis given to community, digital and entrepreneurial skills. In this context, volunteers offer new ways to add capacity and skills. Libraries' role out in the community, reaching vulnerable and excluded people, will extend to popping up temporarily as local circumstances demand and allow. This might involve using vacant spaces, or being invited in to other community services or workplaces to meet particular needs. If the library of the future will look different from those of the past and present, their enduring role and purpose means that some things will feel familiar. A high value will continue to be placed on the importance of quality leadership, professional skills and experience.

Books will sit comfortably alongside digital and other cultural resources in a rich and diverse library collection. Finding the information to answer any question, books to satisfy the never-ending desire for pleasure, learning and knowledge, and the practice of literacy as one of life's basic skills, will remain at the heart of what makes a library, and what will place the library at the heart of the community. Our national role means that we are well-placed to stimulate debate and offer support to the development of public libraries, and we want to work with our partners based on the thinking that has emerged in our research.

How that is reflected locally will be determined by each council based on their own priorities and the needs of their communities. It is this combination of enduring values, new thinking, collaborative leadership and flexibility that will equip public libraries to create economic and social benefits for this country and its communities long into the future.

2

Technology and Public Libraries - Present and Future

INTRODUCTION

There are many quotes and claims that come to mind in discussing the present and future of libraries and technology. For one, there is Santayana's famous admonition that we must study the past or we will surely repeat it. From my long experience, I remember too well one of the profession's mavens opining at the 1973 ALA Library Automation Preconference in Las Vegas that librarians would not have jobs in 10 years unless they became programmers, too.

Having spent more than two decades in virtually daily struggle with the management of computers and related technologies, what I have to say will fit no easy category. Unqualified claims of the printed word's demise in the foreseeable future are idiotic. Yet militantly ignoring technology's offerings and the varied media via which information is conveyed, make the ostrich's sand-buried-head appear to be enlightened.

As; to the claims of the technocrats that we must acquire their jargon, techniques, and protocols if we are to continue in this profession, an especially appropriate response is Ralph Kramden's hearty har, har, har. This speech was prepared on a microcomputer with overwhelmingly greater capacity and speed than the IBM mainframe upon which my work with library automation began in 1968, at a small

Massachusetts company. You do not have to know how to programme, but an understanding of how the machine works and what it can and cannot do are essential if one is going to manage data processing projects in a public library.

Optimally, such an understanding should inform the use of data processing technology, too. No one is trying to set up straw people to burn down with simplistic arguments. The need for a reasonable perspective in viewing technology must be to the point, not the outrageous claims of technocrats or Luddites. Let us now commence the serious part of this palaver with a view of the development and application of technology in contemporary libraries. And we will endeavor to see what courses will be pursued in the next decade. These directions should be yielded from the technological context developed. In this respect Mr. Santayana will be given his due.

TECHNOLOGY ALTERNATIVES

The alternatives will be explored by first reviewing data processing and related technologies in their technological setting.

COMPUTERS

Mainframe, Mini, and Micro computers are high speed data processing devices capable of doing an incredible variety of tasks at extraordinarily high speeds. Computers store, access, compute (*i.e.* process), and display information, and have been used with increasing success by libraries in the U.S., since the 1960's. But it might be noted that the late John W., Cronin as Chief of the Library of Congress Card Service installed International Business Machine (IBM) tabulating equipment as long ago as the late 1930's for fund accounting purposes. Maintaining reasonable definitions and distinctions between these categories of computers is virtually impossible. The most powerful microcomputer of today dwarfs the mini-computer of the early 1970's and many, if not all, of the smaller mainframes of the 1960's. Mainframes, minis and microcomputers will be distinguished by use rather than by strict data processing definition.

MAIN FRAME COMPUTERS

Main Frame Computers are used primarily in large scale applications such as the major North American catalogue networks, *e.g.* OCLC (Online Computer Library Center), UTLAS (formerly, University of Toronto Library Automation Systems), RLIN (Research Libraries Information Network) and others; and some of the very largest libraries, such as The New York Public Library, University of Chicago, Library of Congress and others. These mainframes have been used primarily as cataloging resource utilities. The major exception is the turnkey local system, NOTIS. It was developed and runs on a mainframe IBM computer.

It has been written down so it can run on smaller IBM computers, but basically it was developed for and has been used by large universities and scattered public libraries who use a portion of the resources of the jurisdiction's IBM mainframe. More about local systems later. In terms of economics, the sole ownership of mainframe computers is fiscally beyond the finance of all but a few of the very largest public libraries. What's more, who would want one? They are far more expensive and more complicated to operate than the other computers to be discussed. And beautiful and wondrous applications have been developed to run on machines which the average public library, on its own or in consortium with other libraries, can reasonably afford.

ONLINE CATALOGING NETWORKS

OCLC is the biggest of the online cataloging networks. OCLC is used by over 6000 libraries to search for cataloging copy, to enter individual library catalogue holdings, to obtain catalogue cards and other catalogue products, for interlibrary loan, and to maintain and produce union list of serial holdings (including full serial cataloging). All of the OCLC functions are performed online through interactive telecommunication between the local library and the OCLC computer facility in Ohio. (Recently, CD-Rom products derived from the OCLC database have been options added to the OCLC workstations.

It should be noted that OCLC actually employs a variety of computer devices The database of over several 10s of millions of records has been stored on the original Sigma mainframe computers upon which the network began in the late 1960s, and the telecommunications traffic is handled by Tandem computers, which, depending on their size, can be viewed as mainframes or minis. In the ver near future, unless I missed it already, the Sigma will finally be carted away from OCLC and be replaced by current generation computing equipment.)

Other networks such as Utlas, RLIN, and WLN, have shifted with the times. RLIN will have replaced its IBM mainframe with the CRAY computer, supposedly the single most powerful machine in functional captivity today. Utlas replaced its Sigma mainframes in 1985 or so with Tandem computers. These networks use their behemoth equipment to serve thousands of libraries and store their holdings

ONLINE BIBLIOGRAPHIC DATABASE SERVICES

The online bibliogtapic database services are different. Local holdings generally are not an issue, but what is important is the for-pay access these services provide for a myriad of databases. Mainframe computers are used also for maintenance of, access to, and searching of such online bibliographic database services as DIALOG, ORBIT, BRS, WilsOnline, and others. Such data bases are searched by users from all over the world, typically gaining access via some form of telecommunication device and a local terminal or computer.

Some pros and cons need to be indicated here, and can be elaborated upon later. Even though these databases are online, they are not online in real time the way OCLC and the others are. The individual databases serviced by DIALOG, for example, are updated monthly, quarterly, or even more slowly than that. OCLC is updated instantaneously. When a library enters a holding to the database, it is immediately made available to all 6,000 users. For want of a better definition, this notion of instant updating and record availability is a way of understanding "real time".

A second major deficiency of DIALOG, ORBIT and BRS is that the various databases to which they provide access, all have different search rules (protocols is the fancy word for rules). This means that someone who knows how to speedily and effectively search ERIC may not have any idea how to search Predicasts. On the other hand WilsOnline, being a service offered by a single company for all of its databases-a couple of exceptions notwithstanding-does not require a different set of protocols for each of its databases. This is an important issue and points to a major direction for the future, that is, the normalisation of databases. Lets continue with technology review.

Minicomputers are smaller, but still quite powerful computing devices which have been quite effectively used in local library or regional automation efforts. They have been especially effective in such applications as online circulation control systems for individual libraries (as with many college and university libraries, plus some public libraries), and libraries in combination (*e.g.* public libraries with many service outlets; regional public library systems consisting in many individual public libraries; and consortia, *i.e.* several libraries in combination, sharing a single minicomputer.)

For almost twenty years the MINICOMPUTER has been successfully used to maintain control of all of the books (and other library materials) held by all of the libraries participating in the system. It indicates where they are located (*i.e.* on the shelf, in circulation, or any other status), who has them, reserves or holds them for use by library patrons when they are not immediately accessible; it maintains a complete record of all of the registered library users which includes their name, address and other appropriate information so that the user can be notified if he or she has overdue books, a reserved book is available, or for other information pertaining to library service; it also keeps track of the amount of money owed by individuals who returned their books late.

Individual suppliers of these minicomputer based systems have addressed such applications as online acquisitions; online catalogs [confusingly referred to as PACs (Public Access Catalogs)]; serials acquisitions, cataloging and check-in; film control and booking; and special collection control (an important application for libraries which have special collections such as videos which may circulate only for one or two days at a time).

More and more libraries are using these minicomputer-based systems for full public access catalogue use and complete circulation control. Note well that the precondition for such applications to run on the minicomputer is the creation of a machine readable database of the library's holdings. The conversion of library holdings to machine readable form has been the biggest obstacle to the complete and successful automation of libraries. Invariably the conversion of the data to a form manipulable by the computer is the most problematic, difficult, and expensive part of automation.

MARC

Things would be a hell of a lot worse if there were no standardised format, the MARC format. Because of MARC everyone can use and share the same data for conversion purposes. Of equal importance is that a competitive market exists of automation purveyors, all of whose systems are predicated on MARC-based databases. All of the software for these minicomputer systems is written to operate on MARC records. There is no way to adequately explain within the time constraints how incredibly important this standardisation of cataloging data, the MARC format, is. Let's move on to the most exciting and fun machines to use.

MICROCOMPUTERS are used primarily in single library and single function applications. There are a variety of microcomputers available and in use by U.S., libraries. Microcomputers are being used in such administrative applications as fund accounting, word processing, and data base management. The kinds of microcomputers used to perform these functions typically are based on the Intel chips, that is, the 8088, and the 80286 - 80486 chips which are on the IBM PC, XT, AT, and compatibles; and the Macintosh, which is based on the Motorola 60000 series of chips. From smart toys and hobbyists' enthusiasms, micros have evolved to become devices with as much as 16 to 64 million bytes of random access memory, and which store over 600 million bytes of data on a single hard disc drive. Devices of such monstrous capacity (and smaller ones, too) can support sophisticated local area networks of PCs and/ or terminals.

Microcomputers are being used to perform such library functions as acquisitions, cataloging, serials control, and circulation control. In the last couple of years they have been used, too, as public access catalogs and sophisticated database storage and searching devices. Typically, most micro based systems do not accept, process or output cataloging data in conformity with library standards, that is, the MARC record. However, there are exceptions, and definitely more are coming along.

What has made the big difference in capacity for micros is the storage medium, CD-ROM. CD-ROM stands for Compact Disk - Read Only Memory. The CD-ROM platter is capable of storing over 16,000 pages of information, and is approximately 511 wide. The combination of the PC, a CD-ROM reading device, and a CD-ROM disk with a database on it, have made possible unprecedented extensions of automation, and more specifically have made possible the distribution of databases on to PCs which heretofore could only be stored on mainframe computers with massive disk storage.

With all of the equipment required to use a CD-ROM now costing less than $2,000, a library now has the hardware for storing and accessing the entire U.S. MARC format database. The compaction of data, the relative inexpense of the CD-ROM storage medium, and the reduction in unit cost for data processing as represented by the PC have made it possible to provide the most sophisticated applications to operate wholly self -sufficiently in the most remote and tiny locations. The only requirement is a stable power source compatible with the equipment.

CD-ROM is the extremely powerful solution to the tremendous costs of remote site online telecommunication charges to a host computer. With CD-ROM the database sits out there in Timbuktu. With terminals online, we have to pay the phone company for providing the connection between the terminal where we are and the computer at some remote site. Many public libraries have several databases that are on CD-ROM at their disposal: Books In Print Plus and Ulrich's from R.R. Bowker, Dissertation Abstracts, WilsOnline, InfoTrac, etc

In addition to such bibliographic databases, companies such as the Library Corporation of America make the MARC database available on CD-ROM as well as software to search it and prepare catalogue cards and labels from the MARC records. This particular product is called Bibliophile and it has been very successful in as a source or medium for inexpensively capturing Library of Congress cataloging data.

Bibliophile also provides for the printing of catalogue cards and labels from the Library of Congress catalogue record. No more typing catalogue cards and labels. Through Bibliophile a database of MARC records could be created for the books cataloged. Library Corporation will take the records created locally from its Bibliophile product and create a CD-ROM catalogue of the library's holdings. Public and other libraries all over the country have availed themselves of this service.

MICROGRAPHICS

The two major areas of micrographics employed in libraries today are the traditional photographic micro reduction of hard copy documents, and computer based micro reduction. With photoreduction, the hard copy document is photo-reduced to microfilm, 16×, 24×, reductions all the way down to 75× and 150× in some ultrafiche reductions. Computer micro-reduction is usually 42× or 48×, that is, a reduction to 1/42nd or 1/48th of the size of the original document, had there been one.

Both microfilm and microfiche have been used for storage and/or preservation of: deteriorating materials, infrequently used materials, and those items which suffer from vandalism, misuse, or for some other reason need this protection. The other reason is simply to save space. In addition microform is an alternate and cheaper means of subscription to some materials, *i.e.* many libraries with limited budgets in an inflationary economy find it acceptable to acquire given serials in microform rather than hard copy. The disadvantage is that the serials cannot be received on a timely basis.

COMPUTER-OUTPUT-MICROFORM (COM)

Computer-Output-Microform (COM) is a medium used by libraries since the 1960's which successfully utilises both the data processing and microform technologies. Instead of photoreducing hard copy documents, the information displayed on COM is converted into machine readable copy from hard copy format or directly keyed into machine readable form, thus manipulable by the computer to suit the given library application. The machine readable data, instead of being displayed (*i.e.* printed) in hard copy form by the printer, is input to the COM device. The COM device, also called a "camera" because of its camera-like function, converts the machine readable data into its visual analog format, *i.e.* it displays it on a cathode-ray-tube (CRT) screen in a human readable (not digital) form. The CRT display is then projected through a lens onto reel microform at extremely high speeds. In this manner either 16mm microfilm or microfiche are created. (Note that the microfiche are created as a single roll of film and cut into the individual sheets later.)

There are a large number of libraries in the U.S.A., which have COM catalogs, but since the inception of CD-ROM, their number is diminishing. It is an extremely compact medium, a given sheet of microfiche can contain the equivalent of 224 pages of computer printout. It is relatively inexpensive, as the largest costs are associated with the data processing effort required for organising the machine readable data into the desirable manner of display, *i.e.* the way the catalogue is to look. The costs for the COM master and the copies from which it is made tend to be modest, assuming the catalogue is not too large. Many libraries have found that COM catalogs are a viable intermediate step between the card catalogs which still exist, and. the online catalogs which require far more expensive equipment to use, host computers with online terminals.

Libraries also are choosing CD-ROM catalogs as final options which are replacing the COM catalogue, and eliminating online catalogs as a goal. The cost of online catalogs and the problems of telecommunications have provided the basis for the success of the CD-ROM catalogs in competition with online catalogs. Note that they are not a panacea.

CD-ROM catalogs are always out of date, and the frequency of updating is a function of the size of your pocket book. Getting back to COM, it generally has functioned as an inexpensive storage medium and it has eliminated bulky and comparatively expensive paper listings. It is used best as a disposable product, and is not thought of as an archival medium. For example, many libraries use COM microfiche for current on-order information. Since libraries tend to order, receive and cancel (orders for) books on a frequent basis, a COM listing of the status of the orders must be fairly frequent if it is to be of value. Hence the disposability of the COM on-order file and its regularly being supplanted by a more current edition. It is also the case that libraries use COM as a substitute for any necessary computer generated report that involves a large amount of paper.

Finally COM does not enjoy a great future; as the cost of computing storage and processing continue to drop, the viability of online interactive systems increases, thereby eliminating a major reason for utilising COM. The other major reason COM will further erode as a remote display medium is the aforementioned CD-ROM. Major COM catalogue manufacturers now offer CD-ROM catalogs to customers with increasing success in selling the medium. All of the costs associated with CD-ROM are far greater. As noted the CD-ROM requires a PC and the CD-ROM player. With COM all that is required for display is a $150 – $200 reader. The preparation of the COM masters and duplicates are appreciably cheaper as well. Typically the master costs from $10 - $25, and each duplicate fiche is about $.25 depending on the supplier.

MORE ABOUT CD-ROM

This leads to a discussion of the CD-ROM medium. The more comprehensive term is laser recording and display media. By the use of the laser technology the information is encoded on to a silver platter of varying size and varying storage capacity. There are Optical Disks and CD-ROMs, the two laser media prevalent today.

Optical Disks are relatively new as regards library usage. Experimentation is proceeding with this medium as a storage device capable of holding much more information than is found in microform; two gigabytes (*i.e.* 2 billion bytes or more than 65,000 pages) stored on a single optical disk; they are capable of producing appreciably clearer images on playback or display; and lastly, they are capable of combining on a single optical disk both digital and analog (*i.e.* pictorial) information. The Library of Congress and other major research libraries are studying this closely as another means of preserving deteriorating books.

Since optical disks, as noted, include digital information much work is being done to find applications which will combine the computer's indexing, searching and control capability with the laser disk's capacity for accessing pictorial information through digital data encoded on the disk as well. Note that the optical disk is read or examined by a laser device and displayed on a television monitor or some other form of cathode-ray-tube display device such as a computer monitor.

One company has taken huge medical databases and placed them on optical disks, and reduced the storage device costs of the databases by many factors. Some optical disks are known as WORM disks, *i.e.* WO for Write Once, RM for Read Many times. These applications are usually tied to devices significantly more powerful than microcomputers.

CD-ROM: This disk, to which reference has been made several times, especially in the microcomputer discussion, has become a, hot item in United States library discussions, and its impact is just beginning to be felt. CD stands for Compact Disk, and ROM means Read Only Memory. Each disk can hold about 500 million bytes of information, which means that over 16,000 pages of data can be stored on a single platter. The extraordinary impact of CD-ROM is that it provides the distribution of massive databases, including sophisticated retrieval capability, while at the same time requiring none of' the prohibitive telecommunications costs normally associated with the distribution of databases to remote sites. All that is required for access to a database, such as the Library of' Congress MARC database, is a PC compatible microcomputer with a CD-ROM reader and control card, and the CD-ROM platters with LC' MARC, which is several million records large at this point.

In the past libraries would incur major phone line charges to call the computer upon which resided the database to be searched. Plus the library had to pay towards the cost of storing that database on the computer online. As noted here and earlier, tremendous cost savings are thus realised, and the CD-ROM is sitting there waiting to be used whenever one chooses to use it. Several libraries have chosen the Bibliophile product over membership in OCLC because it is so much cheaper for them to catalogue with Bibliophile.

Many U.S., library systems or consortia, rather than face tremendous telecommunications charges, are putting their public catalogs on CD-ROM, rather than connecting terminals via dedicated phone lines to the circulation system computer. This application strikes one as particularly valuable when one thinks of regional or distributed networks where resources may be scarce and access to sophisticated telecommunications technology may be either limited or prohibitively expensive. If CD-ROM would be the primary distribution medium, there would always be a built-in delay for the time required to create and duplicate the platters from the machine readable data (four to eight weeks).

Most recently, with the help of consultants or specialised in-house staff, libraries are creating Local Area Networks (LANs) which connect several micros and/or terminals to a host microcomputer which has the CD-ROM product. In this way, many people can simultaneously (almost) have access to the single CD-ROM station. This is a high tech way to make the lean dollars of the 90's stretch even further while still providing cutting-edge service.

Perhaps one last point should be made about CD-ROM and its advantages over COM. COM is a much cheaper medium, but one cannot utilise the indexing and searching capability that the computer and CD-ROM provide in combination. Boolean searches on keywords, subject terms, names, parts of names, etc. all are possible with CD-ROM based systems. So the extra cost of CD-ROM versus COM pays for appreciably greater search and retrieval. capability, a capacity far exceeding that of the traditional card or book catalogue. Without further belaboring the CD-ROM technology's virtues, one will now discuss telecommunications, the big giant to which the little CD-ROM seems to be providing an alternative.

Telecommunications is an area of great specialisation and, as a major technology, has its own discipline to be mastered. No attempt will be made to indicate just how complex this area of technology is, nor even to explain the various telecommunications processes. It will suffice to indicate the kinds of roles telecommunications may play in a distributed information network.

The use of telecommunications in the contexts discussed here means the use of phone lines as the means by which a user at a remote site communicates with the central site computer or anyone at another remote site. (Much less frequently, other means for transmitting messages such as satellite, microwave dish, or radio frequency transmitters may be used.)

If there is a phone line specifically established for such communication, and if it is used solely and exclusively for that purpose, then it is called a dedicated line. If a phone line can be used for a variety of calling purposes, one of which is calling the computer from a remote site, then the remote terminal. has dial-up capability.

For both dedicated and dial-up lines to be used, special equipment is required on the terminal and on the computer that will permit the data to be converted into a form that can travel between the computer and the terminal, and then converted back so that it can be displayed on the terminal or processed by the computer-depending on the direction the data is headed.

The telecommunications equipment is expensive, but even worse, the telephone charges themselves are extremely dear. And worst of all, the weakest link of all online systems is the phone line. WLS has non-stop transaction processing equipment, that virtually never goes down. But, our library users are connected to this computer via phone lines which go up and down far too frequently. It is pathetic how much we are at the mercy of Ma Bell.

The library has a telecommunications bill of over $10,000 per month. It would have been double that price if we had been unable to take advantage of a special federal tariff. What is painful to realise is that there is nothing in the actual usage of the lines that has any bearing on the doubling or halving of the charges. It is simply a matter of our escaping the local billing policies and coming under the jurisdiction of the federal tariff.

The telecommunications equipment was approximately 1/4 of the price of the total system, that is $350,000 of a $1.4

million dollar purchase price. The system currently supports 220 terminals at 45 sites, those being all WLS member libraries, plus the Bedford Hills Women's Correction Facility.

These astronomical costs are why U.S., libraries are turning to CD-ROM and other non-phone line alternatives for distributing data. The interesting trend that seems to be emerging is that online terminals are used and will continue to be used where the data must be accessible in real time and must be maintained and current to the moment. Online circulation systems which keep track of who has which books and which books are in or out, are examples of the justification of online communication with the computer. Online catalogs are harder to justify. For example, if a library's database consists of 500,000 volumes, if it adds twelve thousand volumes per year, and its CD-ROM catalogue is updated quarterly, then the most someone will be denied access to will be 1 per cent of the library's holdings. And there are alternate ways of making that three to six months of information available so that it is not entirely inaccessible to the library user. In this way the library is spared the substantial telecommunications bill for online public access catalogs, while the users will still have access to most of the titles held by the library. The discussion of technologies would not be complete without briefly touching upon Video and Cable communications.

VIDEO AND CABLE COMMUNICATION

Video and Cable communication are technologies being used by libraries in a variety of ways:

- Video and cable communication are being used simply as entertainment and educational media within libraries much the same way they are used in the home. Libraries have extended this function by either videotaping, broadcasting or otherwise making available information of value to the local community not otherwise accessible to that community.

- Public libraries have been especially exploiting the home videocassette market by buying and circulating to their clientele entertainment and educational videocassettes.
- The potential for this medium as an information dissemination tool is great. It is not yet being used very effectively in this manner. Libraries have focused on theatrical videos as a boost to circulation. It is hoped that they will find a way to promote the growing wealth of information and programming available on video that goes beyond the box office hits.

WLS uses cable communication as an educational, political and entertainment medium. Guests have ranged from the WLS Board President, to the County Executive an Assemblyman and other politicians, to Arthur Ashe, Roger Kahn, Alan Arkin, Paul Schrader, the President-Elect of NYLA, your speaker tomorrow, and many others. It is shown regularly by the County's several cable companies.

Two-way cable communication has been used by some libraries to enhance reference service. Libraries have placed TVs in public areas, both for cable and video playback viewing. Libraries have also served as Cable Studio or broadcasting facilities This is an extraordinarily powerful information medium that as public library people, we must exploit more fully. We are in the information business, and we must work with all information media.

THE FUTURE

There are a few things that have to be said, now that we have gotten this far:

- First, I don't believe that I will ever read a mystery in bed that is in any form but a book. I do not believe that people will wish to read fiction, poetry, or serious literary or philosophical works in a medium other than the printed page.
- Second, microforms are the worst form of displaying materials in the library. No one in their

right mind, all things being equal, could possibly prefer to view or read anything on microform if the same information is available on a printed page or a CRT display, either of which are incomparably better than the microform picture. It is interesting hoe little the microform display has improved over the last several decades.

As artifacts and as media for protracted use, and not to mention, pleasure, books have a secure place in libraries, and for sure, in my home. Much more can be said in addressing the future in libraries, but I'll make a few more points and turn the floor over to you for questions and comment.

- The database services will reach more and more, and smaller and smaller public libraries, via the CD-ROM medium. Even with the growing sales of the WilsOnline product, there has been no decrease in the number of subscriptions to the parallel print products. Regarding Bowker's products, it would be interesting to know If libraries discontinued their BIP subscriptions once they subscribed to the BIP+ CD-ROM product. In any case, over the next 15 years, libraries will add more and more micro-based products. CD-ROM (and whatever more compact medium succeeds it) will become increasingly prevalent. Depending on the phone lines and the future of telecommunications, it is likely that public libraries will eventually have most of their bibliographic control processes accessible via online terminals. The extent to which these services will be available online to the public will be mostly a function of cost. I would safely predict that there will be a blend of CD-ROM and online services available to the public at the local library. The CD-ROM data is the best backup for the online database, even if it is a bit pricier than COM.
- Cataloging and technical services will fall into even greater disrepute because of the impossibility

of having quality databases without attendant costs. The basest canard is the attack on the catalogers for doing what they are supposed to do.

OCLC suffers from irreversible bibliographic chaos because there is little quality control over what goes in, and all-too-little quality control over what comes out. What catalogers called authority work, and what lay people expect simply as consistency in headings, has been deteriorating at an accelerating pace since the 1960s. It costs a great deal of money for a library to ensure that all works of an author can be presented to the user, or that all editions of a work are related properly, or that all materials on a subject are brought together. With OCLC as the chief cataloging resource for US libraries, with the decreasing numbers of catalogers, and with the increasing determination of library people to have everything online NOW, less and less will be related by human enterprise, and more and more will be lost to the unsuspecting user.

Machine searching power will compensate somewhat, by permitting searches with wild cards or question marks. But how can the computer possibly know that Donald Westlake and Tucker Coe are the same author? To the extent that local systems will have authority files, *i.e.* files of names and topics, and all the appropriate references to and from those names; and to the extent that those files are linked to the catalogue files, the user will stand a better chance of getting all of Westlake's works displayed as the result of a single search.

The sorry story is that libraries will find it increasingly difficult to pay for catalogers to review and revise names and headings for a local database. In addition there still is a long way to go before local systems will be able to readily import the name and topic data for their internal authority files, and there still is much much more to be done to develop local system software which will integrate and refresh all of the locally resident bibliographic records to reflect correct names and topics.

The most positive note is that the unit cost of data processing technology has been decreasing dramatically each year. Computers and related technologies are there for us to use, to enjoy and to deliver essential information and recreational services to our clientele, the citizens of our community. It is essential that the public library continue to be the bulwark of our democracy that provides barrier-free access to its resources, be they print, machine-based, or human. We will continue to need all three if we are to continue to maintain a high standard of service over the next decade.

3

A 2020 Vision and Plan for Library Technology and Service

The New York State Board of Regents challenged the library community to rethink the State's vast array of library services to ensure that they are aligned with modern expectations and the expanded functions needed in today's society, operate with improved efficiency, and are prepared for the future as an essential and vibrant part of the State's educational infrastructure. Working through the Regents Advisory Council, library users, trustees, and staff have spoken out with regard to their libraries, offering not only affirmation of the importance of libraries, but also numerous suggestions for progress and models of success.

PURPOSE

The Board of Regents is responsible for the general supervision of all educational activities within the State of New York. The Board of Regents charters public and association libraries, as well as Pre-K-12 schools, colleges and universities, and cultural institutions, both public and private, which operate school, academic and special libraries as a critical component of their educational programmes and services. The Board of Regents also oversees the New York State Library and the 73 library systems that tie these libraries and other special libraries - located in hospitals, courts, businesses, government agencies, prisons and other public and private organisations - together into a robust statewide network of some 7,000 libraries.

The Board of Regents must also articulate and promote a vision that inspires and promotes excellence in all the educational institutions within its purview. Though the original charge for this effort was for "Vision 2020," we believe that the future of libraries can be found right before us in the remarkable work currently being done by visionary librarians, library staff and trustees who understand the needs of their constituents and respond with innovation and service. Therefore, the primary purpose of this document is to provide the Board of Regents with a clear vision of what excellent libraries should look like and to offer models of success that may be emulated by libraries throughout New York. Specific Regents' policy suggestions that would move this vision forward are noted where appropriate.

LIBRARIES - AN INVESTMENT IN OUR FUTURE

Libraries provide the physical and virtual spaces that are an integral part of an overarching system that provides continuous opportunities for learning from birth to senior age. By offering all New Yorkers the opportunity to acquire the knowledge they need to be informed and engaged participants in an open democracy, libraries empower individuals. Library "profit" is demonstrated through both the promotion of economic enterprise and the social return on investment. Libraries continue to undergo tremendous transition as they move to virtual services in response to changes in technology and the expectations of their patrons, and as they facilitate not only the use of existing information, but also production of new information through online communities and efforts to preserve local history.

One significant change is the increasing convergence among traditionally different types of libraries in the services they offer. Such convergence includes online access to digital resources, the re-tasking of library space, the need for staff skilled in virtual librarianship and collaborative learning, as well as more customary types of service. Because of the continuing centrality, complexity and diversity of today's knowledge creation and information distribution environments, it is important that our students and residents be equipped with both print and digital literacy skills — how to find, evaluate, and effectively use information from a variety of sources and formats.

Literacy - and in particular digital literacy — lies at the heart of the mission of all libraries. Regardless of the many levels of technological change, libraries remain the embodiment of Americans' "right to educate themselves", a critical necessity in a knowledge economy where everyone must relentlessly improve their skills throughout their lifetime.

The library is what makes lifelong learning for *all* residents both possible and practical, including, and perhaps especially, for those with special challenges such as the disabled, homeless and economically disadvantaged. People unable to respond to new challenges and invest in their own abilities are likely to become an economic liability, unable to participate fully in society. Libraries continue to represent a community investment in a vision of a better tomorrow through sharing information, knowledge and, hopefully, wisdom. They are the repositories for the collective memory of our communities, our state, and our nation, and offer us an institution that reflects the American dream of self-help and equity. Today's libraries are busier and more vibrant than ever because of, not in spite of, the dramatic impact of digital technology. But even though they have a well established and well respected brand, libraries suffer from outdated public attitudes based on misperceptions that are limited to their traditional roles, stereotypes and the constant assault of competing commercial information providers.

UNIVERSAL RECOMMENDATIONS - FOR ALL LIBRARIES

The themes of Access, Information Literacy and Sustainability are woven through all libraries in our state and nation. Though each serves its unique community, all share these values.

MODELS FOR SUCCESS

Over six decades ago the State of New York outlined its vision for universal access to information for all residents through its creation of library systems. This remarkably successful model has evolved to embrace nearly all the libraries within our state, creating a framework and foundation for the fulfillment of this dream. The notion that any and every child or adult may follow their curiosity to its fullest extent, accessing resources from around the world, is today a reality for most, but not all, of our state's residents. Vibrant libraries of all types, enjoying the robust support of their community or constituency and working in partnership with their library system and its collaborative systems are able to bring these resources into their communities. We have the potential to fulfill this vision for all.

RECOMMENDATIONS

To assure that tomorrow's libraries continue to be a vibrant and vital part of all New Yorkers' lifelong learning experience, all libraries must:

- Improve the marketing of library services to all clientele and communities by rebranding libraries while addressing the erroneous perceptions about the need for libraries in a digital world.
- Develop better tools for advocacy, and identify library champions at all levels of governance: university and school boards, town and city management, State Education Department, Board of Regents, New York State Legislature and Executive branch.
- Collaborate to integrate services and collections of all types of libraries while developing a transparent and seamless world of library services that are ubiquitous and instantaneous, yet personalised and flexible, serving all ages and needs.
- Seek operational and cost efficiencies in light of technological opportunities, energy efficient facilities, and online service delivery methods.

- Develop economic justifications for the investments that governments, communities, individuals and philanthropic organisations are asked to make in libraries, and enhance the role of libraries as economic drivers for their communities.
- Recruit technologically savvy staff and train current staff in virtual librarianship while influencing higher education to appropriately educate tomorrow's service providers.
- Function at the front lines of e-resources (including e-books) purchasing, licensing, digital rights management, digital curation, resource-sharing, and preservation; and advocate for the delivery of open content as embodied in initiatives such as the Digital Public Library of America or the Berlin Declaration on Open Access to Knowledge in the Sciences and Humanities.
- Actively address issues concerning the privatisation of information and its impact on traditional models of library services, defending residents' rights to free access, free lending and the intersharing of materials among libraries.
- Create collaborative partnerships with all cultural and educational organisations in the state to offer our residents the most comprehensive educational opportunities available anywhere in the world.

SCHOOL LIBRARIES (P-12)

School libraries are deeply engaged in the implementation of the New York State P-12 Common Core Learning Standards. There is a well documented connection between student achievement and effective school libraries. The role of school librarians is evolving as they teach students information literacy to be savvy information consumers, producers and judges of appropriate content in all formats. School librarians increasingly collaborate with teachers in designing curricula, developing learning experiences, and providing technical infrastructure that are ideally placed to support differentiated instruction and facilitate special programmes for the gifted as well as students with special needs. The school librarian is unique in that he/she addresses the depth and breadth of the entire curriculum, and leads in teaching a 21st Century curriculum of enquiry, problem solving and content creation.

MODELS FOR SUCCESS

The best school libraries are fully integrated into the P-12 learning experience and are at the hub of each campus, reaching into every classroom as well as into students' homes. Based on the research findings of the recent Information Brief: The Impact of School Libraries on Student Achievement published by the NY Comprehensive Center, it is clear that with the shift to the Common Core Standards and a commitment to five key elements of the Regents reform agenda, school libraries with certified school librarians play an important role in student achievement, curriculum development and instruction. Information and digital literacy is recognised as a critical aspect of each student's education. The school librarian is a true educational partner with every teacher and administrator in providing the best possible learning experience for each child.

RECOMMENDATIONS

The Board of Regents and State Education Department should formulate policy and regulation that will:

- Adopt and implement a statewide information fluency curriculum framework, aligned with the New York State P-12 Common Core Learning Standards, which, through certified school librarians and a strong library programme, will provide equitable access to information and digital literacy instruction and tools. Such a framework will further the schools' ultimate goal of preparing students, beginning at the elementary level, with the literacy and digital skills and knowledge needed for career or college.

- Expand the existing Commissioner's Regulations to require a certified elementary school librarian in every school to strengthen instructional leadership in meeting the P-12 Common Core Learning Standards, and enforce library staffing regulations in all public schools.
- Create incentives to encourage school districts to actively expand and promote access to the school library collection of online resources, e-books, and Web 2.0 tools, available 24/7, to create learning and enrichment opportunities that reach beyond the school day and encourage yearround learning.
- Create incentives to encourage school districts to adopt flexible scheduling to support full academic day access to school librarians, school library resources and information and digital literacy instruction.
- Create incentives for school libraries to collaborate with other libraries and communities to result in full-time, full-year access to information that will further opportunities for all students.

ACADEMIC AND RESEARCH LIBRARIES

Academic libraries are the engines that support teaching, learning, critical thinking, research, and collaboration on campus. They provide core support for faculty and student research, development offices, campus information technologies and alumni, and are leaders in the digitisation of research resources and the creation of content. Academic libraries are increasingly challenged by digital rights management and digital curation issues, costs of online research resources, and copyright law.

MODELS FOR SUCCESS

The best institutions of higher learning understand that their libraries are the heart of intellectual enquiry. Libraries provide or mediate access to many physical and digital resources for students, faculty and researchers, wherever their location. Libraries also provide digital and physical spaces for collaborative learning and research, free ranging intellectual discourse, cultural expression and housing of historically significant materials. Even in the digital age, the library building as a place – redesigned to foster collaboration among students, faculty and staff – maintains an essential role in academia.

RECOMMENDATIONS

The Board of Regents and State Education Department should formulate policy and support initiatives that will encourage:

- The development of a statewide/national digital library of shared use, freely accessible digitised books and research materials through the *Hathi Trust* and similar organisations.
- Active participation by New York's libraries in the Digital Public Library of America and the Internet Archive's Open Library initiative, in order that New York's freely available but disparate content can be accessed by all our residents.
- The acceleration of digitisation of special collections and their integration into curricula; and making those materials freely available for research.
- The publication of academic research generated by faculty that would be universally available at no cost to the user.
- Leadership in the preservation of digital resources and advocacy for open access and reduced copyright restrictions in the support of digital preservation.
- The continuation and strengthening of collaborations with other communities in support of lifelong learning, information literacy and research.
- Collaboration among all academic libraries in the development of print repositories designed to

reduce redundancies within collections while maintaining high levels of access and stewardship.

- Advancement of the primary role of academic librarians in fostering the integration of information literacy competencies into teaching and learning on their campuses to support student academic achievement and to prepare students for the global information economy that will shape their professional and personal lives.

PUBLIC LIBRARIES

Public libraries provide services that cannot be replicated elsewhere. They provide residents the right to free and equal access to information, a right now under duress with the development of commercial information services. Some of these commercial services are free but of questionable quality; others of high quality but high price; and others are comprised of collections that are no longer owned, but rented. Libraries provide a guide through such a maze of misinformation for the average citizen. They are a beginning point for early childhood literacy, a center for each community's history and culture, a key to the American dream for immigrants, and much more. The public values its libraries as a meeting place, a community center, and a learning place.

Residents desire more business hours; more traditional resources such as children's programmes and print books; and more e-resources such as electronic books. Public libraries are also digital knowledge centers for communities, ensuring residents' equal access to technology. This is especially true as the state transitions to e-government and many residents do not have access to the computers and broadband connectivity. In many areas, especially rural areas, the public library is the only source of broadband internet connectivity for the entire community. The quality of public library service remains unequal across the state. Reasons for this include community wealth, legal structure and lack of political support.

MODELS FOR SUCCESS

Public libraries reflect the highest ideals of the communities they serve. The best public libraries are places where the love of learning is instilled at the youngest age and intellectual curiosity encouraged for all. They provide a path to navigate life's challenges and help new Americans assimilate. As community centers they actively encourage civic engagement and cultural awareness while remembering the past by the preservation of community history. They actively strive to provide access to their facilities and their resources to all residents, especially for those who are physically or mentally disabled, economically disadvantaged or otherwise facing unique challenges in today's competitive world. Their success is grounded in their basis as a truly democratic institution, governed and supported by the people they serve.

RECOMMENDATIONS

The Board of Regents and State Education Department should formulate policy and support initiatives that will encourage:

- The further proliferation of the Regents' *Public Library District Model* to enable all public libraries to become fully funded and governed through citizen participation and public vote.
- All public libraries to proactively create and collect local content and serve as a catalyst for civic engagement to promote civil discourse and confront society's most difficult problems.
- Collaboration with other libraries and community organisations to develop seamless information literacy initiatives, promote cultural understanding and protect local historical and cultural treasures.
- Support state and national digital literacy learning initiatives providing this 21st century skill to people of all walks of life, not just those enrolled in schools and colleges.

- The provision of robust early childhood education programmes and the provision of homework assistance as a core service; the alignment of outreach services with societal priorities, such as teen services and gang prevention.
- The provision of full access to library services by people with disabilities, including accessible buildings, homebound services, and assistive technology.
- Investment in public library facilities in order to be able to respond to the changing needs of communities – rewiring of older buildings, creation of larger meeting spaces and small meeting rooms, flexible storage solutions so that libraries can adjust as print to e-format ratios change and energy efficiency improvements to keep operating costs down.

SPECIAL LIBRARIES (CORPORATE, LAW AND MEDICAL LIBRARIES, HISTORICAL SOCIETY LIBRARIES, ETC.)

Special librarians are invaluable because of their mastery of particular information content; they are charged with the provision of evidence-based, reliable, high quality information in a cost effective way. Historical and museum libraries face special challenges with regard to the digitisation, conservation, and preservation of special collections.

MODELS FOR SUCCESS

Professionally managed and dedicated to the sharing of information, the best special libraries offer unique collections and expertise of enormous value to the social, intellectual and economic life of our state.

RECOMMENDATIONS

The Board of Regents and State Education Department should formulate policy and support initiatives that will encourage:

- Making special library collections available to other libraries and the public.

- Collaboration with other libraries in the development of statewide licensing of electronic data bases and e-resources; participation in a state digital library/ digital repository.
- Innovation in the creation of new services such as the deployment of systems for intelligent processing and correlation of large data sets.
- The collaborative development of consistent, cost-effective digital preservation strategies.

NEW YORK STATE LIBRARY SYSTEMS

New York's network of library systems – school, public, and 3Rs councils – were created to facilitate collaboration and equalise library services across New York, but are not currently being funded by the state at a level to meet even minimum service needs. Systems provide documented economies of scale, but costs continue to rise and new services are in demand. Library systems should assist their members to adapt more quickly to new user expectations, provide the highest quality professional development and training opportunities to system members, encourage and prepare staff to be at the forefront of innovation, consider changes in governance, mergers, and collaborations, and collaborate more with the New York State Library. As library systems have had to ask their member libraries to cover more and more of the cost of services provided to them to make up for long-term underfunding by the state, there is concern that only the more affluent regions of the state will be able to afford superior library services. The new cap on property taxes may make it more difficult for member libraries to increase their financial support for their library systems to the extent needed to ensure that valued systems services can be sustained.

MODELS FOR SUCCESS

The most successful library systems reflect the needs of their membership, providing such services as cooperative purchasing, shared automation services, legal advice, continuing education, collaborative digitisation initiatives, and shared virtual reference. They are highly responsive to changes in the marketplace and the profession and prepared to take entrepreneurial risks to bring new initiatives to their member libraries and their constituents. Tomorrow's best library systems will share and consolidate services across library types, geographic boundaries and other governmental (and perhaps commercial) institutions. Each will excel in its own area of expertise while continuing to demonstrate a statewide model of collaboration, efficiency and cooperation.

RECOMMENDATIONS

The Board of Regents and State Education Department should formulate policy and regulation that will encourage:

- Increasing and providing incentives for collaboration among systems and with the New York State Library, as well as with other state agencies.
- An environment of flexible regional solutions without loss of state funding.
- Library systems to be at the forefront of training, professional development, technological innovation, outreach, marketing and branding, and other high-value services needed by member libraries.
- Library systems to explore models of broader and more intensive collaboration with their members through appropriate membership fee structures or charges for special services.
- Library systems to consider restructuring their governance and initiating partnerships for greater collaboration at the regional and state level; up to and including consolidation.
- Library systems - as with all libraries — to anticipate and develop innovative and entrepreneurial services; and to discontinue out-of-

date services when they no longer provide benefit to their members or the end-users.

- Public Library Systems to proactively encourage and assist their member libraries that are eligible to pursue the Regents' Public Library District model of public governance and support.

STATE LIBRARY/SED/BOARD OF REGENTS

There is a need for leadership at the state level in the areas of advocacy, issues related to the privatisation of information and challenges to the doctrine of fair use, collaborative acquisition and licensing of electronic resources, statewide programmes, and electronic content.

MODELS FOR SUCCESS

The most vibrant and effective State Library organisations are at the forefront of innovation, providing the leadership necessary to implement new technologies and services by leveraging statewide purchasing power and political clout to assist and encourage the advancement of all library organisations within their state. The focus is on creation and development rather than simply regulation and reporting.

This model of success recognises that libraries are essential to the educational, cultural and economic future of the state and are treated as full partners in the lifelong educational process of its residents.

RECOMMENDATIONS

The Board of Regents and State Education Department should formulate policy and regulation that will:

- Reaffirm the importance of libraries in the lives of all New Yorkers.
- Enable the New York State Library to make its licensed electronic resources available to businesses having fewer than 100 employees.
- Mandate public library trustee education similar to that required of School Boards.

- Mandate library staff training; make all Public Librarian Certificates renewable contingent upon ongoing professional development, including 10 hours of annual technology training.
- Remove regulatory and legislative restrictions to intersystem and statewide cooperative purchasing negotiations while empowering the State Library to take the lead in negotiating statewide licensing for e-resources.
- Encourage the New York State Library and the state's library systems to develop statewide delivery infrastructure and to investigate the need for a statewide union catalogue.
- Promote legislation that protects against filtering and other forms of censorship.
- Require the State Library to continuously review and update outdated standards, guidelines, and regulations. Provide clear and relevant standards, guidelines, and regulations designed to improve library services.
- Provide legal assistance for public libraries seeking district library status.
- Create incentives for collaboration, innovation, and shared services among systems.
- Encourage and reward best practices throughout the state.
- Direct the State Library to develop appropriate training, including in the areas of advocacy and development, to be required for all boards and advisory councils to improve governance of libraries and library systems.
- Ask the Governor and Legislature to fully fund the State Library as a part of the State Education Department and as an essential component of the State's educational infrastructure.
- Recognise the Board of Regents' responsibility for its role as statewide library advocate, and avoid viewing library services only through the prism of

P-12 education. Libraries and library systems of all types are essential to raise the knowledge, skill, and opportunity of all the people in New York.

TECHNOLOGY AND THE INFORMATION MARKET PLACE

While library collections may have gone far past the tipping point between physical and virtual by 2020, libraries themselves will continue to evolve as community centers for both technology and intellectual pursuits. Many digital resources, including e-books, are leased, not owned. To counter this, shared cloud or virtual libraries, such as those under development by the Hathi Trust and Digital Public Library of America should be developed to serve as surrogate research libraries. The research community must make sure that valuable content is not locked up by commercial interests. There must be greater attention paid to the development of affordable statewide digital platforms, negotiated statewide licenses for electronic books, periodicals, research databases, and similar materials. NOVELNY or a similar initiative must continue to grow, and libraries of all kinds must digitise local content.

RECOMMENDATIONS

The Board of Regents and State Education Department should formulate policy and support initiatives that will:

- Address copyright, licensing, and digital rights management with one firm voice.
- Encourage the growth of NOVELNY or a similar initiative by adding more e-resources of all kinds for statewide access.
- Identify the current costs of e-resources from all public funds to best determine economies of shared acquisition and use across all schools, libraries, public universities, and state government agencies.
- Foster the development of a common statewide e-book platform and address the particularly high

costs of *STEM* (Science, Technology, Engineering and Mathematics) online electronic resources.

- Encourage branding of all e-content to demonstrate libraries' value to remain visible and relevant to end users, wherever they may be.
- Encourage all libraries and library systems to anticipate and participate in the development of a single, digital library with rich functionality that serves all.

SUSTAINING OUR LIBRARIES

This plan, with its sixty recommendations, many based on successful models already operational, makes it clear that libraries - as educational institutions and community centers - are central to the well-being and economic development of the state. While it is difficult to establish priorities for funding when there is so little available, it makes sense to develop those resources – like libraries and library systems – that are part of the solution to the problems we face as a state and as a nation. The genesis of this planning document was the recognition that significant new state aid for libraries was not imminent. However, it is hoped that this report to the Board of Regents makes it clear that libraries and library systems cannot be sustained and continue to be responsive to the needs of our state's residents without increases in financial support.

The visible and vocal support of the Board of Regents is essential to the success of this effort. As a starting point, the Board of Regents should support full restoration of library funding as outlined in the Education Law. Before it is too late, and libraries are forced to cut even more staff and hours - or close altogether – fair funding for new programmes and services as outlined in this Plan is needed. These recommendations should serve as the basis for specific legislative proposals from the Board of Regents and library advocacy organisations to build a foundation of success for our libraries over the next decade.

4

Library Information Services Using Cloud Computing

SAVING LIBRARIES WITH TECHNOLOGY

There has never been a harder time for libraries: unprecedented public funding cuts, required to cope with a deep economic downturn; the challenge of keeping abreast of rapid change in the technologies of content and search and discovery; and the quiet but insistent questioning of what role there is for public libraries in the modern world. Responses have been varied but predictable. In one camp are those people who cling to the values which led to the development of the modern library service - books, education, self-advancement and personal development - and in the other those bureaucrats who argue that if money has to be saved libraries must be sacrificed in order to divert funds to more pressing social problems. Of course not everyone takes such extreme views, and many feel there is a middle way to be found which protects the best of the library tradition, exploits the existing network of buildings, and doesn't put pressure on rapidly dwindling funds.

Book Industry Communication (BIC) is firmly of this view. BIC is partially a creature of the library sector, having been set up in 1991 by the British Library, the - then - Library Association, the Booksellers Association and the Publishers Association to develop and promote standards for electronic communication in what we now call the supply chain. Its first chairman was Tony Hall, managing director of what is now Capita Software Services but was then BLCMP and subsequently Talis. Its original focus was to bring EDI (electronic data interchange) to the wider book world, but it quickly broadened its outlook to include bar code technology, product metadata, identification standards and subject classification. Much of the book trade - and a significant part of the library supply chain - runs on standards that BIC has developed over the past twenty years.

We believe that, unlike the book trade, the library sector has never been able to leverage available technology sufficiently to gain real cost savings from its deployment. The savings are there to be had, but only a comparatively small number of libraries have taken advantage of the opportunities. There are various reasons for this. One is the lack of the commercial drivers which galvanise interest from the book trade. Another is the lack of technical expertise in libraries themselves. Another is the huge diversity that comes from multiple library authorities making independent investment decisions on the basis of their own needs.

Perhaps the most telling, though, is the fact that the companies which exist to serve the library sector - LMS providers, RFID suppliers, stock suppliers and others - have made too good a living from the non-standard environment which these other factors have allowed to develop. Stock suppliers have made their money from servicing books to the specific needs of their customers rather than from the books themselves; LMS and RFID suppliers have been only too glad to tailor systems to individual needs rather than sell a standard product. These are the costs which BIC believes can be saved; and we are encouraged in this by the growing realisation by the companies involved that better delivery of standard products is in the end a more realistic and appropriate policy to adopt.

BIC's remit is about standards, collaboration and consensus. We believe there are huge wins to be made from eliminating waste in the library supply chain, by using technology and standards in a judicious way to cut away at the cost structures that have been allowed to exist in the public library sector because of its fragmented structure.

WHAT ARE THE KEY COMPONENTS OF THIS STRATEGY

EDI is one. Though the BIC standards are widely adopted by libraries and their suppliers, only a minority of libraries has implemented the full cycle of EDI messages - quotes, orders, delivery notes, invoices - and reaped the benefits of error avoidance, once-only keying and paperless transactions. Fewer still have been able or willing to create electronic links between library and corporate finance offices, so that invoices can flow electronically between approval and payment. EDI may be a little complicated to set up, but all the major library suppliers have invested heavily in standards-based electronic communication, and transaction costs are a fraction of any alternative and repay the investment many times over when it is in place.

RFID is another. This technology is hardly new, having been widely adopted by libraries, primarily as a more sophisticated alternative to bar codes for self-service applications, and where it has been implemented it has been universally acclaimed as a way to enable the more productive deployment of staff, facilitate longer opening hours, and provide a more welcoming environment for users. Now, with the help of the BIC/CILIP RFID in Libraries Group and its support for the new ISO 28560 standard, RFID is expanding its potential beyond self-service to stock management and other functions in the library, reducing workloads and providing ongoing cost reductions.

What is more, the standard enables libraries to invest in the technology, confident that they are not locked in to any specific vendor's software or hardware. BIC has published a UK profile for the standard, which has the acceptance and support of all the major RFID suppliers.

The work BIC has done on RFID has spawned other things too. For many years the required communication between self-service devices and LMSs has been handled by 3M's SIP2 protocol. In response to growing dissatisfaction from LMS providers, BIC has commissioned an entirely new communication framework which both extends the functionality of SIP2 but also defines web services as a mechanism for the transfer of information.

LIBRARIES AND THE CLOUD: EVOLUTION NOT REVOLUTION

From reading both the computing and the library press it seems that "cloud computing", "software as a service" and "hosted services" have become the magic pixie dust that will solve all the library service's IT problems, and make all of our lives easier. Needless to say, the realists amongst us know to take this with a pinch of salt however. Using the "cloud" does have some real advantages for libraries and like all 'new' inventions it's not as 'new' as it portrays itself to be.

One thing is for certain, library users are already taking advantage of the storage that 'cloud applications' provide. If you cast your mind back 20 years, storage on floppy discs was the way to safely transport data from one system to another. These were quickly replaced with CDs, then DVDs and finally flash drives as the need for greater amounts of storage and speed of access grew. Now, a number of applications are born in the cloud, services like Flickr, Dropbox and Google Docs, all hosted in the cloud, holding large amounts of data and being accessed by millions of people over the web, all with huge storage capacity compared to those floppy discs 20 years ago.

These new technologies mean that large amounts of data can be used in a library context and some of the social software like Library Thing (the social cataloguing web application) is an example of how apps can be used in a library context. However, I'd argue that Capita's library business has been using cloud or cloud-like solutions for a number of years. Perhaps the oldest example is Base, the bibliographic database that holds some 30 million bibliographic records. Not only do these hold commercial datasets, but also a large number of records that have been catalogued by staff in libraries and contributed back for the benefit of the library community. It's also always been a hosted service.

The second example is our Resource Discovery System (Prism), which is used by over 90 libraries in the UK and Ireland and was launched four years ago. It's a cloud based system that benefits from regular releases of new features (currently about every six weeks) and libraries can take advantage of these releases immediately. It's an application that allows library services to benefit from the rich data contained within the modern amazon-like interface as well as mobile phone enabled interfaces. All without the need for any additional hardware or overheads for libraries to manage, allowing the technology to provide your users with an intuitive interface to access resources.

The final piece in the jigsaw has been the release of Chorus, the Capita Library Management System (LMS) as a Service. This has all the benefits that you'd expect from a hosted service, including security, reliability, scaling to meet the requirements of the library service as it grows, and also reducing the overall total cost of ownership in providing the LMS that libraries need. It has removed the need for locally deployed hardware on premise and meets the needs of both individual and consortium based library services.

At Capita we see this as the natural evolution of technology which we have been helping our customers with for in excess of 40 years. This isn't about throwing out the experience and rich data that has built up over time within the LMS, but taking advantage of the way in which cloud services can be applied to the LMS for the benefit of those customers who choose to move to this environment. Cloud computing isn't a paradigm shift, it's about evolution and not revolution.

INFORMATION SERVICES USING CLOUD COMPUTING: BALANCING ISSUES AND IMPLICATIONS IN DECISION MAKING

While forecasting the next must-have library information service can be difficult, it is likely that the service will be available in the cloud. Library IT vendors more frequently offer hosting options along software and are developing new systems that leverage cloud architecture to share data and make adoption and management easier for libraries. In addition, open source projects such as DuraCloud and Omeka are using cloud computing to facilitate adoption and generate income. This means that libraries have new choices to make when selecting information services but also means that they must evaluate IT platforms as well as information services. This stage explores some of the criteria that libraries can use to make these decisions and examines the long term implications of the cloud-computing trend.

FACTORS THAT INFLUENCE IT ADOPTION

The choice to adopt a particular IT service depends on a number of organisational, technical, and community factors. Differences in funding sources, IT staff expertise, information service needs and policy and legal issues means that there is no one right solution for libraries exploring whether or not to adopt cloud-based IT services. Before we consider the longer-term implications of cloud computing adoption we will consider each of these factors.

COST

Ongoing service cost and requirements of funding sources can be a major barrier to cloud adoption. Many IT organisations are focused on a capital or one-time investment model for technology assets. On the other hand, libraries have a background with subscription-based financial models and may feel more comfortable with lower capital but higher ongoing costs than their IT department counterparts. A way to understand the differences in cost is to complete a high-level return on investment (ROI) analysis comparing the differences between cloud and local IT services. Reese provides an overview of how to compare ROI on cloud and local IT services including start-up vs ongoing costs, staffing/support costs and direct service vs required infrastructure costs. He suggests comparing cloud and local approaches based on your organisation's capital depreciation schedule to better understand the long term costs. While this enables an apples-to-apples comparison it also masks some of the advantages that cloud platforms offers in service flexibility and scalability.

EXPERTISE

Having a strong understanding of local IT staff expertise and capacity is particularly important when selecting an IT infrastructure. Capacity can be defined as the ability of an IT department to provide technology and staffing resources to ensure quality service. In contrast, expertise can be defined as the technical ability of staff to support a service. While these two factors are often directly correlated (e.g. an increase in expertise results in an increase in capacity) this is not necessarily the case. In my own research many libraries cited expertise as either a motivating factor (e.g. lack of local organisational IT capacity motivated the library to seek external support) or an inhibiting factor (e.g. lack of internal IT expertise limited which cloud solutions were explored).

Expertise and capacity in your organisation can be difficult to quantify but tools such as a time-allocation analysis or skill survey may be useful. If your IT staff's skills typically do not include server or datacentre management skills, then infrastructure as a service (IaaS) based cloud solutions are not likely to be successful. If, in contrast, your IT staff has considerable expertise in software development and tweaking, then platform as a service (PaaS) will provide them tools that may expand their service support capacity.

Defining capacity and current workload can be difficult, but at the least should include understanding your staff's recurring tasks and ongoing workload. Scholars explore capacity planning from a staffing perspective in depth in their chapter on Organisational Structures and discuss tasks including service deployment, ongoing management, end-user support and service decommissioning.

SERVICE QUALITY

Service quality is often where libraries begin their exploration of a new application. Service improvements may include new discovery features, better mobile accessibility, or wider research resources. In deciding whether or not an IT service will be of higher quality in a local or cloud-based platform depends in part on how the data being provided in the service can be managed locally over time.

For example some information services depend on rapidly changing data that can only be managed via an outsourced subscription (e.g. OpenURL resolvers and journal subscription services).

Because many library services feature large data repositories there are a number of services including journal databases, resource linking applications and 24/7 research support services that are often only available as a cloud-based or at least externally supported service.

In these cases, the ability of the vendor to update the database is an important consideration that may sway libraries towards a SaaS versus a locally implemented approach. Other systems, such as digital library applications, integrated library systems, research support and web site services, however, may be influenced more by other factors including expected uptime and reliability, speed and interoperability. Understanding these issues and how they relate to capacity and skill issues can help libraries understand the essential elements of what will make a service successful.

POLICY AND LEGAL FACTORS

Organisational policy and legal factors should be one of the first areas to explore when considering cloud-based services. Understanding the implications of privacy and accessibility laws on information services and having an appreciation of organisational policy can save time by eliminating solutions that are a poor fit. In addition to speaking with organisation experts about service regulations it is important to evaluate Service Level Agreements (SLAs) of cloud providers to ensure that their services are in compliance. When exploring SaaS providers it is also important to understand which cloud platforms these providers are using to provide their services.

While it is important to be aware of these issues, it is equally important to not get bogged down in them when exploring potential IT solutions. Low risk or low sensitivity services may be entirely appropriate for cloud platforms that do not provide bulletproof SLA agreements while services that have private data or management requirements are best in locally managed environments.

WHERE SHOULD LIBRARIES FOCUS THEIR IT RESOURCES

With an understanding of these four factors (cost, expertise/capacity, service quality and policy/legal) libraries can make better informed decions about their IT environments. Libraries operate in a complex information environment comprised of multiple information systems and guided by professional ethics including an interest in ensuring free, open and ethical use of information. Cloud computing provides both an opportunity and a challenge for libraries seeking to hold onto these principles as they adopt new information systems. It is increasingly common to find software vendors and open source software developers that offer systems on hosted platforms. DuraCloud, Equinox and Omeka are just a few examples of open source software offered by non-profit and commercial hosting organisations that also engage in software development. Many commercial developers offer some form of hosted or cloud-based service as well.

This approach has been successful in growing the market for co-operative library services in the US. For example, the Georgia Pines Library system that led the creation of Evergreen not only succeeded in migrating its branch libraries to a new single-ILS platform, it also led the way for other states seeking the opportunities for data sharing and economies of scale. This is good news for open source projects seeking to find long term viability. A recent Ithaka research report discussed the difficulties associated with finding ongoing support for open source projects including new projects, shifting priorities and lagging community involvement. By leveraging cloud-computing hosting, some open source projects are both expanding their community of adopters and benefiting from a revenue stream to enable ongoing development.

My research on cloud computing adoption in libraries showed that it was more common for libraries who had turned to cloud computing to have turned to a SaaS as opposed to PaaS or IaaS platforms. SaaS solutions also pose a long-term challenge for libraries by eliminating local capacity and expertise and ultimately impacting the ability to migrate to new systems. In contrast, PaaS and IaaS solutions provide libraries with tools that level the playing field by preserving local expertise and expanding capacity. Unfortunately, it can be rather difficult, if not impossible, to implement many current commercial and open source systems in a PaaS or IaaS environment.

Many open source and commercial products operate on very specific IT stacks. Although PaaS providers, including Heroku, Cloud Foundry and Google Apps Engine are expanding support for different programming languages and database platforms, library applications have not been developed using these frameworks or deployment techniques. This means that the redundancy, replication and backup features that come with PaaS platforms is out of reach of libraries who either must rely on a vendor-provided SaaS approach or turn to local or IaaS solutions.

Further complicating the situation is the difficulty inherent in migrating to new platforms for libraries using SaaS or IaaS solutions. While PaaS providers may not always support easy migration, by focusing on building applications using industry standard frameworks, vendors and open source communities could make migration more realistic. Unfortunately, few if any commercial or open source library systems operate in these environments. This limits the range of IT solutions available to libraries and can push libraries towards either largely localised or outsourced options.

While cloud computing offers new opportunities for large and small libraries, it also raises the stakes on information service selection. Libraries are increasingly moving towards network-based data and more complex information services. At the same time they are grappling with constrained resources and a new range of IT platforms. In selecting an information system and IT platform, it is important that libraries choose solutions that improve service while also ensuring that their choices are good for the long-term.

EDINBURGH LIBRARIES AND SOLUS

Rather than roll over and accept this, the City of Edinburgh has chosen to harness the very technology cited as a threat and engage with new audiences in new ways. The primary aim has always been to attract physical users to their facilities, however if this is not possible then the next best thing is to engage digitally with their audience. If you think about citizens in a new way, as mobile, digitally accessible, yet unique and focused on receiving the service that they want whenever they want it, technology gives them and you the opportunity to build a new relationship. Once in place, it also enables you to market your services free of charge, increasingly important in these austere times.

Liz McGettigan, Library and Information Services Manager at the City of Edinburgh Council, realised the requirement to engage with developments in web 2.0 services, or risk being left behind in an increasingly digital world. She saw the opportunities for promotion that social media enabled and created a team of people within the library to pull all electronic resources into one location. Finally, she employed the best technology available to engage with Edinburgh's citizens, in facilities, on the web, socially and on the go.

- *Your Library*: the Web Portal – This unique portal unites all digital resources including catalogues, databases and other web sites.
- *Tales of One City*: This is an integrated approach to social media, engaging citizens and local communities with Edinburgh's blog, Facebook site, Twitter feed, Flickr and YouTube sites. It's push and pull communication that connects with their audience.
- *SOLUS*: This gives Edinburgh the power to schedule content from their web-based Content Management System to digital signage, web and desktop video players, a library app and to social media channels.

SOLUS, a member of the Capita Partner Programme, provides Edinburgh with a unique digital communications capability and helps maximise efficiency in a market where cost saving and best value is critical. Jim Thompson, Edinburgh's Development and Quality Manager, stated, "The premise behind SOLUS is the ability to create once and schedule many. SOLUS allows us to use one system to upload a promotional video file to our digital signage network, make it available to view across our desktops, embed it into our web portal and intranet, schedule it to our mobile app and distribute it automatically to all our social media channels."

SOLUS has also fully integrated with the Capita LMS to provide functionality for "Your Library App" and this has enabled additional benefits. Most recently added and most popular stock can now be automatically promoted across other platforms managed by SOLUS, such as digital signage and social media. Neil Wishart, Director of SOLUS, was recently at Downing Street, discussing the potential of "Your Library App" with Nick Jones, Director of Digital Communications for No. 10 and The Cabinet Office. Following the meeting Neil commented:

> "One of the key requirements for government at all levels is to engage more efficiently and

effectively with citizens. The digital citizen is real and their dependency on technology is increasing. Rather than being a threat, it provides libraries with the biggest opportunity in a generation to engage with new users in increasing numbers. At the same time, it will let them do this more efficiently and effectively. For the citizen, libraries can offer easy and immediate access to services that can save them money. If people are cutting back due to their personal budgets being squeezed, libraries can take advantage."

To take advantage, access must be 24/7, slick and with instant gratification. V2 of Edinburgh's Library App will allow users to scan a barcode in a shop and automatically search the library catalogue. This is already reality - the recently launched Haringey Library App, which is powered by SOLUS, allows users to scan, search and reserve within seconds. If they don't know how to get to the reserved item, the app will take them there and if an Ebook is available, users can get that instant gratification!

Of course, the proof is in the pudding and Liz McGettigan has solid evidence to prove this innovative use of technology is working. In the last year digital visits have increased by 135,000, PC usage is up by 145,000 sessions, attendance at events has increased, up 32 per cent, and significantly, the decline in physical visits has been reversed with an extra 30,000 people attending libraries. Wishart stated, "It's a classic case of inbound marketing, where effective online positioning has a direct impact on offline behaviour. It's fantastic for Liz to be able to report back to her stakeholders that she has improved access to services and achieved a direct return on investment, both in relation to time and money."

What's next? Creating an app, using social media and installing a digital signage network are all great foundations, but maximum uptake can only be ensured through effective ongoing promotion. The next step in the partnership between Edinburgh Libraries and SOLUS is to develop a range of collaterals to shout about libraries. Liz commented, "There is no point in having the world's best kept secret, we want as many physical and digital users as we can possibly attract. We are actively working on materials with SOLUS to promote our App and these will be resources that can be shared with other libraries across the UK. There is no point replicating spend - if we can all make further efficiency savings and at the same time develop really exciting material, it benefits the whole library community."

Libraries now lead the way in Edinburgh, with other departments continually looking to implement their successful strategy.

NEW LIBRARY SECURITY AND ASSET TRACKING COMPANY LAUNCHED

Since 1 January, 2012, there has been a new choice in the library security, self issue and RFID market and it's a company made up of a team who can boast many years of experience so can give a solid perspective on optimising security functions to include stock tracking, usage and numerous other functions.

PSP Asset Protection Ltd will be bringing a fresh approach and an exciting new portfolio of products to the library security and asset tracking market, throughout the UK. PSP is spearheaded by Plescon's previous management team of Nick Hunt and Helen Morphew, and all Plescon staff have transferred to the new company.

After both working for Plescon Security Products for over 15 years each, Nick and Helen are the driving force behind the new company and both are extremely excited about the new opportunities and solutions PSP Asset Protection Ltd can offer. "It was important we retained the existing staff to ensure we can continue to offer the best possible service to our customers but both wanted to expand our focus and forge new and closer partnerships so we have the very best possible solutions to offer the market," explained Nick.

"The new company will supply the very best solutions for protecting library book stock using RFID, electromagnetic and radio frequency, while focusing on innovative stock tracking and self-service units. Modern technology has revolutionised library security and given added functionality that saves librarians' time while being able to offer data that will benefit staff, customers and budgets alike. At PSP Asset Protection we believe in a consultative approach and our new partnerships with other companies ensure our customers can get a great choice. Our ethos will be to offer the best of the best with the most up to date products. We now also have an in-house design and technical team who can integrate a solution to match the composition and flow of any library.

Having been involved in such a great company as Plescon Security Products for the last fifteen years has provided me with invaluable experience, working closely with a number of fantastic libraries, librarians and suppliers. The opportunity to build on our existing knowledge while adding new and innovative products has been the impetus behind the decision to start PSP Asset Protection Ltd.

INTRODUCING SIP 3.0

3M introduced the 3M Standard Interchange Protocol (SIP) version 1.0 in 1993. This protocol provided a standard communication mechanism to allow LMS applications and self-service devices to communicate seamlessly to perform self-service transactions. This protocol quickly became the defacto standard around the world, and remains the primary protocol to integrate LMSs and self-service devices.

In 1997, version 2.0 was released, and it provided additional functionality to support check-in, fines and fees payment, off-line transactions, renewals and chargeable loans. Since 2000 various extensions have been published, however in development of SIP 3.0 these extensions have now been standardised and become an integral part of the protocol. Clarification of text fields and additional functionality for managing patrons has also been added.

SIP 3.0 has been developed with input from representatives of the global library community. Libraries,

LMS companies, IT providers, RFID suppliers and other library providers worked in partnership to create the new communications protocol. Due to version 3.0 being built on the same platform as SIP 2.0 and with input from the library community, this new protocol will be well understood and easily implemented from the outset.

Development work on SIP 3.0 has involved more than the addition of new elements and features such as support for patron management and sortation systems. Areas of the protocol have now been simplified and the greater use of mandatory fields has made implementation easier.

- *Is SIP 3.0 an 'open' protocol?:* As with earlier versions of SIP, SIP 3.0 has been designed as a non-proprietary protocol. SIP protocol currently remains the intellectual property of 3M and hence 3M were best placed to manage the development of version 3.0.
- *Is SIP 3.0 backward compatible with SIP 2.0?:* No. A system designed to communicate with SIP 2.0 will not be able to automatically communicate with SIP 3.0. However version 3.0 is built on the same principles and does share much of the same basic message structure, and will therefore be familiar and easily understood by anyone that knows SIP 2.0, ensuring quick and easy implementation.
- *Is SIP 3.0 free to use?:* 3M does not charge for the use of SIP 3.0. The protocol was developed with the library community, for the library community.
- *Can SIP 3.0 be translated to a web service?:* SIP 3.0 is a common data format designed to be easily understood by different types of systems. The term 'web service' refers to the transport mechanism that delivers the data. SIP 3.0 can be transported via a web service if both parties agree on using web services as the transport mechanism.
- *Will SIP 3.0 allow data transfer from a handheld device?:* Any data that is supported by the fields in SIP 3.0 can be transferred.

- *Can SIP 3.0 be used to communicate with other non-library data systems?:* The focus of the SIP 3.0 development effort is to ensure that the needs of today's library community are fulfilled. It was felt that development beyond the scope of the library environment would compromise the ability of SIP 3.0 to deliver optimum usability and functionality for libraries.
- *What is the difference between SIP 3.0 and NCIP?:* NCIP, like SIP 3.0, is a widely used data protocol for use in libraries. The decision over which protocol best suits a library's needs will depend on the functionality required by the individual library. More often than not the choice will depend on which protocol is supported by all of a library's different systems.
- *Can SIP 3.0 be extended in the future?:* Yes. SIP 3.0 is designed to allow for new fields and functionality to be added in the future.

5

Use of Computers in Library and Pro-cognitive Functions

SYNTACTIC ANALYSIS OF NATURAL LANGUAGE BY COMPUTER

The relevance of automated syntactic analysis to library pro-cognitive systems lies in machine processing, and in eventual machine 'understanding,' of natural language text. There is no thought that syntactic analysis alone - whether by man or machine - is sufficient to provide a useful approximation to understanding. On the other hand, there is no doubt that appreciation of the syntactic structure of natural-language text is a part, and an important part, of the over-all problem. Bobrow surveyed the work that has been done, and is being done, towards automation of syntactic analysis of English.

The efforts to automate syntactic analysis have been, essentially, efforts to implement various theories of grammar through the preparation of computer programmes that operate on natural-language text in the form of strings of encoded alphanumeric characters. The output of a successful syntactic-analysis programme is one or more sets of.assignments of the words of a sentence to grammatical categories plus, for each set of assignments, a representation of the grammatical structure of the sentence.

The grammars that have been used as bases for syntactic-analysis programmes include dependency grammars, phrase-structure grammars with continuous and with discontinuous constituents, predictive grammars, string transformation grammars, and phrase-structure transformational grammars. The main characteristics of, and differences among, these grammars are set forth in Bobrow's report.

Although it is too early to say with assurance which of them is best for our purposes much expert intuition favours the phrase-structure, transformational approach. Many of the programmes that have been successful in making syntactic analyses have depended upon a distinction between 'function words' and 'content words.' The distinction is a simple and familiar one.

Function words are words such as 'and', 'or', 'to', 'from', 'a', 'an', 'the', 'neither', 'nor', 'if', and 'whether'. Content words are words such as 'grammar', 'equivalent', 'structural', 'diagram', 'sentence', 'minimum', 'weekly', 'accept', and 'develop'. There are, of course, many more types of content words than of function words. It is therefore reasonable to store in a computer memory very detailed descriptions of the functions, characteristics, idiomatic uses, and so forth, of the function words. The successful analytic programmes have, in addition, employed dictionaries containing, for each content word, the grammatical categories into which it is normally expected to fall. It is the intention here, not to give a complete summary of Bobrow's report, but rather to relate the idea of syntactic analysis by computer to the over-all picture set forth in Part 1. Perhaps the best way to do that is to show in diagrammatic form some of the analyses that are described in detail by Bobrow.

The notion of 'dependency' gives a direction and a hierarchical structure to syntactic relations. Adjectives depend on nouns, nouns depend on verbs and prepositions, adverbs and auxiliary verbs depend on main verbs, prepositions depend on the words modified by their phrases, and so forth. The system of dependency can be represented diagrammatically in the way illustrated for the sentences, 'The man treats the boy and the girl in the park,'

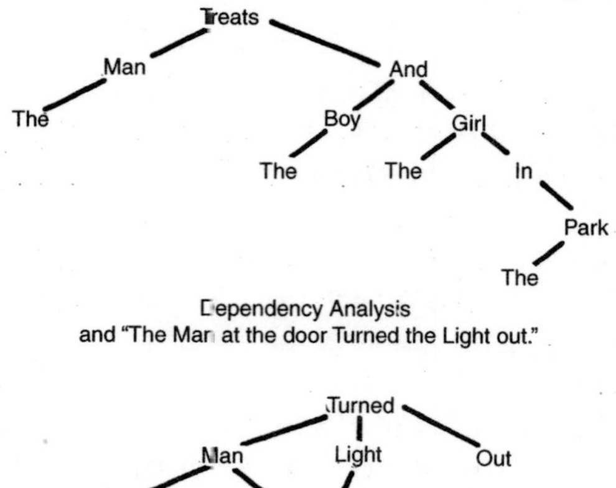

Fig 5.1 Dependency Analysis

This second sentence will be used to illustrate other grammars also, in order to display similarities and differences. Computer programmes capable of implementing dependency analysis have been developed or described by Hays of the RAND Corporation, by Kelly of the RAND Corporation, by Gross of M.I.T., by Klein and Simmons of the System Development Corporation, and by several Russian workers, including Moloshnava and Andreyev. In a phrase-structure analysis that assumes continuous, immediate constituents, t the diagrammatic representation is again treelike, but the nodes of the branching structure are, at all levels except the lowest, syntactic or grammatical categories. At the lowest level, the actual words of the sentence appear. An immediate-constituent analysis of 'The man ate the apple' is shown in the diagram.

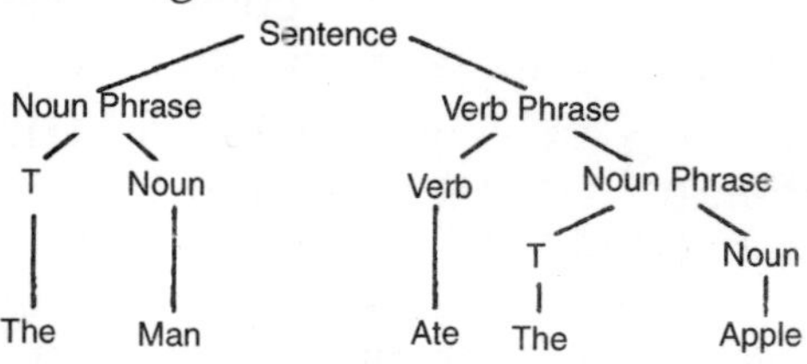

Fig 5.2 An Immediate-constituent Analysis of "The Man Ate the Apple"

The analysis starts at the bottom of the diagram with the string of words and proceeds to discover a superstructure consistent with their grammatical class memberships.

However, the analysis may involve trial-and-error differentiation downward from assumed categories to strings of words. The analysis substitutes for 'Sentence' the two category names, 'Noun Phrase' and 'Verb Phrase.' It then substitutes for 'Noun Phrase' the category names 'Definite Article' and 'Noun.'

For 'Verb Phrase' it substitutes 'Verb' and 'Noun Phrase.' It is then in a position to substitute actual words for three of the category names. 'Noun Phrase,' however, has to be passed through one more stage of analysis before the substitution of actual words can be made. The result of the analysis—the diagram—displays the roles of the individual words of the sentence and, in addition, shows how the several roles are interrelated.

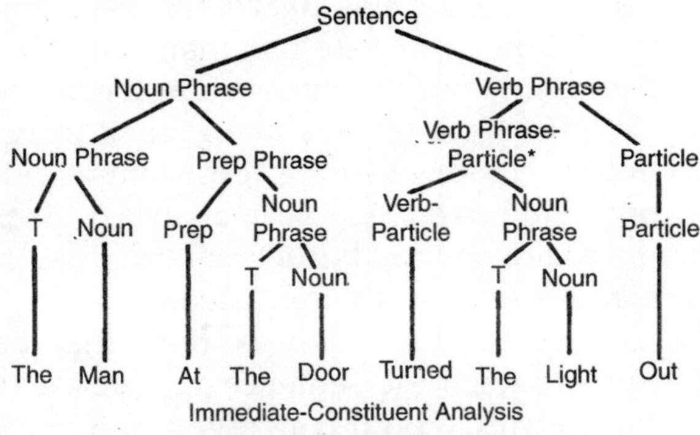

Immediate-Constituent Analysis

* Read the Minus Sigh (Not Hyphen) as "Minus."

Fig 5.3 Immediate-constituent Analysis of 'The Man at the Door turned the Light Out.'

In the foregoing example, the analysis proceeded in a succession of binary branchings. An alternative formulation makes use of multiple branching to produce coordinate structures with fewer levels. Bobrow compares binary structure and coordinate structure in the phrase, 'the old black heavy stone.'

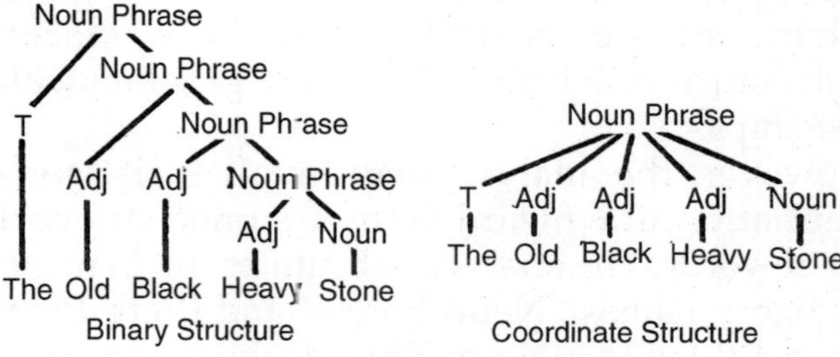

Fig 5.4 Binary Structure and Coordinate Structure

Computer programmes capable of making immediate constituent analyses have been developed or described by Robinson of the RAND Corporation, Cocke of the International Business Machines Corporation, and Klein of the System Development Corporation. Kuno and Oettinger of Harvard have developed extensively the technique of predictive analysis advocated by Rhodes of the National Bureau of Standards. Predictive analysis takes advantage of the fact that, once he has heard the beginning of a sentence, the listener can rule out many of the myriad syntactic patterns into which sentences are, a priori, capable of falling. Predictive analyses keep track only of the alternative interpretations that are consistent with the part of the sentence that has already been analysed. At the very beginning, there are usually but few alternatives, for then the interpretations are not differentiated.

In the midcourse of an analysis, there may be many possible ways in which the sentence can go. At the end, however, the analysis should converge upon one pattern of grammatical categories, or, at any rate, upon a set of patterns among which a choice can be made on the basis of semantic interpretation of the sentence itself and of its context. The Kuno Oettinger programmes determine all the alternatives. Related programmes developed by Lindsay of the University of Texas find only one syntactic pattern but provide diagnostic information on the basis of which it is possible to clear up misinterpretation through 'postediting.' A minor problem for machine analysis is introduced by the fact that two words may together fill a grammatical category without being contiguous in text. This problem is not faced squarely by immediate-constituent grammars. In discontinuous-constituent grammars, however, the problem is recognised, and a special linkage is introduced to connect the separated parts. The diagram illustrates an analysis of 'He called her up.'

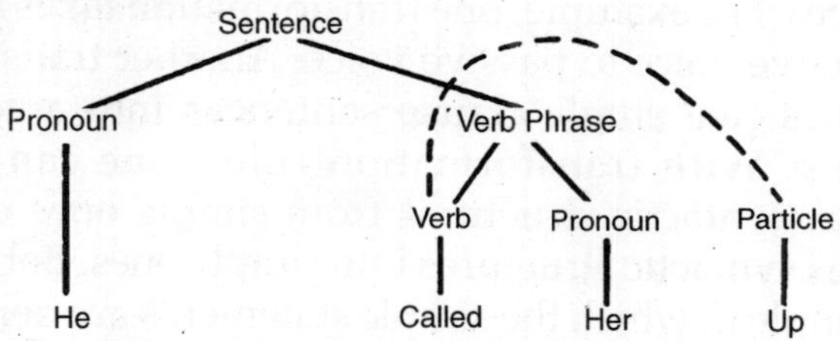

Fig 5.5 Discontinous-Constituent Analysis He Called Her Up

The linkage from 'Verb' to 'Particle' connects 'up' to 'called,' from which it has been separated by 'her.' The diagram shows a discontinuous-constituent analysis of the standard sentence, 'The man at the door turned the light out.'

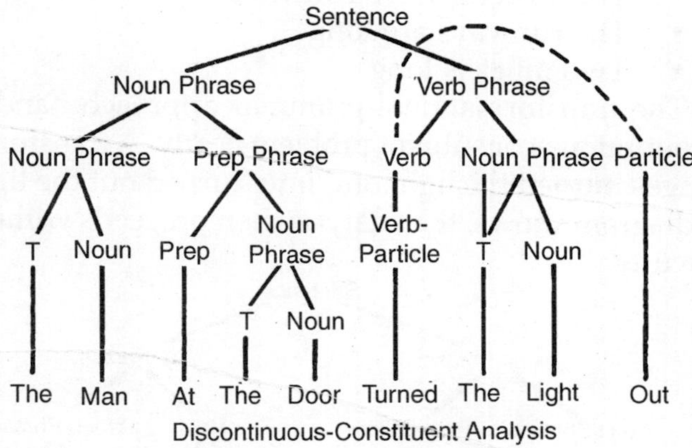

Fig 5.6 Discontinous-Constituent Analysis of the Standard Sentence

For the purposes of library pro cognitive systems, the most important problem in this subject area may well be one raised by Chomsky. Chomsky was concerned that two expressions of the same idea, such as 'The man drives the car' and 'The car is driven by the man' do not have similar phrase structures and do not yield similar diagrams when analysed in the ways we have been discussing. Chomsky handled this problem by setting up 'transformation rules' that transform one sentence into another, or combine *n* sentences into one, or subdivide one sentence into *n* sentences. For example, one transformation takes a sentence from active voice to passive voice. Another transformation combines two single clause sentences into a compound sentence. With transformation rules, one can build up complex syntactic structures from simple ones or analyse complex syntactic structures into simple ones. Bobrow gives an example in which the simple statements are derived from the question, 'What are the airfields in Ohio having runways longer than two miles?' Analysis and synthesis based on such transformations will surely be important for machine-aided organisation of the body of knowledge.

- X's are the airfields
- The airfields are in Ohio
- The airfields have runways
- The runways are long
- Two miles is long

The transformational-grammar approach handles the discontinuous-constituent problem neatly. A transformation changes 'turned the light out' into 'turned out the light.' As the diagram shows, the analysis then proceeds without any difficulty.

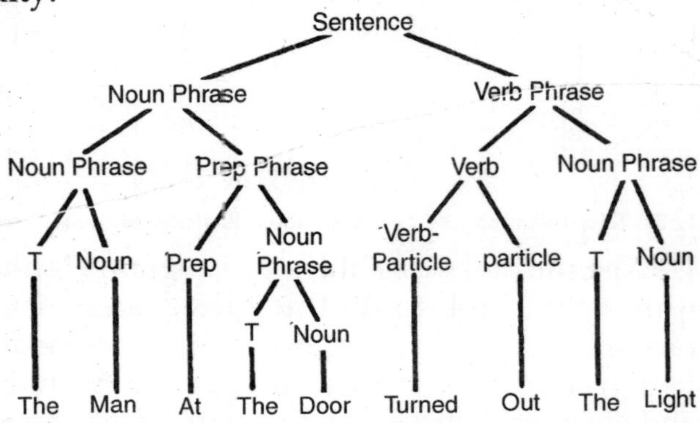

Fig 5.7 Intermediate Stage in Chomsky's Transformational Derivation

Walker and Bartlett of the Mitre Corporation are developing a parsing programme based on a transformational grammar. Harris and his associates at the University of Pennsylvania have developed a method of syntactic analysis that is intermediate between constituent analysis and transformational analysis. Although their method does not lend itself to representation by a tree diagram, a rough idea of its approach is conveyed by relating some of its terms to our standard sentence. In the sentence, the 'string center' is . . . man . . . turned out . . . light.' One 'the' is the 'left adjunct' of 'man,' and the other is the 'left adjunct' of 'light'. 'At the door' is the 'right adjunct' of 'man.' This 'string-transformational grammar' has been implemented in the form of computer programmes. The 'Baseball' programme developed by Green and associates at the Lincoln Laboratory - a programme capable of answering questions about the outcomes of the baseball games played in the major leagues during one season - has a methodological kinship to the Pennsylvania work.

From Bobrow's survey, it is clear that automation of syntactic analysis is possible. Indeed, there are several operating syntactic-analysis programmes. It is equally clear, however, that syntactic analysis is only a part - and perhaps, relatively, only a small part - of the over-all problem. The fact is that even the best analysis programmes produce discouragingly many alternative patterns. Selection among the alternatives has to be made on non-syntactic grounds, and there has not been much progress towards automation of that selection.

Furthermore, it is evident that one is a very long way from understanding what is being said when all he knows is the pattern or structure of syntactic categories into which the words of the message fit. The question was raised in Part I, whether it is desirable, in formulating the basic concepts of this field, to separate syntactic and semantic factors into the two insulated bins of a rigid dichotomy, or whether, as subtler and subtler distinctions are made in the process now called syntactic analysis, that process will start to become semantic as well as syntactic. Although we are not in a position to decide, one way or the other, on that question, we have an intuitive feeling that the latter is more promising as a line of development. We should, in this connection, refer to work that we regard as extremely promising, work being carried out by F.B. Thompson and his colleagues.

RESEARCH ON QUANTITATIVE ASPECTS OF FILES AND TEXT

Two studies by Grignetti deal with quantitative aspects of representations of information in digital memories. The first study concerns the average length of representations of descriptions of documents or, in greater generality, the average length of representations of 'terms'. The second concerns the informational measure 'entropy' - or, to look at it the other way around, the redundancy - of English text considered as a string of _ words. Thus both studies bear upon the amount of memory required to store library information: the first with indexes, the second with actual text.

ON THE LENGTH OF A CLASS OF SERIAL FILES

From one point of view, the over-all organisation and concept of a library or of a pro-cognitive system is a more important thing to grasp, or to improve, than is the efficiency of a low-level 'detail' function. On the other hand, a few functions that appear from one point of view to be mere details, to occupy low levels in the over-all system, are seen from another point of view to be both basic and ubiquitous. One of these functions that looks like a technical detail from one standpoint and like something very basic and general from another is the encoding of elements of information for storage in a digital memory. Let us, for the purposes of this discussion, adopt the point of view from which it seems important. As soon as we do that we may be prepared to examine subcategories, and one of the most conspicuous of these is the subcategory that includes catalogues and indexes. The study to be summarised deals with such files of information. Perhaps the best schema to keep in mind while thinking about this problem is the schema of an index consisting of the names or numbers of the documents in a collection and, associated with each name or number, a list of terms or descriptors that characterise the corresponding document according to some coordinate indexing system. The problem under consideration is how to encode the terms. The object is to be economical in the use of storage space and, at the same time, to make it easy for a computer to decode the representation and determine the names or numbers of specified documents. One of the most widely used techniques for representing terms is simply to spell them out in full or to record readable abbreviations of them. The direct way to encode such representations for storage in digital memory is to assign a binary code to each character in the character ensemble and to store the binary code patterns.

That technique has the disadvantage of using much more memory space than is necessary. A technique that is more economical of memory space is to number all the terms that may be used and to represent in memory in association with each item, not the corresponding terms themselves, but the numbers that were assigned to them. Since there are sometimes several terms per document, it is important not to let the numbers that represent different terms run together in such a way as to preclude subdivision of the over-all representation into its parts. The encodings of the sets of terms associated with different documents must also be kept separable.

In the past, people have kept codes separable either by using special characters as separators or by adding enough leading zeros to the short codes to make all the codes the same length. The prevailing opinion has been that the use of separators leads to more compact files than the use of fixed-. length codes. The first thing Grignetti did was to analyse that comparison. It turned out that, on the average, and under certain reasonable assumptions, the fixed-length code is actually shorter than the variable length code plus separator. If one thinks about this question with simple, schematic examples in mind, he is likely to doubt this conclusion of Grignetti's and to agree with the prevailing opinion that Grignetti finds incorrect. However, Grignetti's conclusion becomes quite obvious as soon as attention is focused upon large filing systems in which the list of legal terms is long. Consider, for example, that, of a list of nearly 1000 terms, almost 90 per cent would be represented by three-digit codes. About 9 per cent would require one leading zero, and about 1 per cent would require two leading zeros to bring them up to the 'fixed' length of three digits. In his work on coding efficiency, Grignetti also examined the notion that products of prime numbers might provide the basis for an effective coding system for the purpose we are considering here. In such a system, each term would be assigned a prime number, and the set of terms associated with a particular item would be represented by the product of the prime numbers associated with the members of the set.

Grignetti was able to show conclusively that the prime-number code is an inefficient code, less good than either variant of the elementary system considered in the foregoing paragraphs. The preliminary enquiries just described led Grignetti to look for a truly efficient coding system for terms. He found one. He calls it the 'combinational code.' It is fairly easy to construct a combinational code. First, one has to decide the maximum number of terms that will be associated with an item, say, five. Second, he examines the list of legal terms, numbers the individual terms, and makes up all the possible combinations of term numbers, taken five or fewer at a time. Third, he orders the numbers corresponding to the terms of each combination in a sequence of increasing magnitude. Fourth, he reorders the list of combinations according to a criterion that takes into account primarily the magnitude of the largest number in the subset but also, secondarily, the number of numbers in the subset. Finally, he assigns integers in increasing sequence to the members of the reordered list. Grignetti gives an analytical procedure for encoding and decoding. He points out that the procedure does not have to be changed, and that existing code numbers do not have to be altered, when new terms are added to the list of legal terms. Finally, he shows that the combinational code is the shortest possible code.

ENTROPY OF WORDS IN PRINTED ENGLISH

Grignetti's interest was attracted to the question of the representational efficiency of direct encodings of the strings of *words* that constitute text by the consideration. That storage of the body of knowledge in processible memories will be an important basis for pro-cognitive systems. In order to estimate the representational efficiency, it is natural to compare determinations of the number of bits required to store a typical segment of text with estimates of the actual information content of the text. The classical estimate of the information measure of a typical word of text is the one made by Shannon in 1951 on the assumption that the frequency of occurrence of word types is sufficiently approximated by Zipf's famous law. Shannon's estimate of the information measure, or entropy, was 11.82 bits per word.

However, Berner using roughly the approximation that Shannon used, calculated that words could be stored, on the average, in 10.76 bits of memory space - with the aid of a compression code that was obviously not optimal. That led Grignetti to examine Shannon's results closely. By a method slightly different from Shannon's, a method that seems straightforward and in which no flaw has been detected, Grignetti found the information measure to be 9.7 or 9.8 bits per word. From one point of view, the difference, which is only 2 bits per word, does not seem likely to have much practical significance. From another point of view, however, the important question is whether or not further work on encoding of text seems to be intellectually attractive. If it seems attractive, then it is possible, and perhaps likely, that a coding scheme will be found that is highly efficient in use of memory space and, at the same time, economical in respect of processing. On the other hand, if further work is not intellectually attractive, there is not likely to be an increase in either the efficiency of the use of space or the economy of encoding and decoding. Perhaps the 2 bits per word will have a stimulating effect. Clearly, the point on which study should now concentrate is the simplification of encoding and decoding.

A MEASURE OF THE EFFECTIVENESS OF INFORMATION-RETRIEVAL SYSTEMS

To some information-retrieval systems, a particularly simple schema is appropriate. The system is a 'black box' that contains a collection or set of items and that, from time to time, either spontaneously or in response to a request, offers a subset of its contents to one of its subscribers and withholds the complementary subset. An item may be thought of as a document. A subscriber may be thought of as simply a criterion: to the subscriber, an item is either pertinent or not pertinent. If one considers a single item of the collection and focuses his attention upon a particular occasion—a particular request from a subscriber or a particular spontaneous offering by the system.

Note that only two of the relative frequencies are independent, for the sum over the four categories must be unity, and the fraction of the items that meets the subscriber's criterion of pertinence is assumed to be fixed. Note, also, that there has to be some way to ascertain the pertinence or non-pertinence of withheld items. Investigating the problem of evaluation of effectiveness, Swets found that eight of the ten studies that met his criterion of pertinence reduced the analysis to two-by-two contingency tables. However, in none of the studies was advantage taken of the fact that evaluative procedures have been developed for, and found useful in, other fields of application in which performance may be summarised in two-by-two contingency tables. Swets therefore adapted some of the apparatus of statistical decision theory to the information-retrieval context and proposed a measure of merit, a measure that quantifies the ability of the system to maximize the expected value of a retrieval trial, *i.e.*, of an offering or withholding of an individual item on a particular occasion. The measure takes into account the relative frequency and the utility of each of the four categories in the two-by-two table. We shall not review here Swets's explanation of its derivation.

Let it suffice to say that an assumption of normality of distribution is involved, that the measure is based on maximum-likelihood statistics, and that, given the relative frequencies of hits and false drops in a particular sample, one can read the value of the measure from an available table or graph. The measure is simple, convenient, and appropriate. It gives definite meaning to the concept, the 'basic discriminating power' of an information-retrieval system. The measure clearly separates discriminating power from mere willingness to yield output, thus avoiding a confusion that has been rife these last several years and that appears to be at the root of many informational difficulties. Moreover, the measure brings with it a well-developed system of procedures that facilitate analysis and interpretation of data. We expect Swets's measure to prove useful in evaluation of information systems. The main obstacle may lie in determination of the pertinence of withheld items. That obstacle is wide. It causes trouble for all the approaches to evaluation of performance in retrieval of information from large collections.

LIBRARIES AND QUESTION ANSWERING SYSTEMS

Marill's Report, 'Libraries and Question Answering Systems,' laid the groundwork for subsequent research on question-answering systems. The report consists of three parts:

- Two Concepts of a Library,
- Question-Answering Systems and
- Semantic Nets: Informal Introduction.

The first of the 'two concepts of a library' is a schematisation of a present-day library. In the schema, the library consists of the collection of documents, the 'tag' system, and the retrieval system that makes use of the tags to retrieve desired documents. The contributions that technology can make within this first concept are acceleration of document handling, automation of the process of 'tagging' and improvement of the retrieval process.

Marill argues that this first concept, instrumented on a modest scale, would yield unsatisfactory results, and that, carried to its logical limit, it would be absurd. The second concept of a library is one in which the primary function is to provide not documents but information. The 'system' of the second concept will be able to 'read' and 'comprehend' the documents themselves and not merely their tags. It will have a high capability for organising the information internally. It will be able to accept questions worded in natural English. If it has the requisite information available, it will answer the questions in natural English. Thus Marill advocates a very sophisticated pro-cognitive system. He is concerned that people may believe the goal unreachable because it will be thought to require that inanimate mechanisms 'think.'

Marill refers to the question-answering system called 'Baseball' to forestall that misconception. In his discussion of question-answering systems, Marill defines the primary concepts: the corpus, the question, and the answer. The corpus consists of a set of quantificational schemata and their attendant predicate definitions, one definition for each predicate in the corpus. Thus Marill immediately seizes upon a predicate calculus as the formalism for representation of the information in the body of knowledge. There are two kinds of questions: questions satisfied by yes-no answers, and questions that require sentence answers. Answers, therefore, are also of two types: yes-no answers and sentence answers. The answer to a yes-no question is 'yes' if the question can be deduced from the corpus - if there exists a deduction that has the sentences of the corpus as premises and the question as the last line. The answer is 'no' if the negation of the question can be deduced from the corpus. There is no answer if neither the question nor its negation can be deduced from the corpus.

A sentence qualifies as a sentence answer if the sentence can be deduced from the corpus and if the schema of the sentence is the same as the schema of the question when the question is in statement form. There can be only one yes-no answer, but there can be any number of sentence answers. Marill's treatment of semantic nets is an extension and formalisation of the discussion of relational networks given in Part 1. Marill takes the view that the proper structural analysis of a sentence is given by the quantificational schema of that sentence, as understood in symbolic logic. To this, he adds the view that the meaning of a one-place predicate is identified, ultimately, with the set of objects of which the predicate is true, and the meaning of a two-place predicate is identified with the set of all ordered pairs of objects of which the predicate is true, and so forth. Finally, he adds the notion that the meaning of an object is identified with, first, the set of one-place predicates that are true of the object, and, second, the set of two-place predicates that are true of it and something else, and so forth. The sets with which meanings are identified are extremely large. The machine cannot be required to prove its 'understanding' of a meaning by producing all the members of the sets. Marill maintains that it is enough for the machine to produce a convincingly large sample. The usual representation of a quantificational schema has the form of a string of symbols. Marill views the semantic net as an alternative notation, equivalent to the string notation, but more promising for computer exploitation. To demonstrate the relation between semantic nets and string-form schemata, Marill starts with three simple statements in string notation and transmutes them, by degrees, into diagrams in which lines tie together the several instances of a variable. The elements of a semantic net in Marill's exposition are the following:

- *Rectangles*—which represent the truth functions corresponding to logical operators and their arguments. Each rectangle has one terminal for each argument.
- *Diamonds*—which represent quantifiers. There are two types, corresponding to 'some' and 'all.'
- *A triangle with point down*—which represents 'sentence.' This triangle contains an 'S.'
- *A circle*—which represents a predicate. The circle has as many terminals as there are places in the predicate.
- *A triangle with point up*—which represents an individual.

Mariu gives six rules governing the combination of elements and the formation of semantic nets. The rules are:

- Connecting a predicate to a sentence symbol forms a sentence.
- Inserting a negation rectangle between the sentence symbol and the predicate negates the sentence.
- To connect two sentences, divert their predicates to a two-place truth-function rectangle and connect it to a single sentence-symbol triangle.
- To add a quantifier to a sentence, insert it in the line between the sentence symbol and its nearest neighbour.
- To terminate an unterminated predicate, attach an individual object to the unused terminal, or connect that terminal to a quantifier that is already in the diagram of the sentence.
- To merge two or more networks into one: for each individual, overlay all the triangles that represent the individual, retaining all the lines that are attached to any of the triangles; associate all the occurrences of the same predicate by connecting them with 'association lines.'

In 'Semantic Nets: An Informal Introduction,' Marill presents diagrams to illustrate the rules and to demonstrate the interpretation of moderately complex semantic nets. Marill's diagrams and discussion make it clear that the semantic net is formally equivalent to the conventional representation of a system of statements in predicate calculus. Marill believes that semantic nets afford a promising path into computer representation and processing of complex systems of relations.

STUDIES OF COMPUTER TECHNIQUES AND PROCEDURES

The following studies are concerned with early steps along the course from present digital-computer system to future pro-cognitive systems. Let us consider the studies in the order of their locations along that course. The first ones were intended merely to make it convenient to carry out some of the functions that are required in research on library and pro-cognitive problems or in the efficient use of large collections of documents. The last ones in the sequence were intended to explore functions that we think will actually be involved in future pro-cognitive systems.

AN 'EXECUTIVE' PROGRAMME TO FACILITATE THE USE OF THE PDP-1 COMPUTER

One of the first needs of the study was a computer programme to facilitate the programming and use of the laboratory's digital computer. The computer is a small but excellent machine, Digital Equipment Corporation PDP-I, specialised to facilitate interaction with users who work 'on line.' The PDP-1 has an oscilloscope display with light pen, several electric typewriters, a set of programmable relays, an analogue-to-digital converter, and an assortment of switches and buttons. Its primary memory is small but it is capable of transferring information rapidly between the primary memory and a secondary drum memory that holds about 90,000 eighteen-bit words. Associated with the computer are two magnetic-tape units. With the computer, it is possible to implement, in a preliminary and schematic way, several of the functions that were described in Part I as functions desirable in a pro-cognitive system. One encounters two main difficulties in trying to do, with the PDP-1 computer, research oriented towards a future period in which information-processing machines will have more advanced capabilities.

First, although the machine is reasonably fast, and although its secondary and tertiary memories make it possible to work with significantly large bodies of information, the machine is not capable of performing deep and complicated operations on really large bodies of text with the speed that would be desired in an operational system. The result is that it may take 30 seconds or a minute to get something that one would like to have almost instantly, that the display flickers on the oscilloscope screen, and so forth. Second, there is not available, at present, on any machine, either a programming language or a man-machine interaction language that makes it easy to do, or possible to do rapidly, many of the things envisioned in the discussion of pro-cognitive systems in Part I of this report. Our approach, during the study, was simply to put up with, and make allowances for, the shortcomings of the hardware system. It was easy to do that in informal experiments conducted by members of the research group; it was not realistic, however, to hope that all the observers of demonstrations would make the necessary allowances, and the shortcomings of the equipment effectively precluded formal experimentation.

Nevertheless, the equipment situation was at least tolerable, in terms of absolute assessment, and it seemed superb when we compared our man-computer interaction situation with any but two or three of all the others with which we were acquainted. The unavailability of highly developed languages and, of course, the interpreter and compiler programmes that would be required to make them useful - was, however, a seriously inhibiting factor. During the period of our study, two good programming-language systems came into being: DECAL, which is a quite elegant and powerful language and compiler of the ALGOL type, suitable for a small computer, and MACRO, which is an ingenious language and assembler system that incorporates several of the features that DECAL lacks and lacks several of the features that DECAL incorporates.

However, neither DECAL nor MACRO was designed for on-line programming, and neither was designed particularly to handle the problems that seem likely to present themselves to users of pro-cognitive systems. Those considerations led to the effort, which was never quite completed, to develop a composite programme oriented and user-oriented system to facilitate our research in man-machine interaction. The system is called 'Exec,' which stands, of course, for 'executive program'- and thus expresses something about the mode of operation: statements of the input language, coming into the computer, are examined by the executive programme, and, depending upon whether or not they fall into the class requiring interpretation, are either interpreted and executed with the aid of a set of subroutines associated with the executive programme or simply executed as machine instructions. Exec was written originally in the symbolic language called 'FRAP' and had, as its main function, simplification of the preparation of programmes and subroutines to be translated and assembled by FRAP.

When DECAL became available, Exec was rewritten in DECAL, and slight modifications were made to facilitate the use of Exec in the preparation of programmes and subroutines to be translated and compiled by DECAL. The original intention - to develop Exec to the point at which it could operate as an on-line language as well as an adjunct to a programming language—was not accomplished. One of the main themes in the work on Exec was to simplify and regularise the 'calling' and 'returning' of subroutines. In most computer-programming systems, and especially in the computer-programming systems that will be required in the implementation of plans of the kind, a computer programme is a complex arrangement of parts. The highest echelon of the structure does little more than represent the chapter headings of the general plan.

The actual work—the detailed processing of data - is handled by subprograms or 'subroutines' that break the task down into successively simpler sub packages at successively lower levels of detail until, finally, there is nothing left for the lowest-echelon subprograms to do but to perform simple, explicitly defined operations upon the few codes or numbers that are supplied to them. In this process of successive delegation of responsibility, the transactions that appear repeatedly are the 'calling' of a lower-echelon subroutine by a higher-echelon subroutine and the 'returning' of control from the lower-echelon subroutine to the higher-echelon subroutine. Calling usually includes transmission of instructions, and also the designation of the arguments upon which the lower-echelon subroutine must operate, from the calling subroutine to the called subroutine. The transmission of information down the line we shall call 'briefing'. Transmission of results up the line we shall call 'debriefing.' In the conventional way of handling calling and returning, a subroutine eventually returns control to the subroutine that called it, but it may first call one or more lower-echelon subroutines. Fortunately or unfortunately, depending upon one's point of view, there are many different ways in which subroutines can be called and briefed and in which they can return control and do their debriefing. As indicated, one of the main purposes of Exec is to simplify and regularise this whole process.

In order to simplify the process of calling and returning, Exec is interposed between the calling subroutine and the called subroutine at the time of calling and between the called subroutine and the calling subroutine at the time of returning. With each subroutine is associated a compact code, that provides Exec with a description of the needs.of the subroutine. Exec can therefore handle in a systematic, centralised manner several of the functions that would otherwise have to be handled by each subroutine. In taking a burden off the routines, Exec takes a burden off the programmers who prepare them. The arrangements in Exec for calling and returning are set up in such a way that the chain of subroutine calls can be recursive. That is to say, it is possible for subroutine *A* to call subroutine *A*, or for subroutine *A* to call a subroutine *B* which, directly or through one of its minions, called subroutine *A*.

To permit recursive operation, one must handle 'temporary storage' - storage of the scratch-pad jottings made by each subroutine during its operation - in such a way that results written by *B*, for example, do not destroy results that *A* calculated before calling *B* and will need to use after *B* returns control. The functions just described have been implemented in a few programming systems - notably in the systems called IPL and LISP. In IPL and LISP, however, one either works wholly within the system or does not use the system at all. Exec extends the basic programming language and provides the new capabilities and conveniences within the structure of DECAL. In implementing the handling of subroutines, we made use of the technique of the 'pushdown list'. A pushdown list is an arrangement for storing information that resembles the spring-supported tray on which plates are stored in restaurants. If one puts a plate onto the top of the stack, it pushes all the others down, and if one then takes the plate off the top, the others pop up again. Exec, itself, employs one pushdown list.

Another pushdown list is available to the programmer or user through simple commands. He has only to give the name of the entity to be stored into the pushdown list or returned from it and to say whether he wants to push it down or pop it up. In the process of handling a call to a subroutine or a return from a subroutine, Exec examines the subroutine's heading code – determines whether or not, and how, to fulfill each of a number of functions, and then carries out those required. These functions include protecting contents of certain special registers of the processor against destruction during the running of the subroutine, finding the arguments needed by the subroutine and displaying them for its use, accepting the results obtained by the subroutine and communicating them to the calling routine, and protecting the contents of various temporary storage registers and 'flag' registers against modification by the called subroutine.

Exec protects information by putting it into the pushdown list. A second general purpose of Exec is to provide the advantages of generality and the advantages of specificity both at the same time and within the same system. If a computer programme is written in such a way as to make it useful in a particular situation. On the other hand, if the programme is written so that for example, it alphabetises or orders any kind of strings of alphanumeric text in any file or table, then he has to communicate to it, or have the routine that calls it communicate to it, that it should operate on words and that it should alphabetise according to a specified alphabet. In Exec, an effort is made to accommodate very general subroutines and to make it maximally convenient to communicate to them the information required to prepare them for specific applications. This is done by setting up and maintaining a description of the prevailing context of operation. In the terms of the example, his description may contain a specification that the currently prevailing string class is the class of 'words.'

It contains the specification that the *x,* in any subroutine prepared to operate upon 'Table *x,'* should be interpreted as 3. The subroutine, therefore, automatically performs on the operation intended by the programmer, despite the fact that the programmer was thinking in terms of abstractions and not in terms of the particular present task. With arrangements of the kind just suggested, Exec makes it possible to use a subroutine that contains the expression, 'next string,' for example, to operate on the next character, or the next word, or the next sentence, or the next paragraph, or the next section, or the next chapter, and so forth. Exec keeps track of three 'string classes' simultaneously, class *u,* class *v,* and class *w.* At any time, the programmer can set anyone of the string classes to anyone of seven levels. He can write, for example, '*SSCU* word,' meaning to *set* the string class *u* to have the value, *word.* From that time on, until the instruction is superseded, all the subroutines that deal with the string class hierarchy *u* will consider the *u* strings to be words.

The procedure for designating tables is similar to that for designating strings. If the programmer would like to have programmes written in terms of Tables *x*, *y*, and *z* operate on the contents of Table zones 2, 5, and 7, he writes '*ntox* 2, *ntoy* 5, *ntoz* 7.' * When Exec sees those instructions, it does more than merely substitute 2 for *x*, 5 for *y*, and 7 for *z*. It finds the descriptions, in its file of table descriptions, that characterise the three numbered tables, and it substitutes these descriptions for the pre-previously prevailing descriptions of Tables *x*, *y*, and *z*, respectively. When a subroutine operates on the contents of the table, it examines the table's description and controls its processing accordingly. This makes it possible to accommodate diverse formats and conventions. Inasmuch as the adjustments are made 'interpretively' during the running of the programme, the user can change his mind and reprocess something in a slightly different way without having to go through extensive revision and recompilation of his programmes. This is an advantage that the present technique has over the technique, based on the 'communication pool,' that has been developed in connection with the programming of very large computer systems—systems programmed by teams so large as to discourage the effort to enforce the use of a single, standard set of conventions and formats.

The part of Exec that we have been describing is approximately an interpretive communication pool. The third set of functions with which Exec is concerned has to do with the display of alphanumeric information on typewriters and on the oscilloscope screen. Although these are very simple functions, they involve enough detailed programming to be a nuisance unless they are handled in a systematic way. Exec makes it convenient to separate specification of the information to be displayed from specification of the equipment through which it is to be displayed. It uses standard programmes to handle strings that are long enough to be considered messages or texts, but it provides special arrangements to facilitate preparation of labels, headings, and the like.

For example, the programmer can call for the typing of any particular character *x* on whatever typewriter is currently specified to be typewriter *b* simply by writing '*type x.*' If the programmer wants the character to appear upon the screen of oscilloscope *a*, he writes '*scpa x.*' With the aid of Exec, the programmer can define in equally short instructions the size of the print, the vertical position at which the text should begin, and other parameters of the visual display.

Exec's arrangements for displaying capital and lower-case letters on the oscilloscope are primitive, but it is a step in the right direction to have both capital and lower-case letters. At present, a 'lower-case' letter is simply a small capital letter. We settled for that stopgap solution only in the interest of economy. The fourth and final set of functions handled by Exec has to do with display, by the computer, of what the computer is doing. One technique developed for this purpose, a technique called 'Introspection,' because it was developed as a separate project. The arrangements described here are integral to Exec. One of the main causes of difficulty in man-computer interaction is that the computer does not give the man any good clues about what it is doing until it completes a segment of processing and spews forth the results.

When the computer is running, its lights flash so fast that they are scarcely interpretable. It seems important to provide a way of having the computer give a running account of its processing. A part of Exec called the 'Reporting Subsection 'an optional part - is brought into play each time a subroutine is called and each time a subroutine returns control to its caller. When the reporting subsection is brought into action, it examines the list of things that it should do. This list can be changed while Exec and other programmes are running. Ordinarily, the first thing on the list is to give the address, and, if it is available in the directory, also the name, of the subroutine that is being called or that is returning control to its caller. Since the subroutines operate very rapidly, the names and addresses would appear to be presented simultaneously, one on top of another, if they were shown in a fixed location on the screen.

Therefore they are displayed in a format corresponding to that of a conventional outline. If a chain of subroutines is called, each one operating at a level just lower than its caller, the names and addresses appear on successive lines of the display with increasing indentation. Then, as the subroutines return control, each to its caller, the names and addresses are displayed again in such a way as to redisplay the outline pattern from bottom to top. To the display just described can be added, at the option of the operator, a display of the contents of the active registers of the computer. In addition, the operator may see the contents of whatever parts of the computer's memory he wants to examine. He designates the various parts of memory to Exec by typing on the typewriter while the programme is running. He can change his prescription at will. The current version of Exec allows him to specify nine different sectors of memory, either symbolically or in terms of absolute addresses. When he indicates that he wants to see 'the subroutine,' Exec interprets 'the subroutine' to mean the particular subroutine that is being called, or that is returning control to its caller. That will, of course, be one subroutine at one moment and another at another moment. When the operator wishes to examine a table or a programme in detail, he touches the space bar of the typewriter. That causes the system to pause in its progression through the sequence of things to be displayed, and to hold the current display until the operator releases it by touching the tab key. The Reporting Subsection provides a few additional conveniences - minor ones introduced from time to time on an *ad hoc* basis - but the foregoing will suffice to give an idea of the existing arrangement. Let us mention a few of the steps not yet accomplished, however. It seems worth while to connect to the Reporting Subsection the 'Introspection' programmes that will be described later.

It is necessary to complete the arrangements that associate the tables that reside in the primary memory to corresponding structures in secondary and tertiary memory and, in the manner of the Atlas computer system, to arrange it so that information structures are automatically shifted up through the memory hierarchy whenever they are addressed. It is necessary, also, to expand the mechanism that associates symbols with machine addresses. That mechanism is only a simple table-searching system, but it is inherently capable of effecting the translation required to make conveniently readable the reports of 'what is currently going on in the computer.' We found it useful to distinguish, in Exec, between 'intrinsic' and 'extrinsic' subroutines. Exec is highly 'subroutinised' and has the partly hierarchical, partly recursive, structure that we have described as essential for pro-cognitive systems. Each sub-function of Exec that appears to have any likelihood of proving useful in future applications is separated out and set into the form of a subroutine. In the process of writing subroutines to handle substantive problems - subroutines that made use of Exec but were not at first intended to be part of the Exec system - we encountered repeatedly several sets or clusters of functions. By associating with Exec the subroutines prepared to handle those functions, we were able to build up a system of considerable convenience and power. The part of the system not intrinsic to Exec was too extensive to be held in primary memory at all times. However, it was clearly desirable to bring parts of it into primary memory - coherent clusters of it corresponding to major functions - whenever required in the execution of a programme. The easiest way to accomplish dynamic storage and transfer of subroutines, and to handle the associated bookkeeping, was to take care of it automatically through Exec's ability to examine calling sequences and subroutine headings. We did not make much progress towards that end during the course of the study.

However, we did work with the problem enough to see the great convenience and power that reside in a coherent structure of computer subroutines and a largely automatic arrangement for calling them and transferring information among them. Evidently, the more sophisticated the arrangements, the larger the fraction of the subroutines that will be intrinsic to the arrangements. We visualise a system in a continual process of development, with a set of intrinsic subroutines, a set of extrinsic subroutines, and a continual flow from the extrinsic set to the intrinsic set as more and more functions are brought within the scope and capability of the system.

ON-LINE MAN-COMPUTER COMMUNICATION

'On-Line Man-Computer Communication' by Licklider and Clark discusses several problems in, and several steps towards the improvement of, interaction of men and computers. These include problems and developments in the use of computers as aids in teaching and in learning and as a basis for group cooperation in the planning and design of buildings. The part of the paper that stemmed from the present study was the development of a pair of programmes, referred to earlier as 'Introspection,' that are closely connected with the last described major function of Exec. The two programmes of 'Introspection' were designed to demonstrate that, although present-day computers are opaque and inscrutable, of all the complex organisms and systems in the world, computers are, in principle, the most capable of revealing the intricacies of their internal processes. We consider this to be an important problem calling for much research. Our two programmes constitute only exploratory steps. The two parts of Introspection are 'Programme Graph' and 'Memory Course.' Programme Graph displays, in the form of a graph relating that quantity to time, the contents of any specified register or registers of the computer.

Memory Course displays the progression of control from one memory register to the next during the operation of a programme. With the aid of these two programmes, the operator can see what is happening, as it happens, within the processor and the memory of the computer. These programmes give him at once both a global view and a considerable amount of detail. They let him see relations among parts of the over-all picture. No longer is he constrained, as he has been with conventional procedures, to peek at the contents of one register at a time, and to build up the over-all picture from myriad examinations of microscopic details. To provide a rough impression of the operation of Programme Graph, it may suffice to describe how it operates when it is set to display the contents of the register of the computer that is called the 'programme counter.' The programme counter contains the address of the memory register that contains the instruction that is being executed. In the absence of 'branching' or 'jumping,' control proceeds from one register to the next, and the contents of the programme counter increase by one, each time an instruction is executed. When a 'branch' or 'jump' occurs, the number in the programme counter changes by some integral quantity different from one, and often the increment or decrement is rather large. Programme Graph plots the graph relating the number in the programme counter to the time. The display presents about a thousand individual quantities simultaneously to view. From the graph, it is easy to recognise the upward-sloping line segments that correspond to non-branching, non-jumping stretches of programme.

When the programme 'loops,' as it often does, branching backward and repeating a sequence of instructions over and over, the display shows a saw toothed waveform. When the programme calls a subroutine, the jump to the subroutine, the loops within the subroutine, and the return from the subroutine are all clearly evident. When Programme Graph is used to display the contents of the accumulator, the input-output register, or one of the memory registers, the interpretation of the graph is, of course, quite different. In general, however, its main value lies in its presentation of a large quantity of information in such a way that relations among parts are easy to perceive. The other Introspection programme, Memory Course, displays only the course through memory followed by the programme under study.

It shows that course as a succession of circles connected by a heavy line against a gridlike background representing the primary memory of the computer. The grid upon which the display of Memory Course is shown consists of 4096 dots, arranged in 64 squares of 64 dots each, and representing one bank of memory. A register is represented by a very fine light dot if the instruction and the address it contains are both zero. The dot is a little heavier if the instruction is not zero. The dot is a little heavier still if the address is not zero. If both the instruction and the address are not zero, the dot is heavy. From the grid, therefore, the user can see which parts of memory are occupied and which are not. In addition, after he has gotten used to the display, he can make out which parts of memory are used to store programmes, and which parts are used to store data. When Memory Course is used to display the 'trajectory' through memory followed by an object programme, the object programme itself is not run in the usual way. Instead, the object programme is operated by Memory Course, which 'traces' the progress of the object programme and displays it on the oscilloscope screen. Each time an instruction is executed, a circle is drawn around the dot that corresponds to the location of the instruction in the computer memory. When a programme 'loop' is traced, the line is set over slightly to one side of the circles it has been connecting. That keeps it from retracing its path backwards and helps it represents the cyclic nature of the course. Memory Course represents loops, as just suggested, by tracing out a closed course. When the programme transfers control to a subroutine, a line jumps out from the dot that corresponds to the call and leads to the dot that corresponds to the beginning of the subroutine.

Thus, Memory Course provides a simple, maplike representation of the programme structure. One can see where the various subroutines are, how long they operate, when they receive their calls, and when they return control to their callers. If an error occurs, either in the computer or in the programme, control is very likely to be transferred to an inappropriate location. If the user knows the structure of his programme, either from having programmed it or from experience operating it, he sees that something unexpected has happened.

He then looks back to the beginning of the unexpected line and determines precisely the location of the register within which the error originated. Having done that, he typically reruns the programme, following its course very carefully as it approaches the critical point. If the error recurs, he reruns the programme once more, this time stopping it at various points ahead of the critical one and using other means to examine the instructions, addresses, and data associated with those points.

A FILE INVERTER

The project to be described next was aimed, like Exec, at increasing the convenience and effectiveness with which the computer could be used in the study of library and procognitive problems. This project, however, had a much sharper focus than Exec. Its aim was simply to implement the operation called 'file inversion.'

A direct file is ordered with respect to its 'items', and usually several terms are associated with each item. An inverse file is ordered with respect to its 'terms,' with several items usually associated with each term. Obviously, both the direct file and the inverse file are aspects of a more general structure consisting of items, terms, and associations between items and terms.

The 'File Inverter' is a computer programme, written in DECAL by Grignetti, that accepts a direct file and produces an inverse file. Since there is no difference in abstract format between a direct file and an inverse file, the programme produces a direct file if it is presented with an inverse one. The file-inverting programme includes a subprogram that alphabetises the entries. If it is used to invert a file consisting of terms associated with alphabetised items, it yields a file of items associated with alphabetised terms.

If the items consist of the bibliographic citations of documents, and if the terms are the key words of the titles of the documents, then the result obtained by applying the file-inverting programme is a kind of 'permuted title index.' Grignetti's programme includes a subprogram that facilitates the selection of key words from titles. The subprogram selects from a string of words all those that do not appear upon a list of words to be excluded. The list of words to be excluded ordinarily contains the 'function' words and, also, words that have been found not to discriminate.

AN AUTOMATED CARD CATALOGUE

Using parts of the file-inverting programme, Grignetti prepared a programme that automates some of the functions involved in using an ordinary card index. The kind of card index towards which the programme is oriented is not precisely the kind used in most libraries. It differs mainly in assuming that each card will contain a series of descriptive terms.

Such card indexes are found more frequently in documentation centers that specialise in laboratory technical reports and reprints than in libraries of books and serials. The 'Automated Card Catalogue' is a DECAL programme for use in exploration of card catalogue problems. The user sits at the computer typewriter and presents his retrieval prescription to the computer in the form of a Boolean function of the terms in which he is interested. A person interested in non-digital simulations of neural processes, particularly including studies made under the heading, 'perception, ' but also other studies in the field of artificial intelligence, might type:

- (Artificial intelligence or perception or neural simulation) and not digital

Using the terms of the Boolean function as retrieval terms, the programme searches a magnetic tape containing the 'card' file. Whenever it finds one of the terms, it looks further within the entry to determine whether or not the function is satisfied. If the function is satisfied, the programme displays the entire contents of the 'card' on the oscilloscope screen for examination by the user. Grignetti's programme makes it convenient for the user to correct his retrieval prescription, to reinitiate a search, to find out just where he stands at any point in his study, and to save 'cards' for future reference.

The programme 'knows' the rules for regular pluralisation and considers the search for a term to be satisfied if either the singular or a calculated regular plural or a given irregular plural of the term is found. In addition, the programme works with a simplified system of spelling, as well as with literal spelling, and is therefore often able to find the desired term on a 'card' even when the term is misspelled in the prescription. In such an instance, it displays, for example,

- Do you mean 'intelligence'?

The user then types y for 'yes' or n for 'no.' The programme remembers this answer and does not bother the user again with the same question. That may be convenient when the user is dealing with names he does not know very well, but it leads to complications that will have to be settled through further programming. Probably it will be better to correct the prescription than to perpetuate the indiscrimination.

A SYSTEM TO FACILITATE THE STUDY OF DOCUMENTS

The two programmes described in the preceding sections are related to, and are intended for incorporation into, a system to facilitate the retrieval and study of documents. The 'study' part of the over-all system is described in a report by Bobrow, Kain, Raphael, and Licklider.

The study system, called 'Symbiont' because we hope to develop it into a truly symbiotic partner of the student, displays information to the student via the typewriter or the display screen. It is intended as an exploratory tool, for use mainly by students who are at the same time experimenters, and it does not yet have the perfection or polish required for realistic demonstration or practical application. However, it does make available, in a single, integrated package, several functions that prove quite useful to a student who wants to examine a set of technical documents, take notes on their contents, compare or combine graphs found in different papers, and so forth. Among the functions provided by Symbiont are the following:

- Present for examination a document specified by any sufficiently prescriptive segment of its bibliographic citation.
- Turn pages, forward or backward, in response to the pressing of a key.
- Permit designation of a passage by pointing to the beginning and then the end with a light pen.
- Accept labels from the typewriter and associate them with passages of text.
- Record as a note, and preserve for later inspection, any designated passage.
- Append bibliographic citations to extracted passages.
- Accept retrieval prescriptions from the typewriter.
- Accept from the typewriter coded versions of specifications of such operating characteristics as, 'Consider a neighbourhood to be five consecutive lines of text,' or 'Consider a search to be satisfied when any two of the three elements of the search have been satisfied.'
- Carry out retrieval searches and display passages in which the retrieval prescriptions are satisfied.
- Compose graphs from tabulated data and present the graphs, against labeled coordinate grids, on the oscilloscope screen.
- Set two graphs side by side to facilitate comparison.

- Expand or compress the scales of graphs, under control from the light pen.
- Change the number of grid lines or the calibration numbers associated with the lines, or both together, and recalculate and redisplay the calibration numbers when grid lines are added or deleted.

The search routines used in finding desired passages of text operate with three sets of retrieval terms. The user specifies the terms of each set initially through the typewriter. All the terms of a subset are considered equivalent during the search, and the search is satisfied insofar as that subset is concerned if anyone of the terms is encountered in the text. The user can specify whether he wants to find a passage in which at least one of the terms of one of the sets occurs, or a passage in which at least one of the terms of each of two of the sets occurs, and so forth. Even though this implementation is primitive, it is evident from preliminary experiments with Symbiont that automation of the function of searching for 'ideas' will be a very powerful aid in technical study. Machine aid in manipulating graphs will also be very helpful.

ASSOCIATIVE CHAINING AS AN INFORMATIONRETRIEVAL TECHNIQUE

Most of the information-retrieval systems that have actually been developed, and even most of those that have been subjected to intensive research, retrieve unitary elements of information, such as documents, paragraphs, or sentences. A basic point in Marill's paper is that for many purposes the retrieval of a unitary part of the corpus is inadequate, and that what often is needed is an answer to a question that may have to be derived through deduction from elements of information scattered throughout the corpus.

When the relation between two items is direct, they are said to be connected by a first-order chain. When the relation between two items can be established only through the intermediary agency of a third item, the first two items are said to be connected by a chain of second order, and so forth. In a report on 'Associative Chaining as an Information Retrieval Technique,' Clapp describes the idea of chaining as a general schema, then shows the correspondence between the chaining schema and certain schemata of graph theory, and finally discusses a programme that traces chains of relevance through corpora consisting of files of sentences.

Chaining, as a technique, is particularly simple and easy to discuss when it is separated from the problem of the nature of relevance. In Clapp's work, the two things - the technique and the concept of relevance - are well separated. For purposes of simplicity and convenience, Clapp considers two sentences to be directly associated if they have one or more words in common. Thus, the sentences, 'The cat is black,' and 'Black is a colour,' are directly associated. They have two words in common, 'is' and 'black.' There is no direct, first-order association between the first two of the following sentences, but only a second-order association through the third sentence: 'The cat is black,' 'Feline animals move gracefully,' 'A cat is a feline animal.' It is obvious, even at the outset, that something has to be done to inhibit associations based on the common occurrence of frequently used verbs and function words. In Clapp's approach, however, whatever is done about that is a separate matter from the development of the algorithm that traces out the chains. Clapp's computer programmes are divided into two sets. The first set of programmes facilitates the preparation of a machine-processible file of information units, such as sentences, paragraphs, or documents. It then prepares, from the file, a series of concordances. Finally, with the aid of the concordances, it determines the set of all first order associations.

The second set of programmes operates upon a retrieval prescription plus the set of first-order associations. The retrieval prescription is a set of words drawn from the vocabulary of the corpus.

The first thing that the chaining algorithm does is to find all those elements of the corpus that contain all the words of the prescription. This is what a 'conventional' information retrieval system would do. Then, however, the chaining algorithm goes on to trace higher-ordered chains through the corpus and to retrieve the information elements that are involved in higher-ordered chains up to some cutoff order specified by the operator.

The programme has been tested and demonstrated only with a corpus consisting of sentences. Except for minor considerations having to do with delimiters - the clues that mark stopping points such as ends of sentences or paragraphs - the chaining programmes are not sensitive to the distinctions among sentence, paragraph, document, and so forth, and it is obvious that the chaining operation can be carried out on textual strings of any class. However, pursuing the technique of chaining based on the common occurrence of words beyond a level of the sentence does not seem to offer much promise. It is evident that every book would be directly associated with almost every other book if the criterion were a word in common and it is equally evident that almost no book would be associated with any other book if the criterion were a verbatim paragraph in common. For the technique of chaining, ordinary sentences seem to be approximately the optimal length. Fortunately, the sets of descriptive terms used in coordinate-indexing systems are of approximately the same length as sentences. The notion of association based on inclusion of common terms is quite appropriate for them. It is in that domain that we think it most likely that the chaining technique, and the chaining algorithms developed by Clapp, will find practical application. In his exploration of the relations between graph theory and associative chaining, Clapp developed the chaining schema in considerably more depth than is reflected in this summary. For example, his development uses the number of parallel links as well as the order of the links in the chain of association. Some of his ideas recognise gradations in the strength of association.

That seems important because, intuitively, one thinks of relevance as capable of variation in degree. The next step in the development of the concept of associative chaining, we think, should be an attempt to define the fundamental relatedness or relevance on which the 'association' is based. Associative chaining has a natural connection with the relational networks and with the semantic nets and question-answering systems studied by Marill and Black. The next step may, therefore, take the form of merging the chaining concept with the concepts underlying the relational and semantic nets and the question-answering systems.

TWO QUESTION-ANSWERING SYSTEMS

Marill's short paper on question-answering systems, described earlier, initiated a series of studies that involved a meld of symbolic logic and computer programming. Most of these studies were carried out by Black, who described them in a series of memoranda and a report. The memoranda and the report share with the corpora of the question-answering systems a tight, terse, logical quality that makes them attractive to the logician and difficult for the non-logician to understand. Following is an effort to summarise, without gross distortion, two of the principal accomplishments of the work on question-answering systems in a freer and less formal exposition. One might justify this aim by quoting a paragraph from Black's 'Conclusions on QAS': A string of words cannot be rephrased without significant loss of facts or ideas relevant to some area. However, if we limit ourselves to certain areas, then the string of words can be rephrased without loss of facts or ideas *relative to those areas.* In the final paragraph of the same memorandum Black goes on to say: Before we can rephrase a string of words without significant loss, we must define our interests precisely.

If we are interested in everything, then we cannot rephrase the string at all. Let us say, therefore, that we are interested in assessing the possibility, and also the technical feasibility, of:

- Representing large parts of the body of knowledge, as well as questions relating to the body of knowledge, in a formal language amenable to processing by a computer and

- Developing a system that will, by processing the questions and the stored corpus, deduce and display COrrect answers.

Black's results attest to the possibility of doing those things. However, Black's programmes take a long time to determine the answers to fairly simple questions. That fact suggests that economic feasibility is dependent upon greatly increasing the processing efficiency of the question-answering system or the processing speed of the computer, or both.

The prediction made in Part I that it is unlikely that there will be great increases in speed in the same computers that have a greatly increased memory capacity, may not bear very heavily on this problem. It may be that as suggested, use procedures that are fast, but not very deep, to retrieve parts of the corpus that are rich in statements germane to a particular question, and then turn to deeper and slower procedures for the derivation of the answer from the rich informational ore.

The first of Black's two contributions to be summarised, the memorandum, 'Specific-Question-Answering System,' February 8, 1963, describes Version III of a system written in the LISP language for the IBM 7090 computer. In this system, the corpus consists of statements that are strings of ordinary words, symbols representing variables, and parentheses.

The use of the ordinary words is highly constrained - so constrained that nothing can be said that could not be said equally well in the shorter, but less widely readable, notation seen in books on logic.

The only variables are *Xl, X2, X3, what, when, which,* and *how*. The parentheses have the effect of forcing the system to consider as a unit the string within the parentheses. The 'questions' asked of the Specific-Question-Answering System may be either statements, in which case they are confirmed or denied by the system, or ordinary questions containing the variables, *Xl, X2, X3, what,* and *when,* etc. The answer elicited by a 'yes-no' question is 'yes,' 'no,' or 'no answer.' The answer to any other question is a list of items that constitute a correct and reasonable reply, or 'no answer'.

The system seeks answers to questions by processing the questions and the corpus in a very straightforward, rigourous way.

It looks through the corpus for a statement that is the same as the statement that constitutes the question or that can be transformed into the question by removing a 'not.' If it finds a match, the answer is 'yes'.

If it finds a negated match, the answer is 'no.' If it finds neither, it looks for a conditional statement in the corpus in which the consequent matches the question. If it finds such a statement in the corpus, it undertakes to determine an answer to the subsidiary question, whether or not the premise of the conditional statement is true. Proceeding in this way, it tries every possibility of deriving the question or its negation from the statements of the corpus. The procedure for processing of questions containing variables is a little more complex than the procedure just described.

It is necessary, in seeking an answer to a question containing a variable, to keep track of all the individuals that can be values of the variable. The process amounts, approximately, to determining the list of individuals that meet all the conditions that are imposed upon the variable. The system is capable of answering not only simple, single-variable questions, but also multiple questions, conditional questions, and even questions containing the names of LISP computer programmes.

In the latter case, there is a rigid format that must be followed in giving the name of the programme and its arguments. All the foregoing structures mentioned as acceptable question forms are also acceptable as forms for statements in the corpus. In the corpus, a programme name may occur even in the antecedent of a conditional statement. We mention these things to indicate that the system has the capability of expressing complex relations and of deriving answers to complex questions. To see approximately what the system does, let us consider a few oversimplified examples and one more complex example.

Suppose, first, that the corpus consists merely of two statements:

- Mercury is (a planet) if (Xl is a planet) then (Xl is a planet of the sun)

The question asked of the system, in statement form, is:

- Mercury is a planet of the sun

To that question, the system says, simply:

- Yes

Suppose, for the second example, that the corpus consists of only one sentence:

- Earth is smaller than jupiter

The question asked of the system and the foregoing rudimentary corpus is:

- Jupiter is smaller than earth

The answer given by the system to that question is:

- No Answer

But now suppose that a second statement is added to the corpus. The corpus now consists of the two statements:

- Earth is smaller than jupiter if (XI is smaller than X2) then (X2 is not smaller than XI)

The question is still:

- Jupiter is smaller than earth

The system is now able to determine an answer. It says:

- NO

The question asked of the system and this corpus is:

- What is a major planet

The answer provided by the system is:

- Neptune
- Uranus
- Saturn
- Jupiter

This last example would be more impressive than it is if the corpus contained a large number of irrelevant statements in addition to the statements shown. The presence of irrelevant statements would increase the length of time required by the computer in answering the question, but the computer has the great advantage, in operations of this kind, that it does not tend to forget the relevant facts already found while it is examining the irrelevancies. For a human being, on the other hand, a problem of the present kind that is difficult but nevertheless within one's scope of capability becomes entirely hopeless as soon as a large amount of irrelevant material is introduced. That fact, we believe, is significant in its bearing on the problem men face in drawing answers from the body of knowledge that is now held in libraries and document rooms.

The other paper of Black's that we shall discuss here is 'A Question-Answering System: QAS-5'. This paper describes in detail the operation of a later generation question-answering system, a descendant of the Specific-Question-Answering System that we have been discussing. The main advances made in the interim between the two papers were advances in the handling of quantification and advances achieved by formalising the language approximately in a way suggested earlier by McCarthy. The advance in quantification makes it possible for the system to deal with problems involving 'some' and 'all.'

The formalisation of the language makes it difficult for the uninitiated reader to understand what is being done, but it reveals the flaws and pitfalls to the veteran in a clearer way than the more readable language does, and, moreover, it suggests what to do to correct or avoid them. We consider the formalisation, therefore, to be a step more in a right direction than in a wrong one - a step that must be taken in order to reach a position from which it will be possible to move forward to simultaneous readability and formal effectiveness.

The mode of operation of QAS-5 is similar in basic principle, though somewhat deeper and more complex, to the mode of operation of the Specific-Question-Answering System. Some of the flavour of the method is given by the following protocol:

- Step 1: The system finds the first match for question 1 in statement 6.

- Step 2: The system forms the backward transform of question 1 and statement 6, giving a new conditional (7) - at (desk, *y*), at (*y*, country) at (desk, country).
- Step 3: The system sets up the first antecedent of (7) as a new question (2) - at (desk, *y*).
- Step 4: The system finds the first match for question 2 in statement 2.
- Step 5: The system forms the transform of question 2 and statement 2, giving the answer to question 2 - (I) at (desk, home).

The latter would be read, as one might possibly guess, 'I am at my desk at home.' The problem to which Black's QAS-5 report is wholly dedicated is a problem posed by McCarthy in 1958 and hitherto not solved by any nonhuman system. It is a well known problem in artificial-intelligence and heuristic-programming circles and is called the 'airport problem.'

The problem, stated here informally, is fairly simple: I am at my desk, at home. My car is in my garage, which is also at my home. I want to go to the airport. The airport is in the same county as my home. I can walk from any point that I would call 'at my home' to any other point that I would also call 'at my home,' because, of course, the dimensions of the area subsumed under 'home' are not very great. I can drive from any point in my county to any other point in my county. What should I do? The answer to the question, or the solution to the problem, is said to be:

> I should go from my desk to my garage on foot and get my car, and I should then drive my car from the garage to the airport.

Having stated the problem and given the solution, we should perhaps repeat that, although the answer is obvious to any adult human being who understands English, no one had succeeded in devising a wholly automatic system that would derive the answer from the description of the situation and the statement of the question. Black's report gives a step-by-step account of the procedure used by QAS-

5 in solving the problem. In addition, it displays, point by point, the minor differences between the notation suggested by McCarthy and the notation employed by Black. The conclusions that we draw from our experience with question-answering systems are summed up in the assertion that the achievement of Black's programme in solving McCarthy's problem is simultaneously a signal advance in automated question answering and a commonplace performance for a moderate intelligence. In greater detail, the conclusions are:

- Clear progress is being made in bringing logical deduction within the scope of automation.
- In the process of programming a system to accomplish a feat such as the one described, one begins to see how extremely deep and complex are the intellectual processes that one accepts as commonplace and undemanding of intelligence when those processes are carried out by people.
- In the running of such programmes, one begins to sense the magnitude of the gulf that separates a demonstration of the type just described from an economically feasible operating system. As the problems become more complex, and as the corpus becomes larger, the amount of time required for processing goes up steeply. This is a discouraging counterpoise to the pattern of growth of the information-processing technology.
- At the same time, one sees, even at this stage, many ways in which processing can be made more efficient, and one senses that there are - waiting to be discovered ways of formulating the procedure that are much more powerful than the ways thus far employed.

In short, it appears to us that the domain of question-answering systems is an intellectually deep and technologically demanding area for research and development. As suggested, there is an extremely long way to go before useful answers can be deduced from extensive information bases at reasonable cost. On the other hand, it may well be that, in this area, each basic conceptual advance will be a long stride towards the pro-cognitive systems we envision for man's future interaction with the fund of knowledge.

AN APPROACH TO COMPUTER PROCESSING OF NATURAL LANGUAGE

This final project was pursued intensively during the first year of the study, but, for reasons not related to its degree of promise, it lay dormant during the second year. Although the project does not appear to be worth continuing in its present form, the following description may prove useful. The approach selected at the outset - to try to mirror in computer programmes the ontogenetic development of the human ability to generate and understand language - was quite different from the approach, then more popular, based upon syntactic analysis. The approach adopted paid more attention to semantics than to syntax.

However, many of the investigators who earlier had concentrated on syntactic analysis have directed their efforts towards semantic analysis, and what seemed to us at the outset to be an unpopulated field is rapidly becoming crowded. That fact, together with our sharpening awareness of the very great difficulty and even greater extent of the task, account for the negativeness of our thoughts about reactivating 'Ontogeny.' At the beginning of the project, it seemed to us to be a good idea to start with 'baby talk' and to try to recapitulate, as closely as possible, the development of the human language process. Recognising the importance of the 'verbal community' in each individual's development of language process, we set up a situation in which an operator at the typewriter played the role of the verbal community and, acting as stimulator, instructor, reinforce, umpire, and protector, presided over the 'shaping up' of language behaviour in the computer.

It was necessary, of course, to provide the computer with basic structures and capabilities corresponding roughly to those that would be inherited by a human being. It was necessary also to set up some domain of discourse that would be potentially 'meaningful' to the computer, as well as to the operator, and that would provide an analogue to the 'environment' in which human beings behave and with reference to which most of their language - that is not about themselves - is oriented. One part of the internal mechanism - of the system of computer programmes - seems worth describing despite the fact that its nature does not in any direct way determine the nature of the over-all system. This part of the programme is concerned with the representation, in the computer memory, of the words and phrases communicated between the operator and the computer. In the input and output equipment, the words and phrases take the form of strings of characters or character codes.

The codes are the so-called 'concise' codes for alphanumeric characters employed in the PDP-1 computer. Each code is a pattern of six binary digits. Representation of words, phrases, and so forth, as strings of coded characters is inconvenient and uneconomical for many information-processing purposes. In a computing machine that has registers of fixed length, it is inconvenient to have words and phrases of variable length. We were at the outset not so much concerned with economy of representation as with convenience of processing, and we adopted an approach designed mainly for convenience. We represented each word, or phrase, or sentence, or string of any recognised class, by a 36- bit code. The code was made up of a 30-bit main code and 6 bits of auxiliary information, which included designation of the class to which the string belonged. A 36-bit code can be stored conveniently in two consecutive registers of the PDP-l memory. The rule for representing incoming words in the computer memory was the following. If the word consisted of five characters or fewer, the concise-code representation is the computer representation; if, on the other hand, the word contained more than five characters, then the computer representation consists of the concise codes of the first three characters, the six auxiliary bits, and, in addition, a 12-bit 'hash code' calculated by a rather complicated procedure from the concise codes of the remaining characters. This representation is capable of discriminating among about 4000 different words with the same three leading characters.

Because the calculation of the hash code is carried out by a procedure akin to the generation of 'random numbers,' one cannot be entirely sure that two different words will not yield the same code. Nevertheless, he can make the probability of a 'collision' as low as he likes by selecting a sufficiently long representation. In the initial stages of the work, we were not much concerned about accidental confusion of one word with another. Children certainly confuse words. Indeed, we were attracted by the hypothesis that some of the confusions that arise in human communication and thinking are attributable to something like a hash-code process in neural representation. The agent that converts strings of text into hash codes is, of course, a computer programme.

First it divides a string of text into words and determines a code for each word. Then it combines the words into phrases, using punctuation as a guide, and determines a hash code for each phrase from the codes for the words within the phrase. Then it determines a hash code for each sentence from the codes for the phrases within the sentence, and so forth. Thus, for each word, for each phrase, for each sentence, there is a 36-bit representation. After the conversion to this internal code has been effected, and until a stage is reached at which it is necessary to generate a response in the form of a string of alphanumeric characters, all the processing is carried out with the internal 36-bit codes. It is easy to transform alphanumeric text into internal codes. To do that, it is necessary only to apply the transformation programmes that calculate the codes. However, to transform in the other direction - to go from the internal code representation to a string of alphanumeric characters - is another matter. Because information is sometimes lost in the forward transformation, it is not possible simply to calculate the reverse transformation. It is necessary to employ a 'table-searching' procedure. However, it is certainly neither necessary nor desirable to store every string of characters received in order to have it ready to type as a response. If one is to respond in a natural way, he must be able to generate sequences of words that he has never received. Moreover, there are too many strings of words to consider storing them all in a computer memory.

The procedure adopted, therefore, is to associate with each internal word code, but not with the code for any string of any class other than word, its complete concise code, *i.e.*, the string of concise codes corresponding to the characters of the word. The association is achieved in the following way. All the internal codes, for words, phrases, sentences, and so forth, are kept together - along with other information - in a table called the 'Hash Table'. One of the entries in the Hash Table, for each word represented in that table, is the address of the register in the Vocabulary Table in which the corresponding concise-code representation begins. That makes it possible, given the internal code corresponding to a word, to find the corresponding concise code and to have the word typed on the computer typewriter.

For those internally represented strings that are not merely words, there is still another table, called the 'Sub address Table'. The entry in the Hash Table that is associated with a sentence the way the Vocabulary Table address is associated with a word, is the address of a register in the Sub address Table. At that address in the Sub address Table, one finds the beginning of a list of 'sub addresses' that are addresses of registers back in the Hash Table. In those registers in the Hash Table are the entries for strings of the next lower class. With each hash code for a phrase is associated the address of another register in the Sub address Table. Going back to the Sub address Table with that address, one finds addresses of registers in the Hash Table.

Finally, in the designated registers in the Hash Table are addresses of registers in the Vocabulary Table. In the Vocabulary Table, of course, are the concise codes of the words. The procedure just described is implemented by programming, so no effort of thought is involved after the programme has been perfected. The programme runs much more rapidly than the typewriter can type, and there is therefore no observable delay. With the system, one can start out with a 36-bit hash code and wind up with a long typewritten sentence. If the initial code is the code of a paragraph, indeed he winds up with a paragraph. We have checked the system to that level of operation. Obviously, nothing stands in the way of representing an entire book with a 36-bit internal code. However, one cannot uniquely represent the individuals of any set of sise approaching $2n$ with hash codes n bits in length.

Our selection of 36-bit codes, and our compromise in the direction of readability by man as well as by machine, was conditioned by the fact that we were working with a 'young' language mechanism that would not be expected to develop a very large vocabulary for some time. It is now doubtless evident that a description of computer programmes in ordinary language encounters serious problems of exposition and endurance. We shall, therefore, not describe the entire Ontogeny programme in as great detail. Let us, nevertheless, explain how the system is designed to keep track of the properties of the various words and phrases and the entities and operations for which they stand. The repository for factual information, in Ontogeny, is a table called the 'Property Table.' One of the entries in each section of the Hash Table is the address of a corresponding section in the Property Table. For convenience, the Property Table records the corresponding Hash Table address and also the internal code of the string with which the properties are associated. The properties themselves are represented by internal codes. When it is necessary to determine the meanings of the property codes, one has to find the codes in the Hash Table and go on from there in the way just described. The structure within which properties are represented in the Property Table is a simple hierarchy, an 'outline.'

The rules for listing properties are loose. In the main, they were made up as problems arose, and indeed a certain amount of care was taken *not* to create a sharp, formal, rigid system. Syntactic and semantic properties are mixed indiscriminately. In the basic system, there is not even any distinction between the symbol and the thing for which it stands. That is to say, under 'table' we might record the property of being used mainly as a noun, the property of being used sometimes as a verb, and the property of usually being made of wood. However, the system would be expected to function without great difficulty if, through happenstance, the arrangement were set up as:

table
material
usually
wood
sometimes
steel

We did not reach the point at which programmes actually operated with that kind of irregularity of format, but we did have search programmes that examined the 'next level down' if they did not find a satisfactory property on the level initially assigned.

From the description thus far, it may be evident that the Property Table is, by nature, full of circular definitions. Everything is defined in terms of something else - except for a relatively few primitives that are associated with subroutines. One of the properties of 'move,' for example, is that move is often used as a verb. Another is that, when it is so used, it is to be implemented by executing a subroutine that is capable of taking arguments that answer 'what', 'by whom', 'from where', and 'to where'. Some of the properties of 'pencil' refer to its capability of serving as an argument. A pencil is 'movable', 'takable', 'bringable', and so forth. We are now almost in a position to turn our attention to the procedure through which an incoming message is processed and responded to by the computer. One more part of the system must be described, however, before that can be done conveniently.

This remaining part is the one that has to do with the 'domain of discourse' mentioned earlier. The domain of discourse is a model room equipped with a few items of furniture. The room has a door that can be opened to various degrees, a window that can be opened or closed, a table that can occupy any otherwise unoccupied position within the room, and a chair subject to the same constraint. There are a book and a pencil, to be manipulated, an active agent called 'Comp', and another active agent called 'Oper'. The discourse involves Comp and Oper and is actually carried out by the computer and the operator. The room and its contents are represented in the computer memory, of course, and they are also represented diagrammatically by simple line drawings on the screen of the oscilloscope. When the door is opened, the representation of the door in the computer memory changes, and the schematic door on the oscilloscope screen swings. The basic subroutines, corresponding to operations in the domain of discourse, are implementations of 'move', 'go', 'carry', 'bring', 'open', 'close', 'put', etc. These subroutines, together with the subroutines that handle the encoding and decoding, the search for properties and the analysis of input messages, were all that we actually prepared and operated. The plan encompassed two additional classes of subroutines. The first of these was to handle the addition, deletion and modification of properties, under the control of input messages. The second was to handle the addition and modification of subroutines, again under the control of input messages. If we had been able to carry through to some accomplishments in the first additional category, we should have been able to increase the verbal capability of the system, but only by adding to its knowledge - to its vocabulary and its fund of facts. If we had been able to move on into the second additional category, we should have had within our grasp the capability of achieving almost unlimited restructuring and reorganisation of the system. But we did not accomplish either of those things, and we mention them here only to indicate that the approach had a higher aspiration than merely to move line diagrams about on the screen of an oscilloscope. Now, at last, we come to the procedure employed in analysing the incoming messages and selecting and directing the actions taken in response to them.

The responses were, as suggested earlier, to move things about in the room, to make replies by way of the typewriter, and - in hope but not in actuality - to add to the internally stored knowledge and to the internally stored behaviour patterns. By knowledge, of course, we mean the contents of the several tables mentioned earlier. By behaviour patterns, we mean the set of subroutines available for use in responding. The problem of interpreting an incoming message is, in the approach we have been describing, to select the appropriate subroutine or patterns of subroutines and to find the arguments that they require under the prevailing circumstances. The selection of subroutines is guided by associating subroutines with verbs. The search is carried out by a part of the programme that examines the internal codes that represent the incoming message and a list of roles that the message segments may play. Records are kept in a matrix during the processing of a message. The rows of the matrix are associated with the words of the incoming message.

The columns of the matrix are associated with the possible roles. In the version of Ontogeny that was carried to the point of demonstration, the processing deals only with words. The first step is to look up each word of the incoming message in the Property Table and place a tally in each cell of the matrix that corresponds to a function that the word can fulfil. When this has been done for all the words of the message, the task becomes one of finding an appropriate and consistent assignment of words to functions and, at the same time, a correspondence between the functions and the argument requirements of a subroutine that goes with the verb. The procedure used to carry out this task starts by 'freesing' the rows and columns of the matrix that contain only a single tally. The next step is to prepare simpler matrix patterns in which each of the words at first associated with two or more roles is assigned to a single role. These simpler matrixes are then considered one at a time.

The subroutines corresponding to the word assigned to the verb category in the first simplified matrix are examined. If one of them has a set of argument requirements that match the roles to which words are assigned, then that subroutine is selected, the arguments are supplied to it, and the response is executed. In an effort to get the system into operation quickly, we satisfied ourselves with the first subroutine that met the requirements. If no subroutine met the requirements of the first assignment pattern, the second assignment pattern was used, and so on. As soon as a suitable subroutine was found, supplied with arguments, and executed, the response was considered accomplished. The programme then simply went into a 'listening' mode and waited for the operator to take the next step. Towards the end of the work on Ontogeny, we were planning a set of subroutines that would operate on higher-echelon strings than words. With this set of subroutines, there was to be associated a subsystem for keeping track, in a primitive way, of the 'situation.' The system was to be capable of asking, on receipt of a message, 'Am I already familiar with this message in this context?' If so, it was to enquire of itself what response it had previously made and how effective the response had been.

If the result had been sufficiently favourable, then-the system would simply have made the same response again and taken notes on its effect. In the likely event that no record existed of previous experience with the over-all message in the prevailing context, then the projected system would work with lower-echelon segments of the message, hoping to find that one or more of them was already 'understood.' In the absence of usable prior experience at each echelon, the system would drop down to the next-lower echelon until it finally came to words. Failing to understand a word, or failing to understand a phrase given experience with the words of the phrase, it would ask for help. Our experience with Ontogeny left us with five main impressions:

- It seems possible, and even likely, that we could store up enough substantive information in a computer memory to handle the analysis of natural language

- semantic as well as syntactic - an analysis capable of supporting 'reasonable' responses, if only the domain of discourse is not very wide.

- It is probably more important to limit the domain of discourse than to limit the length or complexity of the input messages.
- Many so-called semantic properties play roles that are almost indistinguishable from syntactic roles. The distinction between things that are capable of acting with initiative as voluntary agents and things that are not, for example, seems to be approximately as important as the distinction between the active voice and the passive voice of verbs.
- A sympathetic, cooperative, verbal, community is a fundamental essential for the development of a sophisticated verbal mechanism. To develop complex language behaviour in a neutral environment would, we think, take another long-suffering recapitulation of evolution.
- On the other hand, no one seems likely to design or invent a formal system capable of automating sophisticated language behaviour.

The best approach, therefore, seems to us to be somewhere between the extremes - to call for a formal base plus an overlay of experience gained in interaction with the cooperative verbal community.

6

Future Digital Library Management Systems

DYNAMICALLY MAKING USE OF DISTRIBUTED DATA SOURCES

One major goal of grid computing is to establish highly flexible and robust environments to utilise distributed resources in an efficient and transparent way. Due to the highly dynamic nature of such environments where computational nodes may leave or join in, it is essential to bind service invocations to concrete service instances at run-time. This allows to flexibly reacting to changes in the environment. In a service-oriented world, application logic is encapsulated by means of services.

Standards like SOAP over HTTP can be used for the invocation of services, and WSDL for accessing information on the capabilities of services. When several instances of the same service exist in a grid environment, then it should be possible to dynamically make use of as many service instances as possible by parallelising a service call and by submitting requests in parallel to them. The goal of this parallelisation is twofold and depends on the characteristics of the services which are subject to parallelisation.

First, we aim to make use of as many services as possible to increase the quality of the result. This is particularly true for the access to data sources, encapsulated by dedicated services. Second, having multiple service instances accessible opens the possibility to speed up the processing of computationally intensive tasks. Whereas examples for the latter have been presented in detail in and large scale experiments with more than 2500 worker nodes have been demonstrated in using MW class library, this work focuses on the goal of enhancing the quality of the request when accessing data sources by means of services.

The contribution of this work is to introduce architecture of a service seeming to be an ordinary, callable service to the outside world, which is able to adopt its behaviour controllable by optional quality of service criteria, and the resources available on a grid. In short, such dynamic services use Meta information on the currently available service providers and their capabilities and partition the original request into a set of simpler requests of the same service types.

These requests are then submitted in parallel to as many service providers as reasonable, and their responses are finally integrated and returned as the result of the original request. In particular, this parallelisation shall be carried out without the need to modify existing functionality or interfaces, and transparently to the user and developer. Due to its master/slave nature, it is especially suitable for grid environments.

OVERALL ARCHITECTURE

The goal of the architecture we propose is to improve the usability of a single service, as well as to facilitate faster and less error prone development for grid environments. This approach is based on the observation that, following the current proliferation of service-oriented architectures, the number of services and service providers in a grid will significantly increase. Especially services which are provider independent and are not bound to special resources can be distributed fast and widely in a grid environment or be deployed numerously on demand. Although the availability of many congruent services as well as the computational resources thereby offered seems to be within reach, adapting functionality for parallel execution is still necessary and tedious.

The task of partitioning request parameters and re-integrating results afterwards is highly application-specific and, from our perspective, cannot be solved in a generic way. Although we see the potential to identify classes of applications according to the mechanism they partition and re-integrate requests which allows to have pre-built splitter and merger services, an expert in the problem domain will be necessary to tailor them for the specific need or perform some additional, application domain specific work. We name a service, enriched with the capability to partition incoming requests and reintegrate partial results, a dynamic service.

Apart from that we introduce a Dynamiser component, which can be built generically and which is responsible for state management, failure handling, and service discovery. While the latter characteristic is independent concerning the twofold approach failure handling and state management differs. In case of a dynamic service aiming to leverage the result quality, the unexpected absence of a 'worker' service already in charge of a partial task does not hinder in producing a result. If partitioning the request of a computationally intensive task to gain better performance, the overall results rely on each sub task and the Dynamiser is responsible for compensating any failing 'worker' service.

The following logical units can be identified for dynamic services. The box in the center of the left side, labeled 'Payload Service', represents the actual service. It is responsible for providing application semantics, *e.g.*, a genotype/phenotype correlation on a local database. This is usually a piece of business logic that has existed beforehand and is now supposed to be opened to the grid and enabled for parallel execution.

To achieve this goal, it is surrounded by another box, labeled 'Common Interface Wrapper', which encapsulates the 'Payload Service' and enhances it with a common interface.

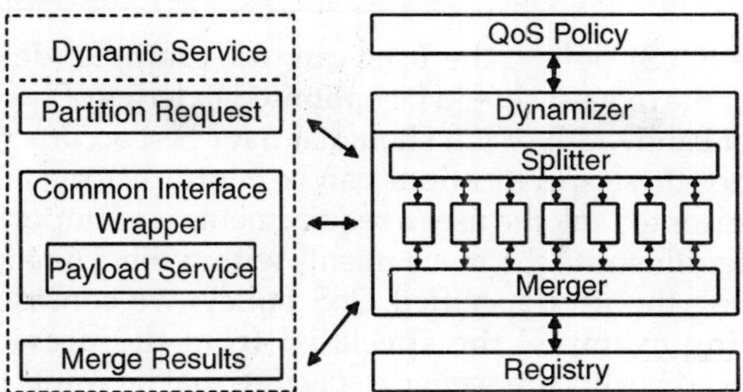

Fig 6.1 Overall Architecture

On top, 'Partition Request' encapsulates knowledge on how incoming parameters for the 'Payload Service' have to be partitioned, so that the original request can be decomposed into numerous new sub-requests. Each of these sub-requests can then be distributed on the grid and be processed by other instances of the originally targeted service. The box at the bottom integrates results returned from the grid to provide the original service requester with a consolidated result. It can therefore be seen as the counter operation to the 'Partition Request' service.

The combination of these elements is referred to as 'Dynamic Service'. To find instances of the originally targeted service, a registry is used. This registry provides information on which services are available, how they can be accessed, and what their properties are. The 'Dynamiser', depicted on the right hand side, makes use of the services. It glues together the previously described services by making the parallel calls and coordinating incoming results. The 'Dynamiser' can interact with all services that adhere to a common interface, as ensured by the 'Common Interface Wrapper'.

It can be integrated in environments able to call and orchestrate services, or it can be packaged and deployed together with specific services. To make the best possible use of the 'Dynamiser', the user can send an optional description of the desired service quality along with the mandatory parameters needed to process the request. In this Quality of

Service (QoS) policy, the user can, for example, describe whether the request should be optimised in terms of speed, in terms of bandwidth or if it should aim for best accuracy.

Since these specifications can be contradictory, adding preferences to rank the user's requirements is of importance. To better illustrate the mechanisms within the 'Dynamiser' regarding the user specified QoS policy, we consider the following example: the specialist from the previously introduced healthcare scenario specifies that he wants to use as many genotype/phenotype correlation information as possible and as affordable within a 300 Euro budget. The 'Dynamiser' finds 7 services with a total of 2 gigabytes of searchable data, each charging 60 Euros per query. Alternatively, there are 40 services available provided by smaller institutions, having just searchable amounts of data starting from 4 megabytes up to 30 megabytes and charging .50 per query. The algorithms on how to reconcile the user specifications, the details of the QoS description language and how to integrate this best with our existing implementation is currently investigated.

INFLUENCE OF REPLICATION ON AVAILABILITY WITHIN P2P SYSTEMS

Peer-to-peer (P2P) digital libraries are highly dynamic as they shall facilitate data sharing among users. The churn rate is high as their peers enter and leave the system frequently. Hence, the dependability of peers is worse than the corresponding characteristics of traditional servers. Particularly, current P2P systems employ small-world topologies, cross-partition pointers, self-organisation and periodic description updates to improve dependability. In summary, these means aim at maintaining the topology and communication among available peers in the presence of failing peers.

P2P systems offer services which are delivered by participating peers. The operation of a service requires access to resources, like databases. Usually, these resources are hosted by the peers who deliver the service. If the hosting peers fail, the service crashes jointly. Hence, means of retaining communication and topology do not suffice to improve dependability of P2P services. Means must address the resources hosted on peers as well. Replication and caching are suitable means to improve availability of resources. Digital library systems provide data and metadata.

Usually, caching is preferred to replication for data like audio and video files as this kind of content changes rarely. However, metadata is subject to replication, because it is updated by users frequently, *e.g.*, to rate content. For example, scholars describe a peer-to-peer digital library which caches content and replicates metadata. P2P systems differ from traditional distributed systems. For example, intermediate peers influence the dependability of communication, and fault characteristics of peers are worse than the corresponding attributes of traditional servers. Therefore, replication has to be investigated specifically for P2P contexts, because solutions for traditional distributed systems may not be appropriate. Our work addresses this issue for the voting-based replication strategies *Read-One- Write-All* (ROWA) and *Majority Consensus* as a first step. Particularly, we explore the availability of read and write operations on replicated resources compared to non-replicated resources.

RELATED WORK

Vanthournot et al. propose small-world topologies, self-organisation, and cross partition pointers as means of fault-tolerance within P2P systems. They simulate P2P systems to investigate the resulting dependability. They focus on failures of peers and connections, but omit the issue of resources on peers. Replication based on rumour spreading is proposed for P-Grid. These algorithms ease consistency conditions to improve availability and performance. They focus on analysing the communication overhead.

THE XPEER ARCHITECTURE

P2P systems which are required to be highly dependable in the presence of frequent updates under a sequential consistency model come into question for voting-based replication. Our current work includes the XPeer architecture for data integration within such systems. XPeer is a logical super-peer architecture which is well suited for digital libraries. It addresses the issue of querying distributed data in a large scale context by realising an integrated schema.

This schema is formed from heterogeneous information sources by classifying data sources into domains and creating user profiles for query optimisations. Information sources are integrated using XPeer's novel concept of super-peer application in a database environment. Super-peers are used to integrate information sources from clusters of interest or similarity. However, these sources are prone to disappear in a P2P architecture, causing problems for the query service and the optimisation process. The Replication Service described here is used to extend the original architecture.

METHOD

The availability of reading a replicated resource must be considered separately from the availability of writing, because the behaviour of replication control strategies may differ for reading and writing. We evaluated the resulting values by discrete event-simulation of scenarios. We developed a simulation model of peers following real-world implementations like Freenet and incorporated techniques of replication. A scenario consists of a P2P system with specific peers, connections, and their availabilities, a replication strategy and a distribution of replicas to peers. The set of all possible scenarios is infinite. We restrict ourselves to a subset of scenario classes for the investigation. The set of all scenarios can be characterised along five main dimensions: P2P architecture, P2P instantiation, faults, replication architecture, and replication deployment.

The P2P architecture describes the conceptual layout of a P2P system. The dimension is subdivided into degree of centralisation, structure, and style of communication. The degree of centralisation determines whether a system may have centralised elements, *e.g.*, index servers. The topology of P2P systems may be structured, *e.g.*, to a ring or small-world topology. The style of communication describes whether peers are able to communicate indirectly by relaying and forwarding messages. A P2P instantiation is a derivation of an actual P2P system from architecture. It describes how many peers participate in the system and how they are connected.

The faults dimension specifies the fault characteristics of peers and connections. We assume an exponential distribution of faults. For our purposes, the mean time to failure and the mean time to repair suffice, because the availability and reliability of peers and connections can be derived from these values. The replication architecture describes the conceptual behaviour of replicas. Several classifications of replication are known. The replication instantiation specifies the actual number and distribution of replicas to peers.

RESULTS

We derived 36 scenarios classes from the dimensions above. We chose decentralised and super-peer architectures with unstructured, mesh-like, and small-world topologies and indirect communication. The mesh-like topology is a special type of a structured topology, whereby each peer is connected to four neighbours to form a net. A small-world topology is characterised by short paths of intermediate peers between any pair of peers. The number of peers is fixed to 49 for each scenario. The connections are chosen depending on the demands of the topology. The range of mean times to failure and mean times to repair is derived from observations of a real-world system. Two simple types of weighted voting are considered for the replication architecture: Read-One-Write-All (ROWA) and Majority Consensus.

The number of replicas is fixed to five for deployment. Their distribution to peers is managed in two ways: They are located on peers with best fault characteristics or are allocated according to a normal distribution. Each scenario class is simulated with a single read or a single write access to acquire the resulting availability. Additionally, each obtained P2P system is simulated with a non-replicated resource to be able to evaluate the relative influence of ROWA and Majority Consensus.

The ROWA strategy requires access to a single replica for reading. We expected that the strategy heavily improves the availability of reading. It has its best influence for availability of reading for scenario class 12 with about 4.25 per sent. The worst influence occurs for scenario class 5 where no influence was measured at all. Not surprisingly, it improves reading for most scenarios. However, for some scenario classes the influence is negligible.

The ROWA strategy requires access to all replicas for writing. Hence, all hosting peers must be available for executing a write operation successfully. We expected that the strategy heavily decreases availability of writing, which was confirmed with relative influences ranging from ‘32.89 per sent to 0.15 per sent. The Majority Consensus strategy requires access to more than half of the replicas for reading and writing. We expected that the strategy improves both availabilities. The influence for reading was expected to be worse than the influence of ROWA, because access to more than one replica is required. It has its best influence for scenario class 8 with a relative improvement of about 3.68 per sent. The worst influence occurs for class 5 where its influence is negligible. In general our expectation was confirmed as the strategy improves availability for reading and writing. The influence for read operations was worse than the influence of ROWA. However, it exceeds ROWA for the scenario classes 2, 3, and 7. It is interesting to see that it does not decrease availability significantly for any scenario class we chose. A broader generalisation of the simulation results is a topic for future work. Even small changes to the scenario may have high impact on the resulting values. However, our results already indicate at this stage that voting-based replication strategies are a favourable replication technique for P2P systems when high consistency is required. Even if the peers of the scenario classes had fault characteristics worse than traditional servers, Majority Consensus improves availability of reading and writing.

ADAPTIVE REPLICATION STRATEGIES AND SOFTWARE ARCHITECTURES FOR PEER-TO-PEER SYSTEMS

The use of replication techniques for data in distributed information systems aims at improving non-functional properties of these systems. Particularly, availability, reliability, and performance should be increased. When considering heterogeneous, autonomy-preserving systems such as distributed digital libraries, the replication techniques employed should be able to adapt to varying proper- ties of the individual systems at run-time. Adaptive replication strategies need to be realised by a software architecture which provides the context for their implementation.

Digital library systems, whose information providers are organisationally closely related, for example under the umbrella of a single institution, should be tightly coupled, in order to allow for a high degree of consistency to be maintained. Other digital libraries, such as those of separate publishers, should be coupled less tightly, to allow for retaining their autonomy. This can be realised by a replication strategy based on peer-to-peer (P2P) techniques which combines intra-institutional and inter- institutional replication strategies. The overall replication strategy is evaluated and optimised at run-time, such that domain-specific requirements are incorporated into a multi-dimensional problem model.

DATA REPLICATION STRATEGIES

Data replication aims at increasing availability, reliability and performance of data accesses by storing data redundantly. A copy of a replicated data object is called a replica. Replication ensures that all replicas of one data object are automatically updated when one of its replicas is modified. Replication involves conflicting goals with respect to guaranteeing consistency, availability and performance. An improvement of one of these properties usually implies a degradation of the others. Replication in a distributed system is realised by a replication strategy, which is often controlled by replication managers. The quality of a strategy can be measured by the correctness criterion it safeguards. The strictest criterion is that of one-copy-serializability: The concurrent execution of a set of distributed transactions is one-copy serialisable, if its effect is equivalent to the sequential execution of the transactions on a non-replicated database.

Besides this criterion a number of other correctness criteria have been defined, which are less strict and thus easier to fulfill. Replication can be performed in an eager or lazy way. In the case of eager replication, when one replica is modified by a transaction, the other replicas of the concerned data object are updated within the original database transaction, as opposed to lazy replication where only the originally accessed replica is updated within the original transaction, while the other replicas are updated in separate transactions. The classification into synchronous and asynchronous replication strategies is essentially equivalent to this classification. Combinations of synchronous and asynchronous replication have also been studied. The concept of an adaptive replication manager was first proposed in. Its goal is to achieve an optimal trade-of between tight and loose coupling of in- formation systems, which is realised by dynamically switching participating systems between being synchronously and asynchronously updated.

PEER-TO-PEER SYSTEMS

Peer-to-peer systems are distributed systems that follow a communication model of equal nodes which communicate directly with each other. In the following we introduce deferent styles of peer-to-peer architectures before we describe the specific benefits of replication within peer-to-peer architectures.

Styles of Peer-to-Peer Architectures

The class of peer-to-peer architectures can roughly be divided into pure and hybrid peer-to-peer architectures. Pure peer-to-peer architectures are completely decentralised. Each peer in the network is equipped with both client and server functionality and the architecture does not contain any central servers at all. Hybrid peer-to-peer architectures combine characteristics of pure peer-to-peer architectures and client/server architectures. Some services are offered by servers and are therefore centralised, whereas other services are based on the peer-to- peer communication model.

Hybrid architectures can further be subdivided into centralised architectures and super-peer architectures. In centralised architectures there are nodes with pure server functionality which offer exclusive services. Super-peer architectures are also called hierarchical architectures and combine the concepts of decentralised and centralised architectures. A super-peer is a peer which acts as a server for a set of ordinary peers and usually interacts with other super-peers. Ordinary peers are typically organised in clusters together with a single super-peer. Super-peer architectures are particularly suited to support both intra- and inter-institutional cooperation because they allow for representing the structures of an institution within the super-peers' clusters as well as the structures among different institutions by connecting the different super-peers accordingly.

Peer-to-Peer Replication

Today's replication strategies often depend on centralised solutions. Replicating heterogeneous, autonomy-preserving information systems, however, requires flexible and well-coordinated approaches. Intra- and inter-institutional replication should be addressed by an integrated approach, where institutions are coupled via a suitable peer-to-peer infrastructure.

We have chosen a super-peer approach because it allows structuring the logical network in accordance with the organisational structure. This architecture is one example of how to model specific organisational requirements by extending peer-to-peer architectures by an additional layer which provides information on the organisational context. The architecture forms a basis for intra- and inter-institutional integration and replication of distributed data resources and services.

Digital libraries together with specialised sub collections as well as individual users are represented by different types of peers. The connections among these peers as shown in the upper right of figure are only one example of how a library may be organisationally structured. Other, non-hierarchical structures are also supported. Documents and also services may be controlled by the digital library as super ordinate institution, by single collections and also by single person peers who *e.g.* can offer their individual metadata or link lists to interesting web documents. The intra-institutional structure is complemented by an inter-institutional coupling with the help of super-peers. The super-peers impose a partition into clusters of organisationally closely related peers, where one cluster may comprise one or more institutions. Super-peers have more responsibilities than ordinary peers. A super-peer stores metadata concerning the structure of the institutions under its auspices and of the data resources and services it provides. Thus, its main task is to mediate between the different clusters.

Within a single institution the overall information system is usually composed of multiple component information systems, which must replicate data permanently due to high availability requirements. An advanced replication strategy is required to facilitate both high consistency and autonomy of the component information systems, each of which must not be vitally impaired when other systems fail. An optimal trade-of between these conflicting requirements can be reached by combining synchronous and asynchronous replication into an adaptive replication strategy. Each system may be replicated either synchronously or asynchronously at any time. Switching between synchronous and asynchronous replication should be configurable and adaptive with respect to the current network configuration status. The configuration is performed using a system of rules, which is continuously evaluated at run-time to ensure adaptivity. The correctness criterion of the replication strategy is evaluated by means of an appropriate consistency measure, *i.e.* a measure of the probability of consistent accesses. A transaction that modifies a replicated data object is called a replication request. It is initiated by any node connected to the peer-to-peer network and is sent to its replication manager: One possibility to determine the replication manager is to use the digital library peer as intra-institutional replication manager, if the initiating node is contained within an institution. If the replication request is not confined to the originating institution, or if the initiating peer is not assigned to an institutional digital library peer, its super peer is used as an inter-institutional replication manager. The process realising an adaptive replication strategy is illustrated for one replication request.

By evaluating the system of rules, the involved nodes are split into two groups, those that are to be updated synchronously and asynchronously, respectively. After that, both groups of nodes are processed. The nodes in the synchronous group are directly updated, while the update requests for the nodes in the asynchronous group are enquired into a message queue. All node updates are performed in parallel within one transaction.

If all synchronous updates were successful, the processing of the replication request is completed and positively acknowledged. If a synchronous update fails, the replication manager checks whether the failing systems may be switched to asynchronous update mode. If this is the case, the corresponding systems are switched and the processing of the replication request is restarted. If some system could not be switched, the replication request fails. Asynchronous replication requests in the message queue are continuously processed in an independent thread of execution. If a system to be updated is not available, the corresponding request stays in the queue until the update has successfully been performed.

Peer-to-Peer Replication for Digital Libraries

Today's digital library systems cooperate in manifold ways. They exhibit a varying internal organisational structure, *e.g.* given by the introduction of specialised sub-collections or by extraction of project-specific reference libraries. Furthermore, different business models also including the ability to count the cost of library access have to be taken into account. Against this background, the ability to map intra- and inter-institutional requirements to the underlying digital library system as presented is of paramount importance. Libraries including resources other than traditional library documents like *e.g.* resource collections in e-science or health information systems emerge. This calls for the determination of detailed strategies not only for searching these collections but also for replication of both resources and services.

DISTRIBUTED SERVICES ARCHITECTURE IN DLIBRA DIGITAL LIBRARY FRAMEWORK

The dLibra Digital Library Framework has been developed in Poznan Supercomputing and Networking Center since 1999. The first dLibra-based digital library (DL) was the Digital Library of the Wielkopolska Region (WBC). It was started in October 2002 and now it consists of over 3000 various publications grouped into four thematic collections: cultural heritage, regional materials, educational materials and music notes. Such number of publications makes from WBC one of the largest Polish digital libraries.

In the end of November 2004 the second dLibra-based digital library was deployed – the Wroclaw University of Technology Digital Library. There are also four other test dLibra installations academic libraries, and in the nearest future three new regional digital libraries will be started. Due to the diversity of mentioned digital libraries, many different aspects must be taken into account during the dLibra development. Each DL has its own specific publications – for example the majority of WBC publications are relicts of writing and old documents associated with social life of the Wielkopolska Region. Such resources are mostly stored in a graphical form, in formats like DjVu, PDF or JPG scans. All that publications consist of quite large files and their content is often not searchable. On the other hand, there are academic DL systems, like one of test dLibra installations in AGH University of Science and Technology, where a typical publication is an academic script stored as a set of HTML pages or small PDF file with searchable text content. Such differences requires support in many areas – from format dependent publication structure analysis during the publication upload process, to sophisticated mechanisms for content indexing and searching, to different publication view and download possibilities. Another important element is the amount of stored publications.

When there are many gathered resources, and a large number of readers accessing it, the overall system performance becomes a crucial parameter. We want to show the way in which we designed the internal dLibra architecture and its basic mechanisms to create an efficient, flexible, distributed and error-resistant digital library system. The structure of distributed services architecture developed in the dLibra Digital Library Framework. We also show an overview of these services functionality. We try to demonstrate our approach to improving the dLibra stability in some extreme situations, like very heavy user requests load or network communication errors. Those mechanisms are an integral part of dLibra services and service management system.

dLIBRA ARCHITECTURE

The initial dLibra architecture and design was based on experiences from previous PSNC projects. We assumed that the dLibra environment should consist of a number of portable, distributed services. Portability was achieved by choosing Java™ as the programming language. Further works and practice from dLibra deployments formed the current dLibra structure.

This structure is based on a set of cooperating remote services. All these services together create the complete dLibra-based digital library. Each service can be started on a separate computer, but they can also be connected into service groups running on the same machine.

When services are started on different hosts, they use Java RMI technology to communicate with each other. Six of dLibra services give together the entire dLibra server functionality.

These services are:

- *The Metadata Server*—gives a possibility to define, modify and remove metadata attributes that are used to describe digital library publications. It also gives access to dictionaries and thesauri with values of all attributes. It is responsible for managing digital library directories and collections. In addition, it allows adding, modifying and deleting publications, and it has possibilities to manage lists of languages defined in the DL system. Moreover, it has a module for performing periodic metadata consistency test.
- *The Content Server*—gives access to all gathered digital content. Before sending content to the client, this service is able to compress it or encrypt and send securely. The Content Server is also used to store the publications content. Resuming is supported during both publication upload and download.
- *The Search server*—allows users to search through all gathered content and metadata. It also contains indexing functionality, which prepares indexes used during search.

- *The Distributed Search Server*—is used to harvest remote dLibra instances by means of the OAI-PMH protocol. It also gives the user a possibility to search through gathered remote metadata. In fact, any OAI-PMH-enabled repository can be harvested and searched using that service.
- *The User Server*—contains all user-related data and allows users authentication and authorisation. It is also used to create groups of users and to grant users different digital library rights, from library administration to simple publication view.

All the services give together the entire dLibra digital library functionality. However, at least two more elements are required to create a fully functional system. There must be a possibility to connect all these services and create an entry point to the system for both external applications and users.

The first of them is a service called the System Services. It can be treated as a broker of services for single instance of the distributed digital library. It allows inter service communication and handles services addresses resolving, connecting and authorisation. For example, when the Search Server wants to refresh its indexes, it asks the System Services for the Content Server and the Metadata Server. The System Service checks if such services are registered, if they are available and if the Search Server is authorised to access them. If all those conditions are met, as a response the Search Server receives references to the requested services. In order to become available to other services, each service must register itself in the chosen System Services. Services registered in one System Services create a digital library. The second additional system level service is the Event Server. It allows services to communicate with the event messaging system. It is very useful when one service wants to notify some other services about a particular event. A good example of this mechanism can again be a process of refreshing search indexes.

Just after start, the Search Server registers in the Event Server for events related with the modification of gathered content and metadata. When a new publication is added, modified or removed, the Metadata Server sends an event notification to the Event Server. Next, the Event Server forwards this event to all services registered for this event type. After receiving such event, the Search Server can decide if index refreshing is required or maybe just some data should be removed from the index.

This corresponds to two additional parts of the dLibra Framework. One of them is WWW Service and the second is the Editor/Administrator application. The WWW Service is designed as a read only entry point to the system. It can be used by readers to access gathered resources. Content browse and searching are the main functionality of this service, but it is also an OAI-PMH data provider, and it has many user-friendly features like RSS feeds with information newly added publications, publications ranking etc. This functionality is realised with the use of all other dLibra services reached through the System Services. The Editor/ Administrator Application is an application for librarians and library administrators. It allows adding and modifying library resources and managing all library items.

IMPROVING SERVICES AVAILABILITY IN dLIBRA FRAMEWORK

The distributed architecture of the described dLibra services requires additional mechanisms for improving system reliability and availability. When one of the services stops responding, the library may become less functional or may not be functional at all - when the User Server or Metadata Server fails. To prevent such situations, a number of mechanisms were introduced. The first of them is the way of service resolving done by the System Services. There is a possibility to create such services configuration, in which multiple instances of the most crucial services are started.

Before the System Services gives one service access to another service, it tests the requested service functionality. When the tested instance of a given service fails, the System Services can return reference to other instance. Such instance switch is transparent to other services. With addition of services load monitoring functionality, this mechanism can also be used for load balancing between service instances. The second mechanism is internal services monitoring. Each service is periodically checked if it is responding or has enough processor time for its tasks. This check is performed by a special service wrapper based on an open-source Java Service Wrapper project. The Wrapper can restart or shutdown the service when, for some reason, it stops responding or when host processors are overloaded for a longer period of time. This service monitoring is done locally so it is independent of the state of network connections. Another reliability improving mechanism is implemented in events sending and receiving parts of the dLibra framework. When service generates an event, it is not directly sent to the Event Server, but it is stored in a persistent storage. This storage is implemented with Hibernate, so it can be based on many types of relational databases.

All stored events are read by a specialised Event Sender thread. This thread tries to send events to the Event Server. If connection to the Event Server is lost, all events stay in the storage until there is a possibility to send them again. On the other hand, when the Event Server retrieves an event, it also stores the event before trying to send it to registered services. Each service, while registering for events, gives the Event Server special timeout parameter. This parameter describes how long the events should be stored in the Event Server, if the registered service becomes unavailable. If the registered service becomes available again, all events stored for this service will be passed to it.

FUTURE WORKS

We think that next dLibra development stages will bring this distributed digital library framework closer to grid technologies. In order to do so, it will be necessary to extend our services model. Each service should gain the ability of describing itself with metadata. On top of the System

Services there must be some kind of a new, much more advanced service - a dynamic distributed digital library services broker. This should allow automated service discovery and creation of virtual DL organisations. Such active organisations of services could be used to create distributed digital collections from resources gathered in heterogeneous DL systems. We can also imagine Information Retrieval Grid services based on different distributed digital libraries. By creating an environment for advanced cooperation of computational grid services, grid data management systems and digital libraries we want to give an opportunity for advanced usage of digital libraries in sophisticated grid scenarios.

INTEGRATING XML DATA SOURCES USING RDF/S SCHEMAS

Digital libraries are collections of resource descriptions that actually describe the catalogue data. In general, these metadata are stored in diverse sources distributed on the Web. One of the main challenges for the digital library community is the integration of such metadata sources in order to provide users with a common vocabulary for searching and browsing them. The Semantic Web offers relevant approaches and standards that can handle these problems.

More precisely, RDF can be used as a common framework for expressing the information by providing a semantically rich representation language for metadata. In this context, a SW integration middleware should be employed for the integration of the heterogeneous and distributed sources. In particular, we propose a SWIM that provides a useful, comprehensive and high-level access to library metadata that reside in relational databases (RDB) or XML sources, by offering a virtual, mediated RDF/S schema. There are many issues involved in the functionality of a SWIM. In particular, a SWIM should facilitate users to formulate queries against the mediated RDF/S schema using declarative languages, as well as, support further abstraction levels using declarative view definition languages. In a nutshell, SWIM should offer the following services:

- Establish mapping rules between XML and RDF and between RDB and RDF,
- Verify the conformance of these mappings w.r.t the semantics of the employed schemas,
- Reformulate RDF/S queries against RDB or XML sources, and
- Combine these queries with RVL views.

In order to address effectively and efficiently the requirements, we should choose a uniform and expressive logic framework to define SWIM integration services. This framework should exploit background theory on conjunctive queries and query containment and minimisation. An architecture based on mediators is highly beneficial for deploying a SWIM. There exist two main approaches for integrating data sources using mediator-based architectures: Global-as-View (GAV) and Local-as-View (LAV). The former provides descriptions of the global schema in terms of the views of local sources and relies on simple query reformulation techniques. The latter considers local sources as materialised views specified in terms of the global schema.

LAV supports easily the evolution of the data integration system by just adding or removing the descriptions of local sources. In our work we advocate a hybrid approach called GLAV, which combines the previous advantages and exceeds the expressive power of both GAV and LAV.

A MOTIVATING EXAMPLE

Let's assume an XML source whose content is described by a DTD or an XML Schema. XML data from this source contain information about Museums, exhibiting some artifacts for which we want to know their creator. Data stored in such sources can be queried using an XML query language like XPath, or XQuery. Now suppose that we add on top of this repository an RDF/S schema from the cultural domain. This mediated RDF/S schema can be queried using RQL and it can be used for defining personalised views with the help of RVL. However, since there are no actual RDF data, we need to reformulate the RQL queries expressed against this virtual RDF/S schema into queries appropriate for our XML source. For example, the following RQL query:

Select X

From {X}exhibits{Y}, {Y}denom{Z}

Where Z = "Louvre".

This reformulation involves several challenging issues. First of all, the schemas employed by our XML sources and the RDF/S mediator are different. Their discrepancies, usually called heterogeneity conflicts, can be classified under three axes: syntactic, structural and semantic. As we can see in our example, we need to view the XML data through the RDF data model, to resolve categorisation conflicts, given that in RDF/S there is a class hierarchy while in XML there isn't, as well as address naming mismatches; for instance the 'name' of a Museum in XML is called 'denomination' in RDF/S.

In order to reconciliate the heterogeneous representations of our data we need to define appropriate mapping rules. Choosing an expressive but tractable logical framework to map data from XML to RDF/S is crucial for the success of a SWIM. These mappings are used for reformulating queries issued against the virtual RDF/S schema into queries acceptable by our XML sources. However, more complex mappings render query reformulation harder. Query reformulation becomes more complex if we take into consideration the presence of constraints capturing the semantics of both the RDF/S and XML data models, as well as, application-specific constraints coming from the schema of XML sources. So, there is a need for a sound and complete reformulation algorithm. Since reformulated queries are evaluated to remote sources and mediator queries resulting from automated manipulation/ generation may entail redundancies, their optimisation is crucial. In particular, optimisation tries to eliminate redundant queries and to simplify queries by removing redundant predicates.

SEMANTIC QUERY ROUTING AND PROCESSING IN P2P DIGITAL LIBRARIES

The digital library community envisions the availability of digital content on a global scale through Digital Libraries (DL) that can be accessed, integrated and individualised for any user, anytime and anywhere. A key point in such a vision is the interaction with multiple DL nodes to support integrated access. We believe that such interaction is far beyond the traditional information integration technologies, which impose restrictions on representation and communication languages used at both the semantic and the structural levels, since:

- DL nodes should be autonomous. Ideally, a node must not have restrictions on how to organise its data and what kind of query capabilities to offer.
- DL services should support decentralised sharing and management of data through a network of DL nodes. In such a network, a DL node must be able to provide data to other DL nodes and, at the same time, to have access to data of other DL nodes.
- The diversity of DL nodes in terms of availability, processing power and interface options, makes a DL network a highly heterogeneous environment in terms of hardware/software setup in addition to the data being provided.
- Finally, the system needs to be evolving in the sense of DL nodes joining and leaving the network at their own will. DL node arrivals and departures affect the data that is available.

Our work explores the application of the peer-to-peer (P2P) paradigm in DL technologies. In particular, schema-based P2P systems exploit schema in- formation to specify what kind of data is provided by the involved peers. The advantages of this approach lies to the fact that:

- More sophisticated than keyword-based queries can be posed and
- More efficient approaches can be developed for identifying peers that are capable of answering the queries.

A natural candidate for representing descriptive schemas of information resources is the Resource Description Framework/Schema Language. RDF schemas offer rich semantics. The primitives of RDF schemas are classes and properties. Classes describe general concepts or entities. Properties describe the characteristics of classes or the relationships between classes. RDF/S:

- Enables a modular design of descriptive schemas based on the mechanism of namespaces;
- Allows easy reuse or refinement of existing schemas through subsumption of both class and property definitions;
- Supports partial descriptions since properties associated with a resource are by default optional and repeated and
- Permits super-imposed descriptions in the sense that a resource may be multiply classified under several classes from one or several schemas.

These modelling primitives are crucial for schema-based P2P systems where monolithic RDF/S schemas and resource descriptions cannot be constructed in advance and DL nodes may have only incomplete descriptions about the available resources. The advanced structuring and retrieval functionality of schema-based P2P systems raises new challenges for view integration, query routing and processing over autonomous, distributed and dynamic networks of DLs. The main contributions of our work presented in this paper are:

- The design and implementation of effective and efficient query routing in P2P DLs, exploiting intensional indexing of DL node views and
- The study of interleaved query routing and processing algorithms in P2P DLs in order to

produce as quickly as possible the first query results.

Related Work

Several projects address query processing issues in general P2P systems. However, they require a priori knowledge of the relevant to a query peers. Mutant Query Plans (MQPs) implement efficient query routing. Unlike our approach, MQP reduces the optimisation opportunities by simply migrating possibly big XML fragments of query plans along with partial results of sub- queries. In indices are used to identify peers that can handle containment queries. However there are no details on how a set of semantically related peers can actually execute a complex query involving vertical and horizontal distribution. RDFPeers is a scalable distributed RDF/S repository which efficiently answers multi-attribute and range queries. This approach ignores RDF/S schema information during query routing, while distributed query processing and execution policies are not addressed.

In, a P2P architecture is introduced, based on the extension of an existing RDF/S store. Although schema information is used for indexing, RDF/S class and property subsumption is not considered. A schema-based P2P infrastructure for the Semantic Web is described in. Their approach involves exact matching of basic class and property pattern and does not consider run-time adaptability of query plans.

P2P DIGITAL LIBRARIES

In order to design an efficient P2P DL infrastructure we need to address the following issues:

- How DL nodes advertise their bases?
- How DL nodes formulate queries?
- How DL nodes route queries? and
- How DL nodes process queries?

Advertisements of DL Nodes

A schema-based P2P DL infrastructure requires that

each DL node advertises its local base content to other DL nodes. Using these advertisements, a DL node becomes aware of the bases hosted by other nodes in the DL. In our approach, we assume that there are global RDF/s schemas for various communities, in which DL nodes have access through the mechanism of namespaces. However, a global RDF/S schema may contain numerous classes and properties not necessarily populated in a DL node. Therefore, we need a fine-grained definition of schema-based advertisements. We employ RVL views to specify the sub- set of a community RDF/S schema(s) for which all classes and properties are populated in a DL node base. These views may be broadcasted to other DL nodes, thus informing the rest of the P2P DL of the information actually available in the DL nodes.

Query Formulation in DL Nodes

In this work, queries and views in a P2P DL are formulated by nodes in the RQL/RVL language. RQL is a typed functional language in the form of OQL. It uniformly queries both RDF data descriptions and schemas. RVL extends RQL by supporting views on RDF/S. In RQL/RVL, class and property path patterns allow users to navigate through the RDF/S schema of a DL node to retrieve resources. RQL queries allow us to retrieve the contents of any DL node base, namely resources classified under schema classes or associated to other resources using schema properties. It is worth noticing that RQL queries imply both intensional and extensional filtering conditions.

Query Routing in P2P Digital Libraries

Query routing is responsible for finding the relevant to a query DL nodes by taking into account data distribution of their bases committing to an RDF schema. The query-routing algorithm takes as input a query and the available DL node views and detects which DL nodes can actually answer the query as a whole or fragments of it. The latter is important, since there might be answers that can be received by joining partial answers from different DL nodes. Our approach exploits query/view sub- sumption algorithms to check whether the classes or properties of the view are subsumed by the respective classes or properties used in the query. In this way, query routing takes into consideration semantic information from the RDF Schemas of the involved DL nodes. Specifically, a fragmentor breaks the given query into subqueries, whose number is bounded by an input variable. The query/view subsumption algorithms of are employed to determine which part of a query can be answered by a DL node view. For maintaining a distributed catalog of views published by the DL nodes in a P2P DL, appropriate DHT structures have been designed.

Query Processing in P2P Digital Libraries

Query processing is responsible for generating query plans according to the results returned by the routing algorithm. If more than one DL nodes can answer the same query fragment, the results from each. "The results obtained for different query fragments that are connected at a specific domain or range class are rejoined". The generated query plan reflects the data distribution of the system and uses it for obtaining at execution time both complete and correct results. The resulting query plan can be optimised. Compile-time optimisation relies on algebraic equivalences and heuristics allowing us to push, as much as, possible query evaluation to the same DL nodes. Additionally, cost-based optimisations based on statistics about the DL node bases enable to reorder joins and choose between different execution policies for the query plans.

A key feature of our approach is that query routing and processing are interleaved in several iteration steps. This leads to the creation and execution of multiple query (sub)plans that when 'unioned' offer completeness in the results. Specifically, starting with the initial query, at each iteration step, smaller sub- queries are considered in order to find the relevant DL nodes that can actually answer them. The routing information, *i.e.*, remote DL node views, is acquired by the lookup service offered by the system on top of intensional DHT structures. The interleaved query evaluation terminates when the initial query is decomposed into its basic class and property patterns.

The main advantage of the interleaved query routing and processing algorithm is that the query results are collected as quickly as possible since they require fewer intra-DL node joins. More precisely, each query fragment is looked up as a whole and only DL nodes that can fully answer it are actually involved in each query processing iteration step.

PUBLISH/SUBSCRIBE FUNCTIONALITIES FOR FUTURE DIGITAL LIBRARIES

We are interested in the problem of *distributed resource sharing* in future digital libraries. We adopt a pure P2P architecture but our ideas can be easily modified to work in the case of hierarchical P2P networks, as in. *Information providers* (DLs) and *information consumers* (users) are both represented by peers participating in a peer-to-peer (P2P) overlay network. There are two kinds of basic functionality that we expect this architecture to offer: *information retrieval (IR)* and *publish/subscribe*. In an IR scenario a user poses a *query* and the system returns information about matching resources. In a pub/sub scenario a user posts a *subscription* to the system to receive notifications whenever certain events of interest take place. In this extended abstract we concentrate on the latter kind of functionality and sketch how to provide it by extending the distributed hash table Chord. *Distributed Hash Tables (DHTs)* are the second generation *structured* P2P overlay networks devised as a remedy for the known limitations of earlier P2P networks such as Napster and Gnutella.

We present a set of protocols, collectively called *DHTrie*, that extend the Chord protocols with pub/sub functionality. We assume that resources are annotated using a well-understood attribute- value model called *AWPS* in. Thus publications and subscriptions will also be expressed in *AWPS*. *AWPS* is based on *named attributes* with value *free text* interpreted under the Boolean and vector space (VSM) models. The query language of *AWPS* allows Boolean combinations of comparisons *A op v*, where *A* is an attribute, *v* is a text value and *op* is one of the operators 'equals', 'contains' or 'similar'. The following is an example of a publication in *AWPS*:

{ (Author, "John Smith"), (Title, "Information dissemination in P2P..."),
(Abstract, "In this paper we show that ...") }

The following is an example of a query:

(Author = "John Smith") $\wedge$ *(Title* $\sqsupseteq$ *P2P* $\wedge$ *(information [0.0] alert))* $\wedge$
(Abstract $\sim_{0.7}$*"P2P architecture have been...")*

This query requests resources that have *John Smith* as their author, and their title contains the word *P2P* and a word pattern where the word *information* is immediately followed by the word *alert*. Additionally, the resources should have an abstract similar to the text value *'P2P architectures have been...'* with similarity greater than 0:7.

THE DHTrie PROTOCOLS

We implement pub/sub functionality by a set of protocols called the *DHTrie protocols*. The DHTrie protocols use *two levels of indexing* to store queries submitted by clients. The first level corresponds to the partitioning of the global query index to different nodes using DHTs as the underlying infrastructure. Each node is responsible for a fraction of the submitted user queries through a mapping of attribute values to node identifiers.

The DHT infrastructure is used to define the mapping scheme and also manages the routing of messages between different nodes. We use an extension of the Chord DHT to implement our network. The second level of our indexing mechanism is managed locally by each node and is used for indexing the user queries the node is responsible for. In this level, each node uses a hash table to index all the atomic queries contained in a query by using their attribute name as the key.

For each atomic Boolean query the hash table points to a *trie*-like structure that exploits *common words* and a hash table that indexes text values in equalities as in. Additionally for atomic VSM queries an inverted index for the most 'significant' query words is used as in. In this abstract as suggested, focus on the first level of indexing and present the sub- scription, publication and notification protocols that regulate node interactions. Protocols for query updating and removal are omitted due to space. The local indexing algorithms we use and their experimental evaluation are thoroughly discussed in.

The Notification Protocol

Once all the matching queries have been retrieved from the database, *P* creates notification messages of the form Q NOTIFICATION ($l(c)r$) and contacts all the nodes that their queries where matched against *p* using their IP address· associated with the query they submitted. If a node *P′* is not online when *P* tries to notify it about the published resource, the notification message is sent to the *successor (p′)*. In this way *P′* will be notified the next time it logs on the network. The modifications to the join and leave protocols of Chord to achieve this functionality originally presented in the non-DHT system P2P-DIET are omitted due to space considerations. To utilise the network in a more efficient way, notifications can also be batched and sent to the subscribers when traffic is expected to be low.

Frequency Cache

In this part, we introduce an additional routing table that is maintained in each node. This table, called *frequency cache* (FCache) is used to reduce the cost of publishing a resource by storing the IP addresses of the nodes responsible for frequent words contained in published documents. FCache is a hash table used to associate each word that appears in a published document with a node IP address. FCache uses a word *w* as a key, and each FCache entry is a data structure that holds an IP address. Thus, whenever *P* needs to contact another node P' that is responsible for queries containing w, it searches its FCache. If FCache contains an entry for w, P can directly contact P' using the IP stored in its FCache. If w is not contained in FCache, P uses the standard DHT lookup protocol to locate P' and stores contact information in FCache for further reference. Using FCache the cost of processing a published resource p is reduced to $O(v + (h - v) \log N)$, where v is the number of words of p contained in FCache. FCache entries are populated as follows. Each time a resource p is published at a node P, P contacts the nodes responsible for storing queries with words contained in p. After this process is over, P knows the contact information of those nodes, and stores it to FCache along with the word each node is responsible for. After that, for each publication taking place at P, P maintains this routing information for the most frequent words contained in resources published to it. Notice that the construction and maintenance of FCache is based only on local information and that the only extra cost involved is FCache misses and the routing information discovered is also cached for further reference).

BRIEF PRESENTATION OF EXPERIMENTAL RESULTS

We have evaluated DHTrie experimentally in a distributed digital library scenario with hundreds of thousands of nodes and millions of user profiles. For our experiments we used 10426 documents downloaded from CiteSeer and also used in. The documents are research papers in the area of Neural Networks and as suggested, refer to them as the NN corpus. Because no database of queries was available to us, our queries are synthetically generated by exploiting 2000 documents of the corpus. The remaining 8426 documents are used to generate publications. Our experiments show that the DHTrie protocols are *scalable*: the number of messages it takes to publish a document and notify interested subscribers remains almost constant as the network grows. Moreover, the increase in message traffic shows little sensitivity to increase in document size.

We demonstrate that simple data structures with only local information can make a big difference in a DHT environment: the routing table FCache manages to reduce network traffic by a factor of 4 in all the alternative methods we have studied. Since probability distributions associated with publication and query elements are expected to be skewed in typical pub/sub scenarios, achieving a *balanced load* is an important problem. We have studied an important case of load balancing for DHTrie and present a new algorithm which is also applicable to the standard DHT look-up problem.

INFORMATION ACCESS IN DIGITAL LIBRARIES

A digital library (DL) system comprises a large, distributed information space, where the objects carrying the knowledge required by the users, live. Setting up and maintaining a DL would be entirely useless if users were not provided with the adequate tools to access the DL information contents. In defining the information access service of a DL, there are at least 3 areas of the information system field which can give significant contributions:

- *Information retrieval* (IR) can contribute content-based methods, that is methods that exploit the signal level of an information object. For textual objects, these include all classical methods based on the statistical properties of language, such as the vector-space method and the probabilistic method. For non-textual objects, in the last decade there has been a fluorishing of methods for similarity-based retrieval of images, video and audio objects.
- The *database* area can contribute all methods for attribute-based information querying, ranging from traditional databases, to semi-structured databases; the methods falling under the last category are especially useful when ad- dressing the *structure* of objects.
- *Knowledge representation* can contribute methods for accessing objects by querying descriptions of their

contents; these descriptions are typically couched in terms of representations of the underlying domain of discourse, or *ontologies* as these have come to be termed lately.

Putting the techniques found in the fields all together at work, requires a conceptual schema which integrates in a unique framework the different aspects of DL objects addressed by each of them. In what follows as suggested, try to sketch such a schema.

A CONCEPTUAL SCHEMA OF INFORMATION ACCESS

We characterise the space of information access by the following, orthogonal dimensions:

- The information access model, which establishes the basic terms of the system/user interaction;
- The information access mode, which establishes the role of the user and that of the system during their interaction.

Information access Models

Similarly to an information retrieval model, an information access model specifies:

- A representation of the objects to be accessed;
- A representation of the user information needs; and
- A function associating a set of objects to each user information need.

Information access models can be categorised according to the options available on each one of their dimensions. For object representation, following we distinguish between simple objects and composite objects. Simple objects cannot be further decomposed, and can be represented along the following dimensions:

- *Content abstractions*: these are representations used to access objects via IR techniques. They are created by IR indexers in an automatic way, by extracting low-level features from objects, such as the number of word occurrences in a text, or the energy level in a certain region of an image);

content abstractions retain that part of the information originally present in the object content that is considered sufficient to characterise the object for access purposes;

- *Content representations*: these are symbolic representations of the meaning of documents, that is descriptions formulated in some suitable knowledge representation language, spelling out the truth conditions of the object. Content representations can be constructed manually, sometimes with the assistance of some knowledge extraction tool, or automatically, for instance via object classification methods. They can be precise or uncertain, depending on whether or not the content representation formulas are expressed in an un- certain logic, such as fuzzy or probabilistic logic.

Composite objects are structured set of simple objects, thus they are typically represented as mathematical *structures*, reflecting their internal organisation. Finally, objects, whether simple or composite, can have a *profile*, that is an attribute-based description of their external properties, such as the author and the publisher of a book, or the data and time at which an image has been taken, and the like. In the context of digital libraries, the 4 dimensions of object representation reduce to 3 only, since content representations and profiles are typically grouped together under the label of discovery metadata. The metadata associated to a DL object can therefore vary from simple records typically adhering to some standardised schema to very complex representations expressed in some knowledge representation language which must be coupled with a representation of the underlying domain of discourse, in order to be properly used for, *e.g.* information access. In summary, as suggested, therefore consider object representation as being categorised as:

- Content,
- Metadata, and
- Structure.

For information need representation, we have 2 options: formal language queries or natural language queries. For the retrieval function, we have 2 options: exact match or best match. Not all combinations of these options give rise to meaningful information access models. Considering the object representation options we have the following:

- Content is typically addressed via IR techniques, based on natural language queries and best-match retrieval function. For instance, users access the content of an image base by providing as a query an image itself In so doing, users are implicitly asking the system to retrieve images which 'looks' similar to the image query, at least as far as the system can tell. For this reason, methods providing access by content are often called *'similarity-based'* access methods. An analogous pattern is found in access models for textual or for audio content. Notice that in some models of this kind, the query may not be expressed in the same medium as the sought objects. For instance, when accessing by content a video database, users may provide an image as a query, and the system is expected to retrieve the scenes sharing visual similarity with the provided image. Similarity-based access models are medium-dependent, in that different media require different techniques, and the possibility of using the same or a similar technique across different media is very limited. In addition, experience has shown that even within the same medium, the effectiveness of techniques is application-dependent: for example, retrieving by similarity sport images requires different techniques from those necessary to establish the similarity of X-ray images.
- Metadata is typically addressed via formal language queries, thus we are in the realm of databases or knowledge representation, depending from the degree of sophisticatedness of the involved representations. For instance, to query a

Dublin Core scheme, one needs a very simple language allowing to state basic relational conditions on simple numeric- or string-based attribute values; instead, to query an OWL representation the ability to state conditions involving taxonomies and navigation of graph structures is required. In general, a query to metadata takes the form of a logical formula, and an exact match retrieval function is employed for query evaluation, grounded in some logical theory. We call these models *semantic* access models. Some retrieval engines allow to exploit information retrieval techniques when accessing objects via their metadata records. This is achieved by seeing metadata records as pieces of text whose words are the attribute values. Such a text is treated in the same way as textual content, and matched against a natural language query as in a similarity-based textual access method. This kind of access model is widely employed on bibliographic records, as it frees users from the necessity of knowing the meaning of meta- data attributes.

- Also object structure can be queried in two different ways:
- Via exact match retrieval functions, such as the one underlying the query language XPath. In this case, the structural query is mostly embedded into a larger query addressing either content or metadata. We do not have therefore separate classes of access models but sophistications of similarity-based or semantic access models allowing also the specification of structural clauses in queries.
- Via best match retrieval functions, which express in a quantitative way the degree of similarity between the structure of each object and a user provided structure class. These models have been investigated in the con- text of XML, and are a structural variation of similarity-based models. We

call the models falling in this class 'similar structure-based access models'.

In summary, we have the following information access model categories:

- Similarity-based access models, possibly with structural conditions;
- Semantic access models, possibly with structural conditions; and
- Similar structure-based access models.

Information Access Modes

Independently from the access model, the information access modes establishes the role of the system and that of the user. Each of these two can be either passive or active. Excluding the case in which they are both passive, we have the following 3 types of information access systems:

- *Query-answering systems*: in this case the user is active, that is, poses a query, while the system is passive, that is it just evaluates the user query and returns the result.
- *Filtering systems*: In which the user is passive, that is, does not pose any query, and the system is active, that is it selects on a stream of incoming objects, those that are deemed as relevant for the user; the relevance assessment is performed by relying on a user profile.
- *Personalised query-answering systems*: in which the user is active, that is, poses a query, and the system is active too, in that it alters the query evaluation process by taking into account the user preferences, represented as a profile. Recommendation systems also fall into this category, since they propose recommendations along with the answer to the query.

CHALLENGES OF DISTRIBUTED SEARCH ACROSS DIGITAL LIBRARIES

The peer-to-peer (P2P) approach allows handling huge amounts of data of digital libraries in a distributed and self-organising way. These characteristics offer enormous potential benefit for search capabilities powerful in terms of scalability, efficiency, and resilience to failures and dynamics. Additionally, such a search engine can potentially benefit from the intellectual input of a large user community.

However, recent research on structured P2P architectures is typically limited to exact-match queries on keys. This is insufficient for text queries that consist of a variable number of keywords, and it is absolutely inappropriate for full-fledged Web search where keyword queries should return a ranked result list of the most relevant approximate matches. This stage builds upon the MINERVA system architecture presented in and brings current challenges to ultimatively making distributed search across digital libraries feasible. MINERVA provides ranked search on data and an efficient query mechanism that adheres to reasonable space and bandwidth limits. Unlike the approach criticised in, we do not spread inverted lists across the directory, but use only pointers to promising digital libraries as compact metadata and utilise these pointers to efficiently answer multiple-keyword queries. We leverage the extensive local indexes to incorporate features that are impossible in the approach studied in, such as phrase matching or proximity searches. Our bandwidth requirements are well within the postulation that a query should send no more data than the size of the documents ultimatively retrieved.

RELATED WORK

Recent research on structured P2P systems, such as Chord, CAN, Pastry, or P-Grid is typically based on various forms of distributed hash tables (DHTs) and supports mappings from keys to locations in a decentralised manner such that routing scales well with the number of peers in the system. We briefly discuss some prior and ongoing projects towards P2P Web search. Galanx is a P2P search engine implemented using the Apache HTTP server and Berkeley DB.

The Web site servers are the peers of this architecture; pages are stored only where they originate from. PlanetP is a publish subscribe service for P2P communities, supporting content ranking search. PlanetP distinguishes local indexes and a global index to describe all peers and their shared information. The global index is replicated using a gossiping algorithm. The system appears to be limited to a few thousand peers. Odissea assumes a two-layered search engine architecture with a global index structure distributed over the nodes in the system. A single node holds the complete, Web-scale, index for a given text term. Query execution uses a distributed version of Fagin's threshold algorithm.

The system appears to cause high network traffic when posting document metadata into the network, and the presented query execution method seems limited to queries with at most two keywords. The paper actually advocates using a limited number of nodes, in the spirit of a server farm. The system outlined in uses a fully distributed inverted text index, in which every participant is responsible for a specific subset of terms and manages the respective index structures. Particular emphasis is put on minimising the bandwidth used during multi-keyword searches. considers content-based retrieval in hybrid P2P networks.

The peer selection for forwarding queries is based on the Kullback- Leibler divergence between peer-specific statistical models of term distributions. In addition to this recent work on P2P search, prior research on distributed IR and metasearch engines is also potentially relevant; see for overviews. However, their work has assumed a relatively small number of digital libraries or databases and a fairly static configuration.

SYSTEM DESIGN

As a detailed description of the system design has already been given in, we only present a brief overview here and refer the interested reader to this prior work. We view every library as autonomous. A conceptually global but physically distributed directory, which is layered on top of a Chord-style dynamic hash table (DHT), holds only very compact, aggregated information about the peers' local indexes and only to the extent that the individual peers are willing to disclose. Every peer is responsible for a randomised subset of the global directory. The global directory consists of aggregated information (Posts) that contains contact information about the digital library who posted this summary together with statistics to calculate IR-style relevance measures that try to estimate the relevance of a particular digital library to a query. These measures are used to support the peer selection process, *i.e.,* determining the most promising libraries for a particular query. If, at query time, the local query result is considered unsatisfactory by the user, a library retrieves a list of potentially useful libraries. Using collection selection methods from distributed IR and metasearch, a number of promising libraries for the complete query is computed from these PeerLists. In we have studied promising and efficient techniques for this purpose. Subsequently, the query is forwarded to these libraries and executed based on their local indexes.

The results from the various libraries are combined at the querying peer into a single result list; this step is referred to as result merging. The goal of finding high-quality search results with respect to precision and recall cannot be easily reconciled with the design goal of unlimited scalability, as the best information retrieval techniques for query execution rely on large amounts of document metadata. Posting only compact, aggregated information about local indexes and using appropriate peer selection methods to limit the number of peers involved in a query keeps the global directory manageable and reduces network traffic. We expect this approach to scale very well as more and more peers jointly maintain the moderately growing global directory.

CHALLENGES

Our work is driven by the question of how a collaborative search across digital libraries can benefit from the unique nature of the P2P paradigm. We want to address the shortcomings of centralised search engines and further benefit from the intellectual input of a large user community.

Democratic Community Search

To overcome the danger of the infiltration of a centralised index by (commercial) interest groups we leverage the indexes from potentially thousands of digital libraries, making it harder to bias the final query results.

Implicit User Feedback

Additionally, we want to incorporate the fact that every library has its own local index, *e.g.*, by executing all queries first locally at the initiating library and using implicit-feedback techniques for automated query expansion.

User Recommendations

We want to incorporate local user bookmarks into our query execution. Bookmarks represent strong recommendations for specific documents. Also, user bookmarks can be considered as compact samples of peer indexes that describe their fields of interest. Queries could be exclusively forwarded to thematically related libraries with similarly interested users, to improve the chances of finding subjectively relevant pages.

Replication

In order to achieve service levels comparable to today's search engines and in order to actually benefit from the infrastructural advantage of a distributed system, we are going to introduce a certain degree of replication to the directory. Currently, as dictated by the DHT-style maintenance approach, a peer gracefully leaving the system forwards its share of the global directory to another peer. Analogously, a library entering the system asks for its appropriate share of the directory. While one approach to ensure a valid, complete, and up-todate directory is to simply rely on the libraries to regularly re-send their Posts to the directory, it is also necessary to replicate parts of the directory to avoid data loss as libraries ungracefully leave the system. Also, replication can serve as a load-balancing measure, relieving the burden from peers that host popular parts of the directory, and increases data availability. Adaptive, self-tuning strategies for choosing appropriate degrees of replication and placing replicas are an open issue in our ongoing work.

Caching and Proactive Dissemination

To further enhance query efficiency, statistical summaries and also the results of queries from across the network may be cached in a way that allows other peers not only to instantly benefit from the existing query results but also to benefit from click streamst that were recorded on the occasion of similar queries. Statistical summaries may also be disseminated proactively among thematically related peers. Finding good strategies to this end is a widely open issue.

Overlap-aware Query Routing

Peer selection has been a research issue for years. Most of the existing literature estimates the expected result quality of a collection, typically using pre-computed statistics, and ranks the collections accordingly. We believe that this is insufficient if the collections overlap, *e.g.*, in the scenario of digital libraries that share an arbitrarily large fraction of documents. We argue for the extension of existing quality measures using estimators of mutual overlap among collections. Preliminary experiments show that such a combination can outperform popular approaches based on quality estimation only, such as CORI. Taking overlap into account during collection selection in this scenario can drastically decrease the number of libraries that have to be contacted in order to reach a satisfactory level of recall, which is a great step towards the feasibility of distributed search across digital libraries.

Benefit/Cost Optimisation

Ultimatively, we want to introduce a sophisticated benefit/cost ratio when selecting remote libraries for query forwarding. For the benefit estimation, it is intuitive to consider such measures.

Defining a meaningful cost measure, however, is an even more challenging issue. While there are techniques for observing and inferring network bandwidth or other infrastructural information, expected response times are changing over time. One approach is to create a distributed Quality-of-Service directory that, for all peers, holds moving averages of recent response times.

DIRECT – A DISTRIBUTED TOOL FOR INFORMATION RETRIEVAL EVALUATION CAMPAIGNS

Digital Library Management Systems (DLMSs) generally manage collections of multi-media digitalised data and include components that perform the storage, access, retrieval, and analysis of the collections of data. The evaluation of DLMSs is a non trivial issue that should cover different aspects, such as: the DLMS architecture, the DLMS information access and extraction capabilities, the management of multimedia content, the interaction with users, and so on.

We are interested in the evaluation aspects concerned with the information access and extraction components of a DLMS ; this interest ranges from measuring and quantifying the performances of the information access and extraction components of a DLMS to designing and developing an architecture capable of supporting this kind of evaluation in the context of DLMSs.

EVALUATION ISSUES FOR THE INFORMATION ACCESS COMPONENTS OF A DLMS

Today, this type of evaluation is carried out in important international evaluation forums which bring research groups together, provide them with the means for measuring the performances of their systems, discuss and compare their work. The most important forums for Information Retrieval System (IRS) are:

- Text REtrieval Conference (TREC),
- Cross Language Information Retrieval (CLIR),
- NII-NACSIS Test Collection for IR Systems (NTCIR), and
- INitiative for the Evaluation of XML Retrieval (INEX).

A wide range of questions are covered by these forums like the quality of the information retrieved, the access of multi-lingual collections of documents, the retrieval of structured documents and the access to Asian-language collections.

In general, these evaluation campaigns follow the Cranfield paradigm giving the participants one or more test-bed collections, a set of tasks to be performed, and a method by which evaluating performances of their systems with respect to the defined collections and tasks. A drawback of the approach followed during these evaluation forums is that huge chunks of textual files are shifted from side to side. Document collections usually reside on a single high-loaded server where all participants connect con- currently in a very short limited time in order to download the collections needed to carry out the experiments. The experimental results provided by participants to organisers usually consist of large text files, containing lists of retrieved documents together with their rank and score, that are numerical data.

The performance figures computed by organisers and returned to participants consist of text files full of numerical data; in particular, the presentation format adopted by TrecEval, the *de-facto* standard tool for computing the performance figures, is not very suitable for direct processing by a computer programme, since it is tailored to be human-readable. These file transfers often requires a mass-mailing between participants and organisers in order to acknowledge the receipt of the files or to correct errors. Moreover, if the performances figures are to be accessed in order to further process them, a lot of textual parsing is needed to transform chunks of text into numerical values, a process which is prone to errors.

Another drawback is that while the performance of IRS are measured by means of traditional IR performance indicators, the analysis of the significance of this results is rarely performed by participants although statistical analysis is a fundamental step in the experimental evaluation, as pointed out by. We identify two main reasons for this: first, the analysis of the whole set of runs submitted is possible only by organisers that collect all the runs, and replicating experiments of other research groups is seldom possible for participants. Second, statistical tools are not easy to handle and the possibility to have non coherent results is high when participants make use of different tools. Moreover, the statistical analysis is burdened by all the textual parsing needed to transform chunks of text into numerical and processable data.

In this chapter, we want to tackle the problem of a new approach to evaluation campaigns, able to take into account the distributed nature of the entities involved during an evaluation campaign: data collections may reside on different servers, participants are scattered around the world, as well as assessors and organisers. Moreover, DLMSs themselves are distributed systems where the services under evaluation can be developed according to different architectural paradigms, such as Web Services (WS), Peer-To-Peer (P2P),. and Grid. Finally, another innovative aspect of our approach is to provide participants with a uniform way of performing statistical analysis on their results. In this way, not only participants benefit from standard experimental collections but also they may exploit standard tools for the analysis of the experimental results. This approach, that makes the analysis and assessment of experimental results com- parable, is quite innovative since up to now participants employed tools built on their own in order to analyse experimental results, making such analyses much more difficult to compare.

An innovative system named *Distributed Information Retrieval Evaluation Campaign Tool (DIRECT)* is being designed and developed to give an alternative to the management of data of these evaluation forums with the aim of integrating the activities among the different entities and giving the tools to make the activities themselves more interactive. The goal will be to create a unified view of this kind of evaluation forums and to propose an innovative architecture able to provide dedicated services and tools to make available data and documents. In particular, the evaluation of information access components of a DLMS will not be calculated by means of standard IR measures only, but also with an integrated tools for statistical analysis available to all participants of evaluation forums. Since we are going to provide and manage the technical infrastructure, both hardware and software, for the *Cross-Language Evaluation Forum (CLEF)* 2005 ongoing evaluation campaign, the possibility of testing and evaluating the DIRECT system in real settings will be exploited.

DIRECT ARCHITECTURE AND FUNCTIONALITIES

Figure shows the architecture of DIRECT. It consists of three layers—data, application and interface logic layers—which allow us to achieve a better modularity and to properly describe the behaviour of DIRECT by isolating specific functionalities at the proper layer. Moreover, this decomposition makes it possible to clearly define the functioning of DIRECT by means of communication paths that connect the different components. In this way, the behaviour of the system is designed in a modular and extensible way.

Data Logic

The data logic layer deals with the actual storage of the different information objects coming from the upper layers. There is a set of 'storing managers' which translate the requests that arrive from the upper layers into *Structured Query Language (SQL)* statements to operate on the underlying *DataBase Management Systems (DBMSs)*. The heart of the data logic is an *Entity – Relationship (ER)* schema that is designed to fulfill the requirements to manage a complex evaluation forums. Note that, due to huge quantity of data to be managed, it may be necessary to split the underlying database across different DBMSs, thus dealing with a distributed database. Finally, on top of the various 'storing managers' there is the *Storing Abstraction Layer (SAL)* which hides the details about the storage management from the upper layers. In this way, the addition of a new 'storing manager' is totally transparent for the upper layers.

Application Logic

The application logic layer deals with the flow of operations within DIRECT. It provides a set of tools capable of managing high-level tasks. For example, the *Statistical Analysis Management Tool (SAMT)* offers the functionalities needed to conduct a statistical analysis on a set of runs; conducting a statistical analysis involves, in the data logic layer, both the *Run Storing Manager (RSM)* to have access to the experimental data, and the *Statistical Analysis Storing Manager (SASM)* to store the results of such analysis. Finally, the *DIRECT Integration Layer (DIL)* provides the interface logic layer with a uniform and integrated access to the various tools. As we noticed in the case of the SAL, thanks to the DIL also the addition of new tools is transparent for the interface logic layer.

Interface Logic

It is the highest level of the architecture, and it is the access point for the user to interact with the system. It provides specialised *User Interfaces (UIs)* for different types of users, that are the participants, the assessors, and the administrators of DIRECT.

P-INDEX – AN INDEX FOR GRAPH STRUCTURED DATA

In the context of the Semantic Web, ρ-operators are proposed in as a mean to explore complex relationships between entities. The problem of searching for the complex relationships can be modeled as the process of searching paths in a graph where entities represent vertices and edges the relationships between them. The notion of complex relationships can be also identified in bibliographic digital libraries, where entities could represent publications and the relationship can represent references or citations between them.

As proposed in, we recognise two kinds of complex relationships. The first one is represented by *a path* lying between two inspected vertices. Speaking in terms of publications this means that one publication indirectly cites or references the other publication – a chain of publications can be built so that one cites another. The second type of complex relationship is *a connection* between two inspected vertices. This symbolises a fact that the two inspected publications indirectly cite one common publication. The knowledge about complex relationships among publications can be used for example for ranking the result of the search for publications.

Another use case can be an automated recommendation of publications based on the preferred set of publications. For that reason, this chapter presents an indexing technique called the ρ-index that enables efficient discovery of complex relationships in large collections of graph structured data.

MOTIVATION

The graph theory proved that a very handy representation of a directed graph is its adjacency matrix because using matrix algebra we can comfortably study the graph's properties. For instance, if the adjacency matrix is powered by two, each field in the resulting matrix contains a number of paths of length two lying between every pair of vertices in the original graph. If the computation continued, the result would contain amounts of all paths of an arbitrary length.

The main difficulty of a matrix representation of a graph is that its use is limited to fairly small graphs, because the matrix grows in the quadratic space and the multisplication operation on matrices has even cubic time complexity. Therefore, we introduce graph transformations to enable the use of the matrix approach to graphs of arbitrary size.

OVERVIEW OF THE *P*-INDEX

The main idea of the approach introduced in this chapter is to identify certain units in the indexed graph such that when replaced by single vertices, they would form a new smaller graph that would be easier to navigate, but yet having the same properties as the original graph had. The aim is to enable the use of the matrix approach on *SG*(*G*) while it is not possible to use it on *G*. And because *SG*(*G*) is also a regular graph it can be again segmented.

Proposed Graph Transformations

The first graph transformation used is *a graph to a forest of trees* transformation. The result of this transformation is a set of trees together with a set of transitions among those trees. A lot of indexing techniques for trees have been developed for efficient navigation inside a tree. We have chosen the tree signatures. They enable fast navigation inside a tree using simple and cheap operation – a comparison of preorder and post order ranks of nodes in the particular tree. The ranks are represented by integer numbers thus the comparison of the particular ranks takes $O(1)$ time. If we take a closer look on the result of this transformation we see that the acquired trees form vertices and transitions among them edges in a new graph. This new graph represents the original graph but in a simplified way.

Certainly, any path that was in the original graph is also in the new graph and vice versa. If the size of the newly acquired graph is small enough to create the matrix representation of it, the job is done. The index would be then composed of the tree signatures and the matrix describing all paths among those trees. However, we would like to index a graph of an arbitrary size. An obvious idea is to use this graph transformation recursively onto the newly acquired graph as long as we get a graph of a desired size. But an evaluation of the recursive application of this transformation in showed that after few applications this method does not lead to a significant reduction of the amount of nodes in the new graph.

Therefore, another graph transformation has to be used to lower the amount of vertices in the new graph. The transformation that we have chosen for this is *vertex clustering*. It reduces the amount of vertices in a graph by collapsing subgraphs (segments) into single vertices. Also in the new graph acquired by this transformation is true that any path in the new graph is contained in the original one and vice versa. This graph transformation represents the graph segmentation, thus, the new graph is a segment graph of the original graph. The reason why the transformation of graph to forest of trees is used is to make more dense graph out of a sparse graph. The tree signatures can be applied to tree of any size. This kind of transformation is used only once as a first step in the process. In all following steps only the vertex clustering is used because the number of vertices in the transformed graph does not decrease in a linear way but rather converges to a certain limit.

Adjacency Matrix of Paths

A path type adjacency matrix is a modification of a usual adjacency matrix. It is designed to represent a graph in a path oriented way. Initially, each field of our matrix contains a path consisting of a single edge whenever there exists such an edge between two vertices in the graph. The convenience it presents over the usual adjacency matrix is that after the transitive closure of the path type matrix is computed, the fields contain not just an amount of paths lying between any two vertices, but also the paths themselves. Naturally, the mathematical operations on numbers + and * are replaced by the respective operations on paths - union and concatenation.

Outline of ρ-index's Structure

Let present a brief example of a three level ρ-index visualised in figure. Firstly, the graph to a forest of trees transformation is applied to the graph that is indexed. Subsequently, a tree signature is created to each acquired tree. The new graph, where vertices represent trees and edges represent transitions among trees, is then decomposed by the vertex clustering transformation.

For each collapsed subgraph, its path type adjacency matrix is created. After that a path type adjacency matrix is created to the newly acquired graph, where vertices represent collapsed subgraphs. Hence, the ρ-index has the following structure. On the lowest level, there are tree signatures of trees obtained by the first graph transformation. Above that is a set of path type matrices describing each collapsed subgraph. And at the topmost level is a single path type matrix used to navigate among the subgraphs.

PRELIMINARY EXPERIMENTAL EVALUATION

An experimental implementation of the ρ-index was built to evaluate its properties. The measurable aspects are the time necessary to build the ρ-index and the time consumed to discover the relationships. Furthermore, a proportion of accessible vertices from the inspected vertex in the indexed graph to the amount of actually accessed vertices in the p-index is measured. Also a total number of accesses to vertices in the ρ-index is recorded. The both graphs used to evaluate the ρ-index properties are a part of the Open Directory Project representing the connections among categories. They mostly differ in the size and density. We have run the tests on a usual desktop computer with a 3 GHz Pentium 4 processor and 2 gigabytes of RAM.

As the total number of edges in each graph proposes, the smaller graph is denser than the bigger one. The evaluation consisted of a set of executions of a path relationship search. Thus, we used the index to retrieve all paths lying between the two inspected vertices. The result of this search was either the empty set or all paths lying between the two vertices. During each execution the total number of accesses to vertices in the ρ-index was recorded to measure the efficiency of designed algorithms. The number of accessible vertices indicates the amount of vertices that can be accessed in the indexed graph from the starting vertex. Number of accessed vertices represents an amount of actually accessed vertices in the ρ-index.

The experimental evaluation concludes that the sparser the graph is the better results we get from the ρ-index. Why is that true indicates the total number of accesses to vertices in the ρ-index. We found out that not every segment sequence that is a product of the transitive closure computation of $SG(G)$ does represent some path on the lower level (in G). And this happens more often in the denser graph causing a huge amounts of these false segment sequences to be checked by the search algorithm.

EFFICIENT AND EFFECTIVE MATCHING OF COMPOUND PATIENT RECORDS

This part provides an overview on structure and content of patient records and motivates our contribution on fast matching in large collections of patient records.

MOTIVATION

Electronic patient records have become an important patient-centered entity in healthcare management. They represent complex documents that comprise a wide diversity of patient-related information, like basic administrative data, billing details, and a variety of medical information. Most of these details are structurally and temporally interrelated, like a

- Particular treatment and
- Medication ordered from a
- Physician on an
- Established diagnosis from patient's
- Reported symptoms at a

* Certain date.

Each item is of a dedicated media type, like structured alphanumeric data, semi-structured text, images, video, time series, and possibly others, like DNA sequence data. State-of-the-art medical information systems aggregate massive amounts of data in patient records. Its exploitation, however, is mainly restricted to accounting and billing purposes, leaving aside most medical information. In particular, similarity search based on complex document matching is out of scope for today's medical information systems.

CONTRIBUTION

As stated in there are many application fields in medicine for content-based retrieval methods. These application fields can roughly be divided into the three domains teaching, research and diagnosis. We believe that efficient and effective matching of patient records forms the rewarding foundation for a large application variety. Data mining applications that rest upon our patient record matching approach will foster enhanced therapy, in general. Specifically, our proposal allows for effective comparison of similar cases to:

- Shorten necessary treatments,
- Improve diagnoses, and
- Guide the proper medication to improve patients' well-being and reduce cost.

Precisely, we introduce a novel matching algorithm that tackles two issues concurrently. On the one hand, we provide a query model that incorporates the particular composition of patient records.

For the time being, we focus on the aggregate structure and different domains. On the other hand, our matching algorithms allows for efficient similarity search with interactive answering times while processing large document collections.

COMPOUND DOCUMENT MATCHING

Health records like any other compound multimedia documents comprise component objects. In contrast to many existing digital libraries, these compound documents do not consist of rather small numbers of objects, but aggregate many multimedia data items over years. For example, the Radiology Department of the University hospitals of Geneva produced medical images more than 12,000 per day in 2002. For a very rough estimation, when all 2197 beds of the hospital are in use, more than five images per patient are generated—on one single day of their life. The Picture Archiving and Communications System (PACS) of Tilak, a local healthcare provider in Tyrol with 2046 beds, has to cope even with 240 Gbytes of new data for a single day, which corresponds to 320.000 images. The aim For this reason, analysing patient records for similarity is more complex than comparing two short documents or web pages consisting of only a couple of paragraphs of text and images. But to illustrate the problem, this might be a good start.

Similarity search on compound documents needs to establish matches of corresponding media objects. Finding these corresponding objects within large sets of objects is a computationally intensive task. A similar problem is prevalent in region based image retrieval (RBIR). That is, regions from two images must be matched to compute an overall similarity score. Two images' overall similarity score is computed by finding best pairs of regions from those two images. This optimisation problem of finding best pairs is a generalisation of the so-called Assignment Problem. Using the Hungarian algorithm, the complexity of similarity computation for two region sets is $O(r^3)$ with r being the number of regions in both sets.

From a query processing point of view, a cubic complexity is unsatisfactory, restricting the applicability to small data sets and few regions. To perform this task more efficiently, proposes a two-stage filter-and-refinement approach. Such an approach can reduce both I/O and CPU costs, *e.g.* in, such an approach is applied to reduce the number of file accesses needed to read feature vectors for content-based multimedia retrieval from disk. For complex queries, the costs of computation become more important and may exceed the costs for accessing the data from storage. In this paper we focus on the CPU cost reduction. The first stage of the approach yields a small number of candidate matches by computing computationally cheap, yet tight upper and lower bounds to the exact similarity score. The second stage invokes the exact distance function on the candidates.

As the cost to compute lower and upper bounds is significantly lower than its exact counterpart, tremendous speed-ups can be achieved. In, authors report a factor of five in query processing time consumption. Like images can be partitioned into regions, compound documents can be divided into their component objects. Figure illustrates this for two documents, consisting of seven and six objects. Calculating the similarity of two compound documents c1, c2 must:

- Establish matches between corresponding objects from both documents and
- Compute the document similarity out of the individual object similarities.

Finding Corresponding Objects

Every component object of c_1 should correspond to exactly one object of c_2 and vice versa. That is, we assign each object to exactly one other object, which is called a complete match. This is a restriction to the simple approach to match each object in c1 straight forward to the object of c_2 which is most similar. This relaxed condition would allow assigning one object in c_2 twice or even to every object in c_1. In general, this is not the correct answer to a compound query document containing several distinct component objects.

In this is explained by requesting an image showing two tigers, but getting results showing only one. For compound documents a similar problem may exist: If we query for a document containing one paragraph about one distinct topic, and another paragraph about one different topic, we may want to retrieve only documents handling the same two topics individually instead of mixing both topics in a single paragraph. With increasing number of component objects, the ability the model this distinction and retrieve only documents fulfilling the complete match criterion gains very much importance.

In contrast to region matching, compound documents may consist of objects from various domains. In figure both documents have objects of the domains text and images. In order to form a complete match, we would need to assign one text to an image. But how can we be sure that the text really relates to the image? To be sure, we would need a similarity function comparing texts to images. In general, no meaningful cross-domain similarity function exists, *e.g.* it is not feasible to match a cardiogram against a CT image of the lung. Even between objects of the same media type, a comparison can be problematic. If we think of medical imaging, DICOM files are generated via various techniques which differ all in the way they represent tissues. Moreover, the screened body function and the spatial orientation of an image have an impact on the object domain, as well. For example, all three images in figure show the head of human patients which were stored in the DICOM file format.

This kind of knowledge can be used to provide similarity functions and judge their significance for application specific problems. Therefore, the structure of a compound query document with regard to its component objects and their media types is one possible feature of the query. An improved approach might even define domains not solely on media types, but whether there exists a meaningful similarity measurement between two objects. The similarity between any two objects is computed using an appropriate similarity function for their domain and the result is normalised to the interval, such that 1 denotes most similar and 0 not similar. We can build a similarity matrix where the rows depict objects from the compound document c_1 and the columns the objects of the compared document c2. The matrix is filled with the similarity score returned by the function for the respective objects. We do not limit ourselves to any particular similarity function. In fact, it is one of the major goals of this approach to be able to use an arbitrary existing similarity measure instead of developing new ones for each domain.

The value N/A indicates that no meaningful match exists. Therefore, we split the matrix into the domain-specific matrices. Since it is not possible to find exact matches in non-quadratic matrices, we extend the split matrices until each has as many columns as rows and fill these new fields with so-called penalty values. In this way, we may penalise missing counterparts in c_2 to objects from c_1.

Notice that any complete match within a domain needs to assign the same number of penalty values. Hence, finding the best complete match of two distinct compound documents is orthogonal to the choice of penalty values. Therefore, the actual values of p_1 and p_2 do not affect the solution to our example. Their values gain only importance when ranking of the similarity between one query document and several other documents is performed and those other compound documents differ in the number of objects within at least one domain.

Document Similarity

Document matching solves an optimisation problem, which is on finding the maximum overall similarity of two compound documents. That is, sim computes two documents' similarity out of their component object similarities. For the time being, we use the unweighted average of the objects' similarities, using a separate similarity matrix for each domain. By defining domains according to the availability of a meaningful similarity measure, we can guarantee that finding the best matches for each domain will also find the overall best match for the complete documents. This is due to the fact that every pair which is not covered within the restriction to domains can achieve only the similarity score N/A – which has to be treated as being worse than any other similarity score including any penalty value.

7

Collection Management

ACQUISITION OF ELECTRONIC RESOURCES DEALING WITH LICENSING ISSUES

The electronic publishing has a very short history, compared to traditional form of publishing. The first known form of e-publishing is in the early 1980s when plain text e-mails were sent to the subscriber via a mailing list. But, the subsequent technological advancements made a tremendous impact on the information cycle process of creation, gathering/production and dissemination of information, which in turn hugely influenced the electronic publishing itself. In 1994-95 the first e-journal was published and the distribution of e-journal turned out to be an instant success. Majority of the journals are now made available in digital form.

The publishers are now offering package subscription to electronic journals at highly reduced price as the publishing charges of e-journals have substantially come down, as compared to their print counterpart, which involved huge cost of printing and distribution. Subsequently, even bibliographic resources were brought in electronic form. Soon, e-books also made their presence. These developments made the libraries to seriously rethink their collection development and information delivery policies. While moving totally to electronic may be a distant possibility, a progressive shift from print to electronic, is being noticed.

MOVING FPOM PRINT TO ELECTRONIC: *A CRITICAL ISSUE*

While the print and online versions have their own advantages and disadvantages. However, to put the subject in perspective, some critical remarks are made here. Print resources subscribed/ bought are physically available in the libraries and form an asset. Online resources subscribed/ bought on one-time purchase can only be accessed by users, as the digital content is held remotely at the publishers' end.

This raises the issue of ownership *vs.* access and is a well debated point in the user and the librarians' communities. The fact, however, is that, in case of online resources, the libraries are currently dependent totally on publishers to access the subscribed/ bought content. This situation made the libraries to think in terms of ensuring perpetual access to the subscribed/ bought content. Of course, publishers too have their own concerns of protecting their content from misuse. It is, therefore, a mutual interest of both the publisher and the end-user to enter into an Agreement protecting each other's interests. This agreement is generally known as License Agreement.

LICENCE AGREEMENT AND ITS TYPES

A Licence agreement is a legal document and contract between the publisher and the institutional library. Both the parties agree to abide by the terms and conditions set in the agreement. There are basically three different kinds of site license agreements according to:

- The type of library,
- Product/ model, and
- Number of sites.

The agreements by the type of libraries include Academic/ Research, Government/ Corporate & Public and generally the variations are in terms of users, fees, etc.; The agreements by product/ model are based on the e-resources, such as E-journals, E-books and Bibliographic Databases. The agreements by site(s) are applicable according to the number of sites, such as single site, multi-sites and consortium. Although, the re-exist some Standard Licensing models, each publisher has his own Agreement and a close look at these indicate that there is a lack of consistency and standardisation. A few publishers have put up the copy of their site license agreement on their web site but others do not do so maintaining it as confidential document. However, signing of License Agreement has almost become mandatory. In fact, a well known publisher has a policy which stipulates that they will raise the invoice for an e-product only after the library signs the agreement. In a way, it is good that the library will know all the terms & conditions before buying the product. Other publishers send the agreement after the purchase order is raised and the payment is made. In such cases, it may be difficult to negotiate any changes in the clauses.

The terms and conditions of the site license agreement are heavily tilted in favour of publishers. However, except a few, the clauses in the Agreement are generally subject to negotiations. The job of dealing with such issues would be much simpler for those Organisations which have a Legal Cell. It is advisable to refer the document to that Cell. But, as is generally observed, many Organisations do not have such Units which make it imperative for the Librarian to take up himself the responsibility of examining the legal aspects in the Agreement. In that case, the librarian needs to be very cautious in studying various clauses in the Agreement.

He/ she must ensure that the interests of his/ her Organisation are protected to the maximum possible extent. After going through the Agreements carefully, one has to first seek clarifications from the publishers on those points which do not seem to be very clear. Possible changes may be suggested to bring in more clarity. If certain terms are unacceptable, it is essential to request for changes/ amendments in the Agreement. Sometimes, it needs a hard bargaining and the librarians need to have strong negotiating skills.

KEY ISSUES IN THE AGREEMENT

Perpetual Access

Perpetual access is ensured by most of the publishers. But some publishers put a condition that the library should subscribe to at least one online journal or any online product of theirs. Otherwise, they will charge maintenance fee/ hosting fee. If the access is provided off-line, then they ask the libraries to bear the cost of production to provide the content on other electronic media, such as CDs/ DVDs, for local hosting. Some publishers prefer to use the term 'Continued Access' in place of 'Perpetual Access'. The terminological difference may have to be clearly understood. As one UK publisher puts it - the 'Perpetual Access' in their terminology refers to a limited period and the 'Continued Access' means indefinite period. Libraries need to ensure that their parent institution will not be put to disadvantage and take precautions to get inserted right terminology.

However, some publishers do not provide perpetual access at all to the subscribed content. If an online subscription is not renewed, the libraries will lose access even to the paid content. If that is the case, then the Licensing document must clearly state it. In such cases, the libraries need to think seriously about an alternative method of archiving either by continuing with print version or get archival year-end CDs/ DVDs, as offered by some publishers.

Withdrawal of Content

Publishers insert a clause that it reserves right to withdraw the content, which it no longer retains the right to publish or infringes copyright or defamatory, etc. While the last condition should be acceptable, the first two conditions may sometime put librarians in a fix. These situations may arise when a journal title is transferred to some other publisher. The new publisher may not permit the old subscribers to access this content, free. It is all the more critical if this content is substantial and/ or directly relevant to their users.

As a remedial measure, one can demand insertion of the following clauses - The publisher will make best efforts to convince the new publisher to provide access to the old subscribers or shall allow local hosting of such content. Also, if the withdrawal is substantial, then the publisher shall refund the amount proportionately.

Restrictions on Usage

Generally, publishers do not permit users to download entire journal issues and e-books. A standard condition to this effect may be found in License Agreement of all the publishers. There are publishers who even put a restriction on the number of pages and chapters printable from e-books. The decision of the libraries to buy ebooks from such publishers depends on how comfortable they are with the restrictions imposed by the publishers. A few publishers do permit the licensee to make an electronic copy and a hardcopy for backup purpose. However, the libraries need to create necessary infrastructure to preserve the content on their local computer server.

Access to Archives through Third Party

In the event of a publisher deciding to wind up his operations or merge with another publisher, it is an obligation on the part of the publisher to make alternative arrangements to provide access to archive of the licensed materials concerned. This is where the third party arrangement comes into picture. Many publishers have made arrangements with some external agencies for the long time preservation of their digital archive. Some examples are LOCKSS, CLOCKSS, PORTICO, and National Library of Netherlands. In a trigger event, it becomes the responsibility of these agencies to grant access to the content to the subscribers. The libraries should insist publishers to incorporate in the agreement a clause specifying the names of the agencies with whom the arrangements are made to provide access to the content in the event of publisher closing his business. Some of these agencies offer paid service, but since the subscribers have already paid for the content earlier, it becomes a debatable point whether the libraries can afford to pay again for the same content.

Inter-Library Loan (ILL)

Providing a copy of an article to another library (not-forprofit, non-commercial) under ILL is generally permitted by most of the publishers, but with varying conditions. While the publishers expect subscribers to observe normal Copyright rules, some put specific restrictions on document delivery system. While one publisher permits only to send copies in print format, the other allows electronic transmission through secure network, but insists that the recipient library delete the file after printing a paper copy. Such clauses are non-negotiable and the libraries need to accept them, so long some form of ILL is permitted.

Governing Laws

Business of digital content is only three decade old. Like any other business, there is a possibility that disputes might arise especially in terms of copyright rules, access problems etc. If such disputes remain unresolved mutually, the aggrieved parties have no option, but to approach Judiciary. This gives rise to the problem of jurisdiction as the two parties belong to different countries. The agreement is generally governed by the laws of the country of origin of the publisher. However, some publishers are flexible on this issue. While some agree to sort out the issue in the court of subscriber's country, others agree to the condition that the aggrieved party can approach their respective countries. Alternatively, some publishers also allow for an independent arbitrator mutually acceptable to both parties.

Fees

Fees charged by the publishers for e-books, online journal packages, etc. varies from library to library, depending upon size of the user community. However, publishers also offer price cap in case a library agrees to go for a multi-year agreement. The base price and the price cap shall form part of the Agreement and as such need to be stated explicitly.

Counter-signed Copy

Original copy of the agreement is generally in duplicate and the two signed copies are exchanged between the library and the publisher. However, the Agreements of some publishers have only the acceptance column which needs to be signed by the Library. In such a case, libraries should keep with them one copy of the agreement.

General Conditions

Some publishers incorporate a clause in the agreement, stating that the content of the Licensed Material is 'subject to change without notice'. If accepted, this allows the publisher to alter the subscribed/ purchased content without notice. In this case, subscriber will be totally in dark about the changes effected, including withdrawal of any content.

To avoid this, the librarians need to insist for change in the clause appropriately by changing it to 'subject to change with prior notice to the licensee' (*i.e.* library). This will protect the end-user from any loss of content, as the user will have time to copy and store the content locally. Some publishers also incorporate a clause that the contents of the License Agreement should not be disclosed to a third party without their consent.

While the publishers urging to maintain secrecy is understandable, it may be difficult for libraries to accept such a clause, especially for those organisations funded by State/ Central Governments, which, according to the Right to Information Act, may have to be disclose the content to those, who seek it. Therefore, it is essential that appropriate changes are demanded in the clauses.

USAGE PATTERN OF INFORMATION RESOURCES AT CSIR

The aim and objective of any Information Centre is to provide pinpoint, exhaustive, and nascent information to readers who use information for a variety of purposes. A library, therefore, is always adjudged good or bad on by its usage. This goal makes the collection development evaluation imminent. Considering the importance of such usage, an attempt has been made in this study to evaluate the current usage of literature at CSIR-National Metallurgical Laboratory, Jamshedpur, Jharkhand (Erstwhile Bihar). The worth of a library collection can be judged through various methods like, circulation of documents, user survey, download analysis of literature, Citation/Reference analysis, etc. The present study, however, evaluates the library usage through reference analysis. Today, citation and ranking information are becoming key aspects of knowledge management in R&D Knowledge Resource Centers.

It helps to examine the changing user needs and products so as to understand and manage the information resources besides responding the user needs better. Effective collection analysis and assessment provides quantitative and qualitative data for evaluating the usefulness and utility of a library's holdings. It assists with determining budget requirements by focusing attention on how well the library's collections in specific areas support the needs of the users and the institution as well. It also points out whether the institution's investment in the collection is being managed responsibly. The aim of such assessment is, therefore, to determine as to how well the collection supports the goals, needs, and mission of the library or parent organisation. The collection (both locally held and remotely accessed materials) is assessed in the local context. Evaluation seeks to examine or describe collections either in their own terms or in relation to other collections and checking mechanisms, such as lists. Both evaluation and assessment provide a better understanding of the collection and the user community. The major problem of research libraries all over the world today is deciding as to which serials should be subscribed to meet the needs of their specialised users without subscribing to any unnecessary journals.

The problem has been further aggravated recently by shortages of funds and subsequent cuts in library book budgets. In order to operate effectively, libraries must identify literature of high utility to their clients, and must acquire and organise the literature in such a way to ensure their optimal use. One of the generally accepted methods of scientific investigation is, indeed, to follow the scientific literature by the simplest means. Various sources are used by scientists to gather information, for example, through regular reading of all available texts, recommendations of colleagues and superiors, and references or citations in other related publications.

RESEARCH METHOD AND DATA

A total of 187 Research papers published in various formats like, SCI, Non- SCI, National proceedings, Internatioal proceedings and book chapters were identified by institutional affiliation.Fig.1 depicts the status of R&D publications, a maximum of 120 papers appeared in SCI was downloaded from Web of Science with complete reference data and the remaining 54 papers were scanned form Non-SCI journals, proceedings and book chapters. Thus, the total number of references cited in the 187 research papers was 3,825.

The average number of references per paper was 20. The availability of references was coded under the following four categories:

- Available in electronic form;
- Vailable in print form;
- Available in the open network; and
- Not available.

The bibliographic references in each article in the sample were first examined by classifying each citation into one of the following nine source categories by format of publications: books/monographs (includes chapters in a book, monograph series, sourcebook), journals (*i.e.* scholarly and academic serials in the form of print or online, articles 'in press' with journal title cited), periodicals (*i.e.* magazines, newspapers, working papers, Newsletters), conferences proceedings (proceedings, seminars meetings, workshops, forums), unpublished (*i.e.* unpublished manuscripts, thesis/ dissertation, documents, reports/documents, unpublished test and short communications), reference sources (*i.e.* government documents, dictionaries, handbooks, encyclopaedias) reports (*i.e.* published reports by institutions or corporations), web documents (documents retrieved from the internet via the worldwide web with Uniform Resource Locator (URL) provided, and others. 'Conference proceedings' was designated for compilations of papers presented at conferences or symposia that were not published as a regular issue of a journal.

CONSORTIA MODELS FOR NETWORKING

SOME ISSUES ON CSIR CONSORTIA

The word consortium has been derived from Latin, meaning association or partnership. In general a Consortium could be described as a group of organisations who come together to fulfil a common objective that usefully requires co-operation and the sharing of resources, and need to have a clear mutual goal in order to ensure their success. Various definitions are there in different dictionaries on consortium but almost the meaning is same in the context of library. An e-journal consortium means the collaborative acquisition of access rights to electronic databases and journals and the aim of is to achieve what the members of the group cannot achieve individually. Journals play a major role in the R&D but unfortunately the number and cost of journals are increasing at very high speed. Number of journals and their costs has increased by threefolds every 15 years and 226 per cent, respectively. During the last 20 years in terms of dollars, this may be further compounded by currency conversion whereas the increase in library 1 budget was only 110 per cent during the same period. In another study by the Association of Research Libraries in USA, it was found that average CPI (Consumer Price Index) for US increased by 73 per cent during 1986-2004, but the research libraries expenditure for journals 2 increased by 273 per cent during the same period due to the increase in number of research scholars, institutions and global competition.

The estimated number of STM (Science, Technology and Medicine) journals is about 25,000. Out of this 15,000 journals are peer- 3 reviewed and 12,000 are in e-form. All types of libraries/information centres are not in a position to subscribe all the information resources required by their users. Not even a single library can meet the thrust of knowledge required by all the readers from its stock of information to the full extent.To solve this, libraries have started library cooperation, *i.e.* inter-library loan (ILL), resource sharing, and library consortium, etc. For the past four centuries, dissemination of information was done through print media alone, but now the electronic media has taken over this mean of communication. Basic purpose of the consortia is sharing of resources, money, and manpower. In the digital context, it is the access to information rather than holding information. 'Collection building' concept has changed to 'Connection building' with the help of Information and Communication technologies (ICT). Access to the e-resources and the subscription amount is shared among the participating libraries. Significant price reduction can be achieved through consortium and individual libraries in the consortium will have collaborative acquisition of access rights to databases and e-journals. Library consortia's have become powerful negotiating parties and incorporating their own clauses in the contracts with the publishers and just no longer signing the standard contract texts provided by the 4 publishers.

TYPES OF CONSORTIA

The types of consortia identified are generally based on various models evolved in India in Variety of forms depending upon participations' affiliation and funding sources.

- *Open Consortia*: This type of consortia is very flexible and it is the wish of members of consortia can join and leave any they please. INDEST Consortium is an example to this.

- *Closed Group Consortia*: This kind of consortia emerges either by affiliation and collaboration among them like CSIR, DAE, IIM Consortium. The formation and operation of the consortia guidelines and its administration are fairly simple and easy.
- *Centrally Funded Model*: In this model, consortium will solely depend on the parent body. A few examples are CSIR, INDEST, UGC-INFONET and ICMR Consortia, etc.
- *Shared-budget Model*: In this model the participating libraries take the lead and form the consortium. IIM and FORSA are examples of this model.
- *Publisher Initiatives*: The Emerald Full-Text Library published by the Emerald Publishing Group (formerly MCB University Press) is recent example. Here, the consortium members will get deep discount price to the participating libraries.
- *National Consortium*: This is a model perceived at national level which includes member libraries from one country.

BENEFITS OF CONSORTIUM

Some of the important advantages of the proposed library consortium are as follows:

- Main advantage of e-journal consortium is, it checks the space problem, shelving, binding, lending, and related aspects of member libraries.
- Instead of user coming to the library, the library is available at the user's desktop/laptop virtually all the time (24/7). Available 24 hours a day, 7 days a week.
- It saves the time of the user since instant access will be available after every updating unlike the shipping time, missing issues, and mutilations. etc., which prevail in respect of print media.
- Consortium builds communication among different libraries and avoids duplication of core journals.

- Consortium provides high quality literature and faster document delivery service, *i.e.*, it provides a wealth of relevant resources readily available and helps in facing the challenges to have a meaningful presence in this digital era to its users.
- It is easy to assess the areas of interest of users so that efficient services can be provided by the concerned librarians through usage statistics given by the publisher.
- The consortium have been offered better terms of licenses for use, archival access and preservation of subscribed electronic resources, which would not have been possible for any single institution and facilities to build up digital libraries.
- Helpful to provide better library services like CAS and SDI.

BOTTLENECKS OF CONSORTIUM

- Absence of a printed copy of Journals and lack of archiving and back files availability.
- Require training of staffs in handling electronic documents etc.
- A consortium requires high initial investments in licensees and infrastructure, internet connectivity, and other accessories.
- Copyright problems. Problems like copyright/ excess downloads from the publisher.
- Content provider/publisher combines both essential and non-essential journals as a package. Whereas in print collection, the selection is done by subject expert(s) and only journals of core area are subscribed. Therefore, measures have to be taken to avoid unwanted items and recall the most relevant items.

GROWTH OF CONSORTIA IN INDIA

The new technology or the modern information technology has made the task of resource sharing very simple and convenient. The new technology brings forward to the information field many products and services which have changed the nature of fundamental library objectives and operations.

Over the last 2 decades, the libraries have witnessed the impact of information technology that has been affecting the structure of the services to a great extent. Library networks have grown mostly during the last 30 years in different geographical environment in order to cater the specific needs of the users. In the U.S., there has been a proliferation of them. In the developed countries, resource sharing networking was started long back, *e.g.* the growth of the network in the U.S., can be traced from mid 1960. USA is the birthplace of library networking and by now libraries in each state are networked to local, regional and national network.

On the other hand, the growth of library networks in India can be traced to the initiatives made by NISSAT in establishing 6 CALIBNET in 1986 and DELNET in 1988 and other networks like UGC/INFLIBNET has established UGC-INFONET Consortium, Digital Library in Engineering Science and Technology (INDEST) Consortium of all Indian institute of Technologies (IITs), Indian Institute of Science (IISc) and a few other institutions which include RECs, NITs, IIMs, etc., the Forum for Resource Sharing in Astronomy and Astrophysics (FORSA) is a consortium of Raman Research Institute (RRI), Indian Institute of Astrophysics (IIA), Tata Institute of Fundamental Research (TIFR), Inter-university Centre for Astronomy and Astrophysics (IUCAA), National Centre for Radio Astrophysics (NCRA), and Physical Research Laboratory (PRL) subsequently.

CSIR CONSORTIUM

The Council of Scientific and Industrial Research (CSIR), a public-funded organisation, is India's largest R&D organisation established in 1942 with a chain of 37 National laboratories and institutes. CSIR is carrying out the research work in various disciplines all over the country.

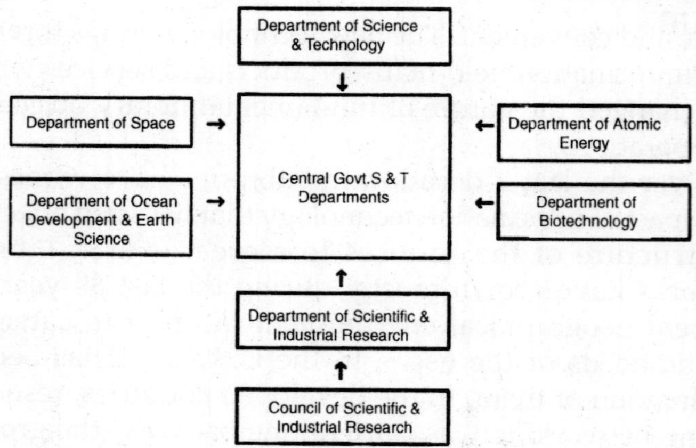

Fig 7.1 CSIR Orgnisational Structure

NEED FOR THE CONSORTIUM

There has been a constant decrease (66 per cent) in the journals base of CSIR laboratories over the last decade, which necessitated its libraries to find out alternate solution to make available R&D information.While laboratory size, areas of work and number of researchers vary, it is desirable to have comparable and adequate information 7 resources irrespective of the size or strength of the laboratory.

OBJECTIVES OF THE CONSORTIUM

- The primary objective of the overall programme focuses on enhancing the visibility and impact of CSIR research output internationally in terms of papers and patents.
- This will be attempted by providing access to maximum possible e-resources to the researchers.
- To provide CSIR & S&T staff electronic access to global knowledge with continues to subscribe existing e-resources.
- To expand the information base of CSIR and provide divergent nature of contents of information to CSIR users subscribe to additional e-resources.

E-JOURNAL CONSORTIUM

The Director General set up a study group in April 2001 to collect/study and compile information to the journals subscribed by the CSIR labs. After several deliberations the eth journal Consortium project finally took shape as a Network Project of CSIR under 10 Five Year Plan with a budget layout of Rs 11.79 crores for the plan period 2002-2007 targeting to access 4500 e-journals. E-Journal consortium is being coordinated centrally by CSIR's National Institute of Science Communication and Information Resources (NISCAIR) as nodal agency for implementing the Consortium, with a task force team established with senior scientists from CSIR laboratories and also negotiation committees to negotiate and finalise the agreements with the publishers in providing required e-journals, databases, etc., for CSIR's constituent laboratories.

The heads of the libraries of the participating labs are designated as 8 the nodal officers to implement the Consortium access to e-journals at their respective labs. CSIR e-Journal Consortium strengthens its library resources by pooling, sharing and providing electronic access services like e-journals and international databases to its scholars and scientists. On 10 June 2002, CSIR signed an agreement with M/s Elsevier Science to 9 access around 1500 world class e-journals.

NISCAIR has coordinated well by constituting different committees like Core Committee, Negotiating Committees, etc., for effective implementation of the consortium. 'Electronic plus' price model was chosen to maintain the print collection of the individual institution libraries irrespective of the duplicate and triplicate subscriptions from the same publisher and paying an extra amount of 9 per cent of the print to ScienceDirect at the beginning of the project.

This extra amount is varied subsequently in the following years based on effective negotiations by the concerned committees. Usage statistics is being provided by the publisher to the individual institutes for effective monitoring of the consortium. Archival issues pertaining to past five years are also being provided by the concerned publisher as per the agreement. E-Journals and other document requirements of the constituent laboratories have been put forth by the nodal officers to coordinating agencies.

The coordinating agency prepares the financial document and gets the money from CSIR negotiation committees to allocate this money to different publishers based on the suggestions received from the nodal officers. In this way it receives 10 more than 4000 e-journals. CSIR Consortium has proved to be a great success and its impact can be measured in terms of revenue savings, usage of e-journals in terms of downloads and contribution of articles in international journals, etc. Substantial revenue has been saved, and significant growth in number of papers and IF (Impact Factor) have been achieved.

Quantitative as well as qualitative improvements have been achieved in the years following the access to e-journals through the Consortium. Continual and steep increase in the number of downloads has also been recorded. In this way CSIR became a leading institutions of the world and the contribution of CSIR researchers in international journals have raised. The 11 National savings on this account is around Rs. 535 crores. Upgrading the CSIR information system is proving effective in meeting its researcher's divergent nature of information requirements.

ELSEVIER CONTEXT

To fill the lack of information in the CSIR laboratories, decided to subscribe e-journals of Elsevier by individual laboratories and sharing these resources among the CSIR laboratories. The coordinating agencies suggested subscribing only the unique journals and avoiding for the duplication for maximum possible so that sharing of e-journals shall be easier through the CSIR network. As scientific literature is exploding, publishing has become an increasingly profitable enterprise.

The competition in the publishing world is very fast, with even old scientific societies turning to commercial publishers, to bring a degree of professionalism of producing and marketing their journals. As journals multiply and costs increase, libraries must worry about budgets and coverage. Problems are compounded by growing costs of maintaining both print and online subscriptions and issues related to continuing electronic access to back files.

Large publishing houses like Elsevier Science and Springer-Verlag are beginning to monopolise the world of science journals, which arises a situation that 12 promotes a seller's market. CSIR Consortium did not agreed to the price hike proposed by publisher and termed it as unreasonable and gave a counter proposal for consideration of the publisher.

However, access to ScienceDirect was stopped in April 2008 as the agreement was not renewed between the CSIR Consortium and the publisher due to failure of negotiations with the regard to price hike by the publisher. In this way after 2008 CSIR laboratories were felt the necessity for a strong networking among their constituent laboratories.

SUBSCRIPTION TO JCCC@VIC: *J-GATE CUSTOM CONTENT FOR CONSORTIA*

After this CSIR entering into JCCC for exchange of holdings of individual CSIR laboratories on inter library loan basis but problems with JCCC are it is a platform which is common to all for accessing information which becomes a great problem to serve the users. As CSIR laboratories are scientific in nature so their members are also dealing with scientific field, but it is difficult to analyse the member of JCCC. It becomes a question mark in their authenticity in identification.

NAL CONTEXT

For possible solution NAL (National Aeronautics Limited) compile a union catalogue for CSIR laboratories and it has come forward flood the updated union catalogue with the cooperation from the member CSIR libraries, an alternatives mode to avoid JCCC.

EXPERIENCE NETWORK WITH DST

After seeing the experience of CSIR consortium with the publishers, DST (Department of Science and Technology) has also decided to join with CSIR consortium for their e-journal subscription.

NATIONAL KNOWLEDGE RESOURCE CONSORTIUM FINAL SOLUTION

Open Consortium- Consortium of S&T institutions, will help to expand the information base will strengthen the negotiating power, develop uniformity across different departments.

NISCAIR should perform a leading role to bring other S&T organisations under Consortium. CSIR going to interconnected all the scientific laboratories with powerful computer networks with one CSIR slogans and the solution is formation of National Consortium of Scientific Departments and named as National Knowledge Resource Consortium (NKRC).

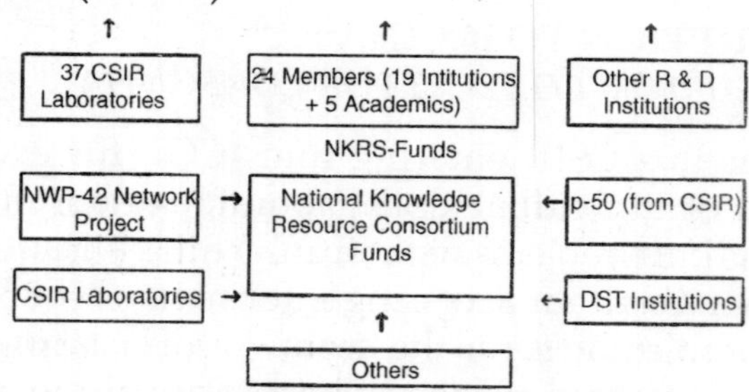

Fig 7.2 National Knowledge Resource Consortium

COLLECTION DEVELOPMENT AND MANAGEMENT POLICIES

The libraries are now functioning as Information or Knowledge Centers, resource centers, which disseminates required pinpointed information to the users. Libraries collect the information published in various forms *e.g.* books, periodicals, thesis, patents etc. and organise it in helpful sequence. The heart of the library is in its collection. The main purpose of the collection is to serve the needs of users and organisational aims in better ways. Libraries have to develop the collection keeping in view the users need and demands and hence the collection development in the library must be proper.

Traditional Libraries have some set of rules framed for the collection development but not operative, but now due use of ICT, revolutionary changes have been observed in the library practices including collection development. The framed rules are not appropriate and suits to the changing practices and hence majority of the libraries in the developed countries have formulated the collection development policies to build the proper and useful collection in the libraries which supports to the needs of the users. Similarly the change in format from print to digital made the issues to develop new policies or to amend the existing policies to suit the environment.

In digital media acquisitions the process is different due to change in format and pricing structure as compared to previous methods followed in libraries. Collection development is the main activity of any library and hence librarians are now focusing more in this area. To maintain the proper collection in libraries there is a need to develop policies or amend to the existing to suit the emerging trends in publications and acquisition methods. The increase in digital media publication and usage the collection development policies for the digital information resources are required to be developed.The process of the collection development covers selection and de-selection of the resources.

Collection development or management involves activities like collection management programme, collection development policy statement, collection assessment, funding and budgeting, selection and de-selection, preservation, and resource- sharing projects. It is very clear from the statement made by Verzosa that collection development process is a complex process involving various activities but its advantages are more to have a proper collection.

WHAT IS COLLECTION DEVELOPMENT

The purpose of collection development pointed out by Melvil Dewey was to provide 'The best reading for the largest number at the least cost'. ALA defined a very suitable definition for collection development as "A term which encompasses a number of activities related to the development of the library collection, including the determination and coordination of selection policy, assessment of needs of users and potential users, collection use studies, collection evaluation, identification of collection needs, selection of materials, Planning for resource sharing, collection maintenance and weeding."

ALA Glossary State that "Library Collections will contain all types of registered information, including printed materials of all formats, audio-visual materials, visual material, materials used with computers, graphs and three-dimensional materials and ways to access the electronic information" Harold Libraries Glossary defined "collection developments as the process of planning a stock acquisition programmed not simply to cater for immediate needs but to build a current and reliable collection over a numbers of years to meet the objectives of the services." These definitions clearly indicate the need of collection development in information growing age. If libraries need to provide qualitative services then qualitative collection is to be made available in the library irrespective of forms and formats.

WHY PROPER COLLECTION DEVELOPMENT

Collection of the documents in the library is the prime task as it is the power house of information resources. There are many factors involved to have proper collection development like.

- Information explosion and Information overload
- Limited and shrinking library budgets

- Increasing users demands for pinpointed qualitative information resources due to specialisation
- Multiple forms and formats of the information resources including digital
- Increase in prices of documents all the times
- Shift in demand of users from collection based services to information and access based services
- More usage of Internet based e-documents

Since digital, internet resources, databases and e-publications are increasing and simultaneously the use in academic and special libraries are also increasing continuously. Growth in literature made necessary to manage proper collection.

Objectives and Purpose of Collection Development

The main objectives and purpose behind collection development are:

- Fulfil the user needs by proper collection
- To support the teaching learning and research endeavors
- Periodically review the collection for weeding
- To provide nascent and relevant information
- To acquire the best and useful literature to the core group of the users

Collection Development policies allows the library personnel's to develop proper collection and based on this value added services can be provided to the users. The purpose of the collection development policy is to provide guidelines for day to day acquisition and withdrawal decisions, resource allocation and long range planning of collection needs keeping in mind the library mission, activities, organisational needs and interest etc.

TECHNIQUES FOR PROPER COLLECTION DEVELOPMENT

For proper collection development for any library, a detailed written collection development policy is necessary.

The policy clearly specifies the organisational requirements, goals and the user needs in specific. The Library committee formed for the proper development and progress of the library consist of the expert members from the various faculties who can contribute in formulating the proper collection development and designing the policies. It is also necessary to look in to the policies formulated by the other libraries and the policies prepared by LC and ALA etc. Library collection development policy should be in clearly spelt out in a written form. The American Library Association's collection development policies assumed that a written collection development policy is a desirable tool that enables selectors to work with greater consistency towards defined goals. The following aspects need to be considered basically while developing policy:

- Users needs and demands
- Review the organisational needs and objectives
- Review the standard, core, border and peripheral subject areas
- Conduct use and users studies for user behaviour and need analysis
- Try to cover the sources which disseminate maximum access to current information in the area
- Take the help of techniques like citation analysis, impact factor, bibliometrics and scientiometrics studies, information audit, information behaviour of users etc
- Resource Sharing practices be initiated at various level including consortium
- Evaluation techniques must be adapted
- Trial access for the databases for certain period and get the feedback from the users before subscription
- Initiate the OA and IR project for protecting IP of organisation
- Analyse strengths and weakness of the collection regularly
- Apply management techniques for quality procurement

Many libraries have developed collection development policies but these are informal in nature and no concrete policies are developed except larger organisations. The collection development policy is required due to multidisciplinary subjects, procurement of epublications. Policy is a guideline to act on. To prepare a policy for any library a review of different standard collection development policies becomes useful to draft a policy.

REVIEW OF EXISTING COLLECTION DEVELOPMENT POLICIES

The basic elements while formulating the collection development policy for any library was discussed in the conferences also and the output presented in the National Conference on "Putting Knowledge to Work: Best Practices in Librarianship" 1-2 May 2009 151-152 highlighted following issues.

- *Organisational Objectives*: The nature of the organisation, its function, objectives and the purpose must be considered at the initial level.
- *Users*: It is necessary to review the needs of the users of the library especially from the organisation, their main area of concern, projects under taken, information resources covering the general aspect about the stream as well as the specialised needs of the users in the area of research. Real and potential needs of the users must be covered.
- *Level of collection*: The collection may satisfy the needs of the experts as well as a common man whose interest is to read for the entertainment and knowledge addition. (Maslow's need based triangle). There is a need to focus on the current and future needs of the organisations.
- *Subject Coverage*: It is necessary to fix the core subjects in which organisational collection must be deep and updated. The peripheral subjects can be developed based on the priority as well as need based collection or even can be shared with other

organisations (Resource Sharing). Hence collection assessment must be evaluated based on the area and subjects of core importance.

- *Type of Information Sources*: While selecting the information recourses it is necessary to provide the access to the literature published in the area which is covered by the secondary information sources. It is necessary to provide maximum access to the users rather than owning the information resources. To make the collection economic on demand acquisition can also be preferred in case of peripheral area or can be obtained from ILL.
- *Budget*: Allocation of the budget must be proper and as per the usage. The budget of any library is not adequate to get all the literature published and hence policies must be fixed keeping in mind the usage and cost effective factors. Resource sharing activity will also help in reducing the expenses in case of peripheral research area.
- *Forms in which material must be acquired*: It is necessary to fix the form in which documents can be acquired. A policy stating the forms (print, digital, non print etc) to be procured must be detailed. However the acquisition must always be cost effective to adjust in the budget allocated.
- *Services provided*: Many libraries provide services to the users from the organisation as well as from different institutions. For this purpose the acquisition must be qualitative.
- *Users and use studies at frequent Intervals*: It is necessary to evaluate the usage of the acquired material. If the material is less used it must be weeded or stacked in parallel.
- *Policies for the preservation of the resources*: Preservation of the literature is the objective of the library. The heritage of the knowledge is useful for the future generation and hence modern tools and techniques may be used.

IFLA POLICY FOR COLLECTION DEVELOPMENT

The IFLA suggested following points in its collection development policy:

- Must be a written Policy covering procedure for selection, de-selection planning (future), public relations, weeding, retaining, preservation etc
- Covers general, narrative and subject profiles
- Use of collection evaluation methods
- Use of collection depth indicators
- Language (English, Primary and predominantly used as per need and country language)
- Policy implementation and revision

The first elements of a collection development policy will be a mission statement of the library, the purpose of this policy and the audience to whom it is addressed. General area covers current focus or also retrospective acquisitions; the resource types (monographs, periodicals, theses, gray literature, maps, etc.); languages; formats (printed, nonprint or electronic); special sources of funding (a grant or gift from a donor); the policy regarding gifts and any special policies regarding maintenance (weeding, discarding, preservation) of the collection; and size of the collections.

Collection evaluation is based on quantitative and qualitative measures:

- Quantitative Measures reveal size, age, use, costs and other numeric data. Examples of quantitative measures include inventory, or shelf list measures to determine actual title or volume counts, by segment or subject area. Median age or similar measures indicate the currency of the materials. Amount expended for acquisitions in a segment or subject area per year illustrates the ongoing commitment to develop that area. Percentage of titles owned by a library when compared to a standard list shows the breadth and depth of the collection. Use statistics (including internal library use and ILL) are both collection and client-centred.
- Qualitative measures are obtained through

subjective evaluation and involve the professional judgment of librarians, appraisal from subject experts, or the opinion of customers. These techniques include impressions of the condition, character and appropriateness of a section of the collection. Another qualitative technique is the judgment made by comparison of one subject in the collection to a similar subject in another library, or to a subject bibliography.

Collection depth indicators indicated are: current collection level, acquisition commitment and collection goal. Indicators define out of scope, minimum information level, basic information level, study and instructional support, research level, comprehensive level etc Each institution, including its community and other constituents, is unique. Therefore, its policy statements will be unique. The policy statements should reflect this particular library and the community it serves.

ALA POLICY

ALA covers following standard elements in its policy developed for academic libraries (College)

- *Standards* 1: Mission, Goals, and Objectives of institution
- *Standard* 2: Collections: including print materials in all formats, audiovisual materials, sound recordings, materials used with computers, graphics, and three dimensional materials. A formula is also presented in terms of collection development in the policy
- *Standard* 3: Organisation of materials: Library collections shall be organised by nationally approved conventions and arranged for efficient retrieval at time of need. The processing methods need to be applied for this purpose.
- *Standard* 4: Staff: The staff shall be of adequate size and quality to meet the library's need for services, programmes, and collection organisation. A staff formula is also presented in the policy

- *Standard* 5: Services: The library shall establish, promote, maintain a range and quality of services that supports the academic programme of the institution and encourage optional library use.
- *Standards* 6: Facilities: The library building shall provide well-planned, secure and adequate housing for its collections and personnel; secure space for users and staff, and space for the provision of services and programmes. A formula is also presented to calculate the space for per vol/Per Sqft.
- *Standards* 7: Administration: The college library shall be administered in a manner which permits and encourages the fullest and most effective use of available library resources.
- *Standard* 8: Budget: The library director shall have the responsibility for preparing, defending, and administering the library budget in accord with agreed upon objectives. These standards provide the guideline for formulating the policy.

UNIVERSITY GRANT COMMISSION (UGC) COLLECTION DEVELOPMENT POLICY

The UGC policy stated following points for collection development:

- Library Committee and its constituents (Chairman, member secretary, members, student representative)
- Library Collection norms based on courses, students and faculty
- Technical Processing.
- Library Finance
- Library Services
- Library Personnel
- Physical Facilities

AICTE COLLECTION DEVELOPMENT POLICY FOR ENGINEERING COLLEGE LIBRARIES

All India Council for Technical Education (AICTE) has formulated norms or policy for development of library collection including number of titles and their volumes, number of national and international journals including e-resources made available through INDESTAICTE. The main elements covered with formulas are:

- Collection of Books and Journals (Print Reading Material)
- Collection of Electronic Resources (e-journals and e-books etc)
- Library Personnel and Library Building

LIBRARY OF CONGRESS. COLLECTION DEVELOPMENT POLICIES

The Library's Collection Development Policy is a guide for materials to be added to the Library's permanent collections. The Collection Policy Statement (CPS) governs the Library's collection development and acquisition efforts. The statements implement the Library's responsibilities to serve. The policies provide a plan for developing the collections and maintaining their existing strengths.The highlighted points in to this policy are:

- *Collecting Levels*: Out of scope no need to buy, minimum level, basic information level, instructional level, research level, comprehensive level
- *Collection Overviews*: Scope, research strength,
- *Selection Guidelines for Electronic Resources*: Evaluate contents, add value, server reliability, judicious use of multimedia, adherence to copyright and fair use guidelines, provision of links to source for the plug-in-software, organisation and ease of navigation, presence of search and help features, procurement of Standard Fee based resources with permanent retention.

From the analytical study of the collection development policies it is understood that minimum components to be considered are:

- *Selection*: Covers purpose (free or purchased) teaching, learning, research and needs of staff and students; responsibility (Staff and librarian), Format (Print or digital), Language, special collections

- *Allocation of resources*: Considerations based on need based requirements and on demand procurement and provide more access to information than possession.
- *Collection maintenance*: Retention policies considering usage, main stack, parallel stacking, compact storage, weeding, retro-conversion etc are properly applied for better management and reduction in cost.
- *Preservation*: Rare and useful collection is to be retained for longer use and needs proper preservation manual or converting to digital
- *Access*: open access or authority permitted to consult in case of rare and confidential.
- *More use of e-publications*: The print media is shifting to e-publications and databases and more use is observed in the present generation.
- *Network based resources and consortium arrangement*: These are also to be considered while planning collection economically
- *Resource sharing and IR initiatives*: Open access and IR and resource sharing initiatives need to be considered

There is a need to develop proper collection in different forms. Collection development policies are to be framed for digital collection also as these documents may increase in the collection including acquisition and resource sharing policies.

The policies need to be revised regularly. Policy supports to customer-focused needs, so that library users have access to current, relevant and authoritative information in their preferred format.

8

The Future Role of the Academic Librarian

INTRODUCTION

In 2005, the decision of the University of Wales at Bangor to make all of its subject librarians redundant caused shock and terror throughout the academic library world, both in the United Kingdom and beyond. Was this an aberration, or was it a straw in the wind? The future of the liaison librarian in the university is an issue that currently occupies many minds. It is naturally of prime concern to the liaison librarians themselves, but it is also a significant issue for library managers. There is an interesting range of opinions on the subject, all claiming to plot emerging trends by extrapolating from current observations, and all pleasantly unhindered by empirical data. One study, at least, is candid enough to admit that "the future is difficult to predict".

It is normal now to find comments in the press along these lines: "with users switching to electronic access to resources instead of books, and using search engines instead of librarians to track down information, libraries face a struggle to remain relevant". Not surprisingly, the library profession's view of the future is largely positive, with rallying cries such as: "there are no limits for academic librarians in the 21st century, there are, however, endless opportunities". We can only polish our crystal balls and guess at what the future may hold. It is nonetheless interesting to see what the profession has to say about its future, and this survey will review some of the recent writing on the subject.

INFORMATION LITERACY

As many traditional library roles began to disappear in the early 1990s, the profession seized upon information literacy as its salvation. Academic librarians began the often painful process of reinventing themselves as teachers who would guide students through the complex process of information discovery and evaluation. To many, this is still seen as a key role. Rader, for example, in describing the work of liaison librarians, says that "above all, they strive to ensure that all students learn appropriate information skills to help them achieve information fluency and become productive members of the information society." But do the students want to be taught? A recent survey of undergraduate students in the United States found that "respondents generally say they have 'good' to 'very good' skills for... the university's online library system."

However the researchers warn that "this response is likely overstated, considering that the literature on self-assessment of skills finds that students overrate their skills in general, men more so than women". There seems no reason to think that this will change. As Reyes puts it, "students want to be self-sufficient and have unmediated, immediate access to information. The very changes in our information technologies have changed this information seeking behaviour, giving the control that once belonged to libraries over to the users."

Perhaps the more important question is: how do academic staff view the role of the librarian in educating students to find and evaluate information? A recent survey in the United Kingdom found that "the great majority of librarians see teaching information literacy and offering subject-based expertise as core roles for them, and central to what they do; researchers are generally supportive, but more equivocal about whether these are core as distinct from ancillary roles for librarians". A 2000 survey of academics and librarians in Canada found that "in the area of teaching/ instruction, there was a sharp contrast between the librarians' willingness to collaborate and the faculty's lack of interest".

Could it be that the material we are presenting in our classes is too elementary to meet the needs of our students? As Reyes remarks, "it is no longer sufficient to teach the mechanics of a single database. We can now move on to make correlations between keyword searching and rhetorical analysis in order to illustrate the use of language in scholarship." But are we really ready to move on? Asher argues that

- what a librarian can't do... is teach students to extract information from resources, theorise, or locate meaning. Teaching students to analyse data, evaluate ideas, and develop a philosophical understanding framed within a subject discipline are elements of information literacy that lie outside the expertise of most librarians. Universities hire academics to do that.

REFERENCE WORK

Many university libraries have reported a steady decline in enquiries at their reference desks, presumably because many students are now independently finding enough information for their needs. As Markey concluded "although research findings demonstrate that end users are not conducting sophisticated online searches, the vast majority are satisfied with their searches. In fact, percentages of users who express satisfaction with the results of their searches reach into the high seventies and beyond."

The consultation report that led to the redundancy of liaison librarians at the University of Wales at Bangor put it more bluntly "the process of literature searches is substantially de-skilled by online bibliographic resources". The recent literature repeatedly calls for more flexible delivery of information services. For example, a report from the United States asserted that "future librarians will increasingly need to take their skills to the clients that need assistance. That model, sometimes referred to as 'place as library,' could be virtual or in person in remote site classrooms or offices, but the organisational model will change to accommodate the 'traveling' staff model". One American librarian has gone so far as to suggest that "librarians could even be assigned to live in dorms, in exchange for room and board, so that they are truly available, visible, and a part of the college student's world".

Presumably only young, single librarians need apply for these positions, and this also suggests that there may be problems in recruiting staff to provide these innovative outreach services. When the library at George Mason University in Virginia opened a new information commons, it specially recruited staff to work in this very different environment. Even so, some staff were dissatisfied, especially because of the long opening hours. The manager suggested "perhaps we should begin to look to the retail environment for our recruits". Clearly she has a point: to refugees from Wal-Mart, any library must look like a pleasant work environment.

It remains to be seen whether the refugees from Wal-Mart will make good librarians. The previously cited IMLS Task Force report suggests that virtual reference services could be outsourced. In a similar vein, the director of the Law Library at the University of Colorado at Boulder has suggested that in the future faculty can expect round-the-clock reference and research assistance. However, they should not be surprised if their midnight reference questions are answered by someone on the other side of the world. Computer tech support has already moved overseas, pioneering the way for other services to follow. Why shouldn't libraries form worldwide consortia to provide 24/7 research assistance, for practical and for financial reasons?

This could be a boon when you have a request in the wee hours of the morning that calls for a straightforward answer, such as the identification of the source of a quotation, but it could mean less quality or less precision in responses requiring more complex research. A university librarian in England has argued that university libraries have not put sufficient staff resources into dealing with enquiries. He has developed plans for providing increased support for users, but admits that his plans are "not fully funded".

RESEARCH SUPPORT

If undergraduates are now finding much of the information they need via Google and Wikipedia, surely there is still a need for experienced librarians to meet the more advanced information needs of researchers? A recent survey of researchers at Deakin University in Victoria reported that "a recurring theme of the interviews was the need for research assistants to undertake information seeking, in particular library-related information seeking. While this was commonplace with many senior researchers, it was a very attractive proposition to those without such assistance and/or those with limited research funding". Funding is indeed the key issue here and many libraries will be unable to afford to provide experienced, highly qualified librarians to provide in-depth research assistance to all postgraduate students and academic staff. Brookman and her colleagues discussed the advantages of having an "informationist" attached to clinical teams in a UK hospital trust, but concluded that "funding is not available for the full implementation of the informationist model". On the other hand, there are areas where funding is more generous, and in these situations it may be possible to provide high level research assistance. Bintliff sees her law library providing such services in the future:

- Faculty can expect more customized information coming from the library, more information that is tailored to support an individual's specific scholarship and teaching. Faculty will find more information 'pushed' at them even before they ask for it, as librarians use 'faculty interest databases' to track and anticipate faculty requests. Librarians will capitalise on the ever-faster ability to receive, assemble, and disseminate information via electronic communications. In addition, librarians will work with faculty to compile an array of information and sources adapted to their specific needs.

Even where funding is available, there is still the question of the level of disciplinary knowledge required to provide research support at an advanced level. The study of clinical librarians conducted by Brookman and her colleagues looked at the possibility of librarians going beyond information retrieval to evaluation and appraisal and found that "those who argued against having the C[linical] L[ibrarian] evaluating the literature, put forward the argument that to critically appraise the sources it is necessary to have a clinical background and real knowledge of the context of the work."

Pagel reports that, for liaison librarians at Emory University in Georgia, "subject expertise is becoming the norm." Advanced subject expertise, probably at doctoral level, will be necessary if liaison librarians are to convince academics that a librarian can be a real partner in the research process. When Ducas and Michaud- Oystryk surveyed academics at the University of Manitoba, they found that, on the question of collaboration with librarians on research projects, "performing a literature search... was [an] area where both groups saw potential for collaboration. In all other areas, faculty were much less receptive to collaboration with librarians." A recent survey of academics and librarians in the UK found that both groups agreed in not seeing a core role for librarians as "subject-based experts embedded in departments or research groups".

INFORMATION TECHNOLOGY

- Librarians and library staff have to be very tech savvy, especially given the popularity of information commons and the ubiquity of

> information workstations... The major challenge will be retraining the staff member who prefers to keep doing what he/she has been doing in the same way it has been done, who sees their value to students and researchers as one shared with their traditional mode rather than be attuned to actual values perceived by the younger generation of students and faculty who have been educated within a technological environment.

There is general agreement in the literature that liaison librarians of the future will need sophisticated IT skills. A survey of an international group of senior academic librarians revealed that, with regard to skills of future academic librarians, "IT and communication skills remain at the top". That is not to say that liaison librarians will need degrees in information technology, but they will need to be highly skilled at keeping abreast of developments which will be of use to them and their clients:

- University libraries, both in teaching and in research institutions, can no longer provide core services without assistance from and cooperation with central Information Systems departments... Learning to work with those cultures and seeking collaboration at every turn is essential. Learning to evaluate technology and make technology-based decisions is critical for the university library staff in every functional area.

Burnett and Bonnici have examined some of the questions that this raises for the training and accreditation of librarians. They argue that "the future of librarianship is seriously implicated... by the demonstrated inability of the discipline of information studies... to establish its claim to a unique body of abstract knowledge." These concerns are perhaps vindicated by Ducas and Michaud-Oystryk, whose survey of librarians and academics at the University of Manitoba found that "in the area of information technology, both librarians (49 per cent) and faculty (43 per cent) ranked assistance with retrieving an electronic document the highest." If retrieving an electronic document is the acme of their IT skills (real or perceived), liaison librarians definitely have cause for concern.

OTHER ROLES

There are a range of other tasks that are seen as being important for the liaison librarian of the future. A UK study reported that:

- There are... a number of additional roles that librarians are interested in developing: providing specialist advice in copyright and I[ntellectual] P[roperty] R[ights] issues; managing non-technical metadata issues; acting as technology specialists in facilitating access to electronic resources; and – most importantly – managing institutional repositories of digital information. With respect to copyright advice, some libraries already employ specialist lawyers; others told us that they had taken the role into the library from other places (*e.g.* the registry) where it had previously resided".

A recent American report on the top ten assumptions for the future of academic libraries stated that "there will be an increased emphasis on digitising collections, preserving digital archives, and improving methods of data storage and retrieval... Librarians should collaborate with disciplinary colleagues in the curation of data as part of the research process". The same report predicted that "distance learning will be an increasingly more common option in higher education", and a recent UK study found that many librarians saw the facilitation of e-learning as a core role for the future, although academics did not appear to share that opinion.

The recent literature has surprisingly little to say about collection development, but at least one study maintains "that the importance of research library collections only continues to increase".

Phipps however is less certain: "will we continue to 'build' collections? Oh, I know, there will always be books.

And for at least five more years the dominant form will be print. Then what?" Some academic library managers have forecast a more extreme scenario where "libraries may be replaced altogether by a single net collection operated by government or other institution". This latter scenario may not be far-fetched: in Germany the federal government has already negotiated nation-wide licences for databases from Emerald and Springer. Barry makes an interesting point about career structure:

- A challenge for the profession is the need to create job structures so that the only way to progress financially in the field is not through management positions. Administrative work takes time away from the continued skill development needed to stay current with the rapidly evolving information environment. Placing high performers in these positions often does nothing but waste the time and energy required for maintaining currency and effectiveness in their positions.

CONCLUSION

From reading the literature, a composite picture emerges of the liaison librarian of the future. It shows a young, outgoing professional who is comfortable hanging out in campus cafes and student halls of residence and able to communicate easily with undergraduate students. At the same time, he or she will be a subject expert, with advanced knowledge of the literature of one or more disciplines and able to work closely with academic staff and postgraduate students. On top of this, our liaison librarian will be extremely proficient with technology and an expert with various software packages used for teaching and research. Clearly there is nobody who fits this Identikit picture. It is easy to see why so many of our current liaison librarians feel under stress. We cannot go on pretending that liaison librarians can provide such an impossibly wide range of services. So what will become of the liaison librarian's role? Perhaps it will split into a variety of roles, each re-aligning itself with other roles to create a new range of professionals. In the university of the future, we may see a group of Learning Support staff, who provide undergraduate students with training and support in a range of study, information and writing skills. We may see another group of Research Support staff, who combine an information specialist role with a more conventional research assistant role and are attached to academic or research units throughout the university. And we will certainly find IT staff who specialise in applications used in teaching, elearning and research, probably as part of the university's central IT support infrastructure. The final word belongs to a reference librarian at Queen's University in Ontario:

- For librarians, two scenarios loom on the horizon. The optimistic or allencompassing future demands that librarians be enthusiastic and flexible enough to create a dynamic learning environment. These librarians will be adept at creating an intellectual landscape densely populated with electronic information sources and rich with a variety of services tailored to shifting needs. The pessimistic future is a passive one where our services and spaces are underused and irrelevant to students and faculty. This future is likely to evolve unless librarians respond creatively to the impact of electronic resources in academic libraries. Administrators who fail to make the transition will see their institutions fall far behind their counterparts. Librarians who cannot or will not make the transition will witness the loss of their workplace as they know it and lose their roles in it.

Bibliography

Beales, G.: *The Evolving Roles of Information Professionals in the Digital Age*, New Delhi: Long Life Publication, 2003.

Bertozzi, S.: *Special Libraries,* Maharashtra: Pune Publication, 2006.

Bloom, B. S.: *Key Concepts in the Architecture of the Digital Library,* New Delhi: Concept Publishing Company, 2003.

Brook, A.: *Technology and the Changing Role of Teacher-Librarians,* New York: Cambridge University Press, 2004.

Browne, K.: *The Electronic Library: Slouching Toward the Future or Creating a New Information Environment,* Princeton: Princeton University Press, 2003.

Gibbs, G.: *Library Management and Information Technology*, Cambridge: Cambridge University Press, 2006.

Harris, J. L.: *Training for Change: New Skills for the Electronic Library,* New Technology, New Librarians?, London and New York: Longman, 2005.

Hey, A.: *Issues of Libraries in the Digital Era,* Chicago: University of Chicago Press, 2006.

Hunt, M.: *Electronic Journals: Promises and Challenges in Indian Academic Libraries,* Amritsar: Guru Nanak Dev University, 2006.

John, V.: *Putting Content onto the Internet: The Library's Role as Creator of Electronic Information,* Aisawl: Mizo History Association, 1995.

Mayston, E. L.: *Cybrarians: The Information Professionals of the 21st-Century,* New Delhi: Oxford University Press, 2004.

Meadows, D. H.: *The Impact of Online Information on Traditional Library Services and the Distance User,* London: Cambridge Perseus Publishing, 2006.

Menzies, E. P.: *The Electronic Document and its Impact on the Information Chain Professions*, London: Kogan Page, 2000.

Mukherjee, N.: *Digital Libraries: Principles and Practice in a Global Environment,* New Delhi: Concept Publication, 2005.

Pickering, G.: *Role of Information Technology in Managing Organizational Change and Organizational Interdependence,* New Delhi: Oxford University Press, 2002.

Rodrik, D.: *Care and Handling of CDs and DVDs: A Guide for Librarians,* London: Yale University Press, 2007.

Salmon, B.: *The Impact of Electronic Publications on Promotion and Tenure Decisions,* London: HMSO, 2005.

Singh Chandrika: *Introducing and Managing Academic Library*, New Delhi: New Delhi Press, 2001.

Sinha, A. C.: *The Management of Library and Information Studies Education,* Mumbai: Manaktalas, 1999.

Snow, C.P.: *Restructuring Academic Libraries: Adjusting to Technological Change,* Cambridge: Cambridge University Press, 2008.

Sreen, S. K.: *Opportunities in Library and Information Science,* New Delhi: Oxford, University Press, 1999.

Stott, N.C.H.: *The Librarian as Publisher: A Case study of a World Wide Web Publishing Project,* New York: Cambridge University Press, 2004.

Thapar, R.: *The Impact of Digital Reference on Librarians and Library Users.,* New Delhi: Oxford University Press, 1994.

Index